Tony Adams is a senior sports writer for the *Daily Telegraph* who has won awards for his coverage of football and rugby league. On weekends, when he's not at the footy, he has been spotted on sports fields around the eastern suburbs of Sydney, coaching son Dean at soccer and basketball.

Other books by Tony Adams

Hit Men

MASTERS
OF THE GAME

Coaches who shaped Rugby League

Tony Adams

IRONBARK
Pan Macmillan Australia

First published in 1996 in Ironbark by Pan Macmillan Australia Pty Limited
St Martins Tower, 31 Market St, Sydney

National Library of Australia
cataloguing-in-publication data:

Adams, Tony, 1959–   .
Masters of the game: coaches who shaped rugby league.
ISBN 0 330 35853 7.
1. Rugby League football – Australia – Coaching. I. Title.
796.3338

Typeset in 11/14pt Palatino by Post Typesetters
Printed in Australia by Australian Print Group

To Dawn, Dean, Cassie and my parents

FOREWORD

THEY weren't always 'Masters of the Game'. Prior to the '70s it was the *players* of rugby league, Clive Churchill, Reg Gasnier, John Raper, John Sattler, Norm Provan and Arthur Summons, to name a few, who were the prime focus of the general public and the media.

Coaches went about their task quietly and with plenty of enthusiasm, while the media, mostly press and radio in those early days of the infancy of TV, were more inclined to cover the game as they saw it and not through the eyes of the coaches.

Although conscientious and hardworking, rugby league coaches in the main were not as knowledgeable and dominant as they are today.

Back in the '50s and early '60s most clubs commenced training a few weeks before the first trial. Weight training, sprint training, drills to improve skills and flexibility exercises were unheard of. Club officials were in fear of players burning out prior to season's end if they trained too hard.

Game plans and tactics were a rarity. At my old club when I played advice on diet and nutrition was limited to 'A steak three hours before kickoff and don't drink much water on game day'. It's a wonder we got through the 80 minutes of football.

Injury treatment was archaic, i.e. soak in a hot bath with a couple of spoonfuls of washing soda immediately you arrived home to fix corked thighs, then rub in plenty of Dencorub. Ice was only thought best for keeping the beer cold.

When Norm Tipping, coach of the first of St George's 11 straight premiership victories in 1956 was sacked in favour of Ken Kearney, there was barely any mention in the press. Imagine a parallel situation today. Coaches were really the back-seat drivers in those good old days.

Into the 1970s rugby league entered a new era—TV coverage spread the gospel of the game, professionalism made its entry via thinking and innovative coaches. The catalyst was the American football connection.

'Winning isn't everything, it's the only thing'—Vince Lombardi.

In 1970 at a General Motors-Holden management conference in Melbourne I saw a motivational film called *Second Effort* featuring the legendary gridiron coach Vince Lombardi.

I was enthralled Lombardi put into words all the things about football, business and life, that I knew were true, but no coach or manager had ever conveyed to me before.

He talked about discipline, sacrifice and self-denial, pride, respect for authority, the reality that hard work was essential to success, goal setting, and most important of all, mental toughness.

I arranged for Jack Gibson to see the film in 1971. He said after viewing it, 'It's the hottest thing I have ever seen.'

Jack was coaching St George at the time, and they were going through a slump having lost several games on the trot. He showed the film to the three grades the following Tuesday night instead of training them on the paddock. Club officials were distraught; they thought the teams should have been training harder rather than having a night off to watch a 30-minute film.

Such was the impact of Lombardi that St George didn't lose a game in any grade during the following seven weeks.

It was the beginning of Jack's regular pilgrimages to the States, leading to the building of a great friendship with Dick Nolan, coach of the San Francisco 49ers and later coach of the New Orleans Saints.

Other coaches followed his lead as we all began to look for an 'edge' on our opponents. Giant steps were taken in off-season and pre-season training; weight training and sprint training programs were introduced. We wanted our footballers to become super athletes as well as ball players and the way to achieve it was in the physical preparation of our teams.

Suddenly we all had club conditioners, many of them disciples of George Daldry of City Tattersall's fame. George had made a study of aerobic fitness and strength training, had trained Olympic athletes and was very professional in his attitude.

'Winning did become everything'—motivational films were used in the mental preparation and some clubs started using sports psychologists in their efforts to improve individual performances. Trainers were employed to supervise injuries and in later years nutritionists, sprint trainers, skill coaches and others were added, all under the direct control of the coach.

Through the 1970s and into the '80s we saw a far greater emphasis on and influence of football coaches on the destiny of their teams and their clubs.

By now video replays of your own game and your upcoming opponents' games were available. Not only could you pinpoint weaknesses in your own team that had to be eliminated, but you could devise game plans to nullify your opponents' attack and observe their weakness in defence.

Tactics, which had been a minor part of rugby league in the 1950s and '60s, was now a major key to success.

The half and five-eighth in rugby league had now taken the equivalent of the quarterback's role in American football. The quarterback was the organiser, the on-field puppeteer. He put into play the game plan and every team member knew what was expected of him. And so it became with the rugby league halves.

Increasingly through this period coaches were given the responsibility of team selection, the hiring and firing of playing personnel and backup staff. The performance of the team became the coach's responsibility. He lived or died by the results he achieved and that is the way a modern-day coach wants it—no-one else to blame for failure except himself.

The only certainty in rugby league for any coach is that one day you are going to be sacked, but it's a price you are prepared to pay for the joy and excitement, the stimulation you receive when your team performs to the guidelines and standards you have prepared for the game. When they stick to your game plan against adversity, have shown you the mental toughness, total commitment and the discipline necessary to win against the odds—that's what modern coaching is all about. It's on those days that football coaches really are 'Masters of the Game'.

Terry Fearnley

Terry Fearnley was at the cutting edge of the new wave which changed rugby league coaching forever in the 1970s and '80s. With Jack Gibson, Fearnley was the first coach to investigate the American football scene, casting a wide net for bold new ideas. In 1976–77 as coach of Parramatta he brought the Eels, after 30 years, to football respectability, and their first grand finals, laying the foundation for the success ahead. In 1977 he coached Australia to win the World Series. Then, in 1985 he was at the helm when NSW won the State of Origin series for the first time and in the same year steered the Australian side to a 2-Tests-to-1 win over New Zealand in a highly controversial series.

CONTENTS

Preface   xiii

The Master   Jack Gibson   1

Bush Lore   Chris Anderson   25

The Old Fox   Harry Bath   45

Bookie Bob's Winning Ways   Bob Bax   65

The Quiet Man   Wayne Bennett   81

The Little Master   Clive Churchill   105

Bozo   Bob Fulton   125

The Man From Otahuhu   Graham Lowe   145

The Sultan of Slap   Roy Masters   167

The Iceman   John Monie   189

Sticks Provan Walked Tall   Norm Provan   209

The Kid From Castleford   Malcom Reilly   229

Playing Wazzaball   Warren Ryan   249

Sweet Shine of Success for Mr Sheen   Tim Sheens   273

Mr Precision   Brian Smith   295

PREFACE

COACHES are the lifeblood of modern rugby league. They make or break clubs, decide the fate of star players, dictate how the game is played and what rules are to be adhered to or broken. But it wasn't always that way. Back in league's innocent days in the seasons after it all began in 1908, most clubs didn't even have a coach. In fact, they were lucky to have a trainer. Then, the burden fell on the team captains to formulate team policy, get the players fit and supervise training. All that began to change in the 1920s when Arthur Hennessy, one of the game's founding fathers, held the reins as coach of South Sydney. A man ahead of his time, Hennessy's tactical insight was a major factor in the Rabbitohs' golden run that produced seven premierships for the club in eight years in the late '20s and early '30s. Hennessy saw league as a running and passing game and thus had a strict rule—no kicks! Anyone who dared to break that rule would often be greeted with a stint in reserve grade and a kick himself—up the backside courtesy of Hennessy. Generally regarded as the father of modern coaching, Hennessy introduced a radical attacking formation that included a five-man pack with two five-eighths.

But it wasn't until nearly half a century later, with the ascent of Jack Gibson, that coaches really arrived in rugby league. A bold innovator, Gibson put coaches on the rugby league map. 'The Master Coach' changed the face of the game forever, combining his own insights and experiences with ideas borrowed from American football. Suddenly, the coach was a man the league public wanted to know. Gibson's witty one-liners saw the coach become a popular man to be quoted, in the limelight for the first time.

In Gibson's footsteps have followed many fine coaches in their own right. In the '70s came Norm Provan, a superb player with St George who graduated from the captain-coach ranks to a fine off-field coach in his own right. Clive Churchill, the man behind the great Souths sides of the late '60s and early '70s, was very much from the old school. Churchill was never one to worry too much about structuring his team's play or technical moves; Churchill knew he had the talent to win premierships. He kept the players happy and everything else fell into place.

Into the 1980s Warren Ryan showed just how powerful an influence a coach can have on the game. A master of tactics, Ryan introduced a ruthless defensive style—dubbed by his critics as 'Wazzaball'—that forced administrators to bring in a host of rules changes. Almost as dominant a figure was Roy Masters, who will be forever remembered for bringing the class struggle to the game plus a notorious, televised face-slapping exercise at Western Suburbs club.

The past decade has seen the emergence of a new breed of coach—men such as Tim Sheens, Bob Fulton, Brian Smith and John Monie. Well spoken, street smart and knowledgeable, they have all played their part in the league revolution in the '80s and '90s.

Selecting the line-up of coaches for this book wasn't an easy task. As every realistic coach will tell you, a coach is only as good as the talent he has under his wing. One can't help wondering how good a coach Tim Sheens would have been without players like Ricky Stuart, Brad Clyde and Laurie Daley at his disposal. Or whether Wayne Bennett would have succeeded without Allan Langer, Steve Renouf and Glenn Lazarus. In nearly two decades in rugby league, I have met many fine coaches who would doubtless have succeeded had

they had the talent at their disposal that the men in the following chapters enjoyed.

Ultimately, success and failure dictate the fortunes of any
coach—and the records of achievement formed an essential
part of the criteria for selection in this book. With 25 premierships between them over the past 33 years, the men whose
stories I hope you will enjoy are thoroughly entitled to be
called 'masters of the game'.

Tony Adams
March 1996

The Master

JACK GIBSON

CLUBS
Eastern Suburbs 1967–68, 1974–76,
St George 1970–71,
Newtown 1973,
South Sydney 1978–79,
Parramatta 1981–83,
Cronulla 1985–87.

PREMIERSHIP RECORD
Games 394, won 245, lost 139, drew 10.
Winning percentage 62.2%.
Semi-finals
1967–68, 1970–71, 1973, 1974–76, 1981–83
Grand Finals (6)
1971, 1974–75, 1981–83
Premierships (5)
1974–75, 1981–83

OTHER COACHING ACHIEVEMENTS
Coached New South Wales 1989–90. Games 6, won 2, lost 4.
Coach of the Year 1973, 1975, 1982.
Dally M Coach of the Year 1982.

Jack Gibson, OAM, is the man who modern coaches can thank for putting them on the pedestal on which they find themselves today. A trend-setting coach who all but revolutionised the way league was played in the 1970s and early '80s, Gibson enjoyed amazing success at a variety of clubs. A tough front-rower with Easts, Wests and Newtown in the '50s and '60s, Gibson played one match in the engine room for New South Wales. But it was when he turned his hand to coaching in 1967 that he really began to make his mark. Gibson stunned the league world by taking an Easts side that hadn't won a match the previous season to the semi-finals—and repeated the effort in 1968 for good measure. He then took a two-year break from the game—one of several spells during his coaching career—before taking on St George in 1970, guiding the Dragons to the grand final the following year, which they lost to Souths. In 1973, Gibson had a year at Newtown, steering the team into the finals and winning the only club championship in the Jets' long history. Gibson returned to Easts the following year, where he won the Roosters' first premiership in nearly 30 years. A superbly drilled Easts side, led by Arthur Beetson and containing brilliant attacking players like Russell Fairfax, Ron Coote and Mark Harris, swept aside the Canterbury challenge 19–4. But better was to come in 1975 when the Roosters made it back-to-back titles, winning the grand final by an awesome 38–0 against St George.

Gibson's only sour coaching experience came at Souths, where he coached the Rabbitohs with some success in 1978–79 but was shown the door after a dispute with club management. A man who had little time for committees or officialdom, Gibson often fell foul of the men in power. But it was the showdown with the powers that be at Souths that led to Gibson's appointment as Parramatta coach in 1981—and the beginning

JACK GIBSON

of a golden era for the Eels. Parramatta won three straight titles under Gibson from 1981–83, with the master coach moulding one of the greatest club teams in premiership history. He had something of a 'no frills' pack with the Eels, but a magical backline containing Peter Sterling, Brett Kenny, Steve Ella, Mick Cronin and Eric Grothe. Gibson's victory speech after the Eels finally won their first premiership—against Newtown in 1981—is part of league folklore. After years of struggling to prove their worth, the battlers from Sydney's west had broken through to take the crown. Amidst joyous scenes at the Eels leagues club after the match, Gibson accepted the microphone and uttered just six words: 'Ding Dong . . . the witch is dead.' Star halfback Sterling will never forget the moment. 'It's frozen in my memory and recalling it sends chills down my spine,' Sterling wrote in his autobiography several years ago. 'When Jack got up a profound silence fell over the room. Jack's aura reached out and brushed every person there. After he spoke those six words, he turned on his heels and walked away. There was pandemonium—the crowd went berserk.'

Gibson spent three short but memorable years with the Eels, taking out a hat-trick of titles—the only one in rugby league since St George's amazing 11-premiership run in the 1950s and '60s. After another break, Gibson had a mixed spell at Cronulla, before finishing his career with a term as NSW State of Origin coach and a stint as manager at Easts—the club that was closest to his heart. Gibson is now a highly sought-after motivational speaker and was a huge success as a guest commentator during Channel Nine's State of Origin coverage for several years.

Jack Gibson is a football philosopher, a man who has kept company with prime ministers, celebrities and movie stars.

Journalists eagerly awaited his post match interviews, which were often reported along the lines of sermons from the mount. Unashamedly influenced by American football, he brought a new professionalism into rugby league. A man of strong principle, Jack Gibson is a champion of the one-line retort and has been a tireless worker for charity. After the death of son Luke who suffered from schizophrenia, Gibson and wife Judy have raised countless thousands of dollars for research into the illness. Pride and discipline were key words in the Gibson coaching philosophy. In an age of lawlessness on the field before trial by video, Gibson condemned foul play and insisted his teams played by the book. He made great use of video in the '80s to study his rivals, but was way ahead of the field in the early '70s before video was available. He often sent a 'spy' to watch the team he would play the following week. The 'spy' would sit in the grandstand with a tape recorder, and describe the team's attacking and defensive formations throughout the match.

Preparation was everything to Gibson, as he suggested in his book *Winning Starts on Monday*. He explains: 'Winning starts on Monday, not ten minutes before the game. It's confidence all week long, and it's confidence for the month before that, and the year before that. People can't get motivated on a five-minute speech before they run out onto the football paddock. It's something you have to wake up with—knowing that your preparation was right. Having the confidence that whatever comes up, you are ready.'

It may well have been Gibson's disenchantment with some of the 'dinosaur' coaches he played under during his own career that prompted him to think he could offer something better. Several years ago, Gibson recalled one of his earliest experiences in first grade. 'I'd just come into the team and was a kid feeling my way,' he said. 'One day I was up against this old hard-head in the front row and he was giving me a real hiding. He was putting it all over me and our coach gave me a real roasting at halftime. He said this bloke was an old sheila and he couldn't believe he was getting the better of me. Things didn't improve in the second half and I remember that really dented my confidence. It took me a long time to recover from that. I kept thinking, "Well if he's an old sheila, what does that make me? This bloke is murdering me".'

Many regard Gibson's success with the no-name Easts team in 1967 in his maiden year of coaching as his greatest achievement. The Roosters were the joke of the league the previous season, finishing on the bottom of the ladder without a point to their name. The 1967 season proved a landmark year for the game, with the introduction of a rule that would forever change the game—the limited tackle rule—and Gibson's introduction to the coaching ranks.

Ironically, Gibson actually applied to coach Easts in 1966 but lost out to Englishman Bert Holcroft. 'An official got up at the meeting when I applied for the job and said, "It's no use putting square pegs into rounds holes",' Gibson recalled. 'To this day, I've never forgotten it, even though I've got no idea what he meant. Was I the square peg or the round hole?' Gibson admits both parties were taking a gamble when the rookie coach came to the club in early 1967. 'People say I took a gamble coaching such a poor side, but they took a risk too,' Gibson explained. 'They hadn't won a game the previous year . . . but neither had I.' The young, inexperienced Easts side provided Gibson with an excellent opportunity to kick off his 'keep to the basics' coaching philosophy. 'I thought if I could get the players to simplify it a bit and not make fundamental mistakes, it would be the quickest way to improve them,' he said.

'If I couldn't change their minds, at least I thought I would be able to minimise their errors . . . that alone would make them better footballers. Hopefully they would finish in front at the end of the contest. And I thought I could do something on defence. I concentrated on defence. Throughout my playing career, we never trained on defence. If we trained for 90 minutes, it was all on offence. The only defensive practice was verbal and that doesn't work.'

Much of Gibson's early success in defence came down to his use of inner tubes to refine tackling technique—one of many innovations he brought to the game. 'We practised on the tubes and used them to good effect,' he said. 'It was fairly radical but I divided the time equally between offence and defence. With the defence, we had an advantage. I made all my major awards for defence. I wouldn't allow any outside people to make awards; often when they did I found the player they chose wasn't good enough to play first grade the following week. To avoid that clash, I made my own awards and made them for tackling—the best hit, most number of tackles—that sort of thing. I put the emphasis on defence and the players responded. It doesn't matter what game you play, once your defence starts to break down, there's no way you'll win. In business or any other part of life, the same principle applies. If your defence holds up, you can't lose. The worst you can come up with is a draw.'

Former Kangaroo halfback Kevin Junee, currently an Easts board member, stuck with the Roosters through good times and bad. He was there in 1966 when the club lost every game but stayed on to experience semi-final glory under Gibson in the two following seasons. 'People often ask how it felt to play in that Easts team of '66 and I can honestly say it wasn't that bad,' Junee said. 'We were young guys in the main and just wanted to go out there and play football. In most games, we were right in there at halftime but couldn't maintain our intensity for the 80 minutes and that proved our downfall.' Junee remembers the arrival of Gibson in 1967 as a breath of fresh air. 'To be honest, most of us didn't understand a lot of what Jack said or where he was coming from,' Junee admits. 'Remember that we were just a bunch of kids and he was hitting us with all these new expressions that most of us had never heard before. Jack always spoke very cryptically but even if you didn't understand exactly what he said, you knew the basic message. The stuff he said was so different from the clichés all the coaches of that era used. And it got you thinking. Most of all, I remember Jack entertained us. Training was never boring, he always had plenty of one-liners and new techniques. Before games he'd bring a gramophone into the dressing room and play his old records . . . at halftime he'd give us tea. One afternoon it was bitterly cold and we were playing badly. At halftime he served up the tea and commented, "It's not too hot out there today." The meaning was obvious to everyone. Another time one of our second-rowers kicked the ball during a game and it was a shocker. Jack gave the guy a ball at the next training session and made him do the whole session holding the ball. Then at the end of the session he told him to kick the ball. The player did and Jack said, "Now you've kicked it . . . that will be the last time you do that this season."

Junee believes fate played a major part in Gibson's success with Easts in 1967. 'That was the year the League introduced the four tackle rule and that really revolutionised the game,' he said. 'In the previous years we'd done okay for a while against the good sides, but a strong team like St George would get a roll on and under the unlimited tackle rule, we couldn't hold them out. They would just wear us down. But the combination of the four tackle rule, which really suited a young, mobile team like us, and Jack's arrival, saw everything fall into place. There's no doubt in my mind that Gibbo was the first true thinker in the modern game. He made maximum use of the four tackle rule, got us to cut our errors and concentrate on the things we were good at. His personality was so strong that he gave you the confidence to do things on the football field. His maturity and vision took us a step forward and we had a couple of great years.'

The Roosters defied the experts by reaching the finals in both 1967 and '68 but were bundled out in the big games by the more experienced Canterbury and St George respectively. Veteran journalist Bill Mordey paid just one visit to a Gibson dressing room before a match—the 1968 elimination semi-final clash with Saints—and still recalls an amazing Gibson speech to his players. 'Easts were rank outsiders—they were just a team of kids who shouldn't even have been there,' Mordey recalls. 'Saints' 11 straight premiership run had been broken the previous year but they were still a great team. They had a host of internationals—great players like Graeme Langlands, Billy Smith and the like. The Easts players were shaking in their boots—literally—when I entered the old Sydney Cricket Ground dressing room about half an hour before kickoff. I'll always remember the noise of the players' studs rattling on the floor—it was like a machine gun they were so nervous. There were blokes running to the toilet, others throwing up—they were in for a beating and they knew it. But then big Jack started to talk and all of a sudden you could have heard a pin drop. He walked around the room, giant man that he was, with the program in his hand, open to the two teams, and he seemed to dwarf the players. He started by walking up to his fullback—I can't remember who the young kid was—and said to him, "Billy Bloggs—you're up against Graeme Langlands". Jack let out a dry laugh before continuing. "He's played so many internationals and is one of the all-time greats. What hope have you got against a great player like him, eh?" Jack went through the entire team like this, basically paying out on his own players and telling them how good the opposition was. With a couple of the forwards he even said, "You've missed 50 tackles this season—I hate to think how many more you'll miss by the end of today's game." He went on like that for a good 10 minutes and you could see the players' nerves replaced by a determination to win and prove Gibson wrong. Finally, he said, "I've told you every reason why you can't win" and with that he screwed up the program and let it drop to the floor. "Now go out there and win—and don't come back here unless you do."'

Inspired by the Gibson outburst, the Roosters put up a gallant showing against the experienced Saints side before ultimately going down 17–10. 'Considering the opposition, it was a great performance by Easts,' Mordey recalled. 'And when they did go back to the dressing room, Gibson was proud of the way they performed.'

Despite his phenomenal success with the Roosters, Gibson packed his bags and left after that last game of the 1968 season. 'The club didn't want to give me any more authority or any more money,' he explained. 'I got $1000 in my first year and $800 in the next . . . I thought if I stayed much longer I'd end up owing them something. I couldn't go any further without them giving me more authority. The officials thought they were more involved in winning football games than I was . . . I couldn't convince them otherwise so it was time to move on.'

Gibson admits that despite his marvellous coaching record, there were plenty of hiccups along the way. 'I've lost count of the mistakes I made. But as a coach, you make more decisions than anyone else so it's probably natural you'll make more mistakes. The important thing is to be able to recognise those mistakes quickly and to do something about them. I think I was reasonably smart and had smart people around me who were able to give me the good information at the right time. Mistakes . . . let's see . . . I remember I wanted nothing to do with conditioning the players. I wanted to coach them, I thought they should get fit at home. That was one area I had to change my thinking in. Then I used to spend a lot of time coaching the young juniors in the club and left the senior players to their own devices to a large extent. That was another mistake. The seniors want more coaching and expect more attention than young players on the way up. In coaching, you stay with your veterans. The rookies to a certain extent, you should let them find their own way, with help. I've been burnt a few times by not sticking with my vets.'

Another mistake came with team selections. 'When I first started coaching, I didn't want to select the team; I was happy to leave that to someone else. After 12 months I realised what a mistake that was. We had seven selectors at Easts in the early days and I thought they would automatically come up with the best team. But I soon found out they didn't and it took me a while to get the job of sole selector. I wasn't going to be right all the time, but I knew I'd make a lot fewer mistakes than the seven-man panel. I wanted to be the boss of the whole shooting match—to pick my first, reserve and third grade teams—so I could work my players' potential. I knew I needed smart people around me so I wanted to employ my own staff but again that was something Easts didn't accept easily. I had to earn that by winning some football games. Once I did that, it increased my bargaining position.' Gibson always placed great emphasis on his support staff and either took a solid team with him to every club he coached, or built one from scratch. People like coordinator Ron Massey, conditioner Mick Souter and ambulanceman Alf Richards were familiar faces in the Gibson organisation. Close friend John Singleton jokes that Gibson has made more mistakes than anyone he knows. 'Jack's philosophy is to take the risks, but to realise your mistakes and flick them forever,' Singleton said. 'Similarly, realise your winning ideas and milk them and milk them until the whole cow disappears.'

Massey, Gibson's right-hand man for the best part of two decades, believes communication was the key to Gibson's success. 'He got through to the players by the way he spoke,' Massey explained. 'He had the knack of getting players to perform to the best of their ability. There was an aura to Jack when he spoke and you could see it with the players. He used to get motivational speakers and psychologists to talk to them occasionally and after five minutes, the players would be fidgeting and looking around the room. But when Jack spoke, every eye was on him; no-one moved and you could see they were hanging on his every word.' Massey said another of Gibson's strengths was his ability to influence the players off the field as well as on it. 'I think it's fair to say that anyone who Jack had contact with became not only a better footballer but a better man,' he said. 'He taught them lessons for life as well as the football field. He saw that they needed discipline in their lives from Monday to Friday if they were going to perform to their best on Sunday. He helped a lot of players to get their lives in order.' Massey swiftly rejects the critics who claim Gibson was a defensive coach. 'Jack was a trendsetter and realised you need to have a good defence to win football games,' Massey said. 'He used to say, "What else are you going to do when you don't have the football?" But he never sent his teams out there to bottle a game up or play negative football, unlike some modern coaches I could name. You've just got to look at the records of his great sides at Easts in the mid '70s and Parramatta in the early '80s to realise that Jack Gibson liked to play attacking football. His aim was to get the ball out to the likes of Russell Fairfax, Mark Harris, Eric Grothe or Steve Ella as much as possible. Jack knew mistakes could make or break a team and so he tried to keep those to a minimum, but that's hardly being defensive.'

Massey rightly sees Gibson as a trendsetter. 'He introduced videos, tackle counts and game balls—they are part of every coach's work now,' he said. 'I remember we started filming with a little black-and-white camera in 1975 and the quality was so poor you couldn't tell Arthur Beetson from "Bunny" Reilly. But the technology improved and everyone else started getting in on the act, videoing their own teams as well as the opposition. Jack also insisted the coach has the final say on selections which is something I'm sure all the current coaches are thankful for. Even our reserve and third grade coaches were given the last say on their teams. Jack would disagree with them at times over selections, but in the end he'd say, "You want him, you've got him." And I'm sure that modern coaches all got better paid as a result of Jack and his influence.'

Despite working together for the best part of two decades, Massey and Gibson rarely disagreed. 'We thought the same way and there weren't many times we didn't see eye to eye,' Massey said. 'We rarely differed on who we thought we could play the game—probably over only two or three players in all the time we worked together. And when that happened, Jack got his way. He was the boss and my job was to support him. I didn't want his job and he certainly didn't want mine.

Ultimately, I was always happy to bow to his way because he knew what it took to win.'

Gibson's departure from Souths at the end of 1979 remains one of the few low points in his coaching career. 'The year before I came to Souths, they won just three games,' he said. 'In my first season, we won nine with basically the same players apart from a few inexpensive recruits I brought to the place. Their most expensive player—winger Terry Fahey—was on just $17,000. Yet we won the pre-season, came second in the club championship and put 100,000 on the gate for the year. The next year we won nine games again—it was a similar season with some success—but our crowds were down around 15,000 on that high figure in '78. That was one reason they had for letting me go. I probably could have stayed if I'd dug my heels in, but they wanted to take some of my authority away. I walked out and was going to sue them but never got around to it. I had a year off and then went to Parramatta . . . so it all worked out for the best for me . . . but maybe not for Souths.'

Gibson is reluctant to compare the many fine teams he has coached, but does admit a partiality towards the Parramatta outfit of 1981 for the massive hurdles it cleared to win the club's first title. 'Everything changes; even Miss World may not win the title the following year,' he quipped. 'But the team that overcame the most adversity, without fear, was that 1981 Parramatta team. They were the mentally toughest team I coached. We had a very traumatic season that year and had to triumph over a lot of factors. They handled it very well. Referees like (Greg) Hartley and (John) Gocher didn't realise we were trying to do something for the game; they were just in it for themselves. We put the game first.' The Gibson–Hartley feud was among the most bitter the game has known. Respectively the number one coach and referee of their time, the pair developed an intense dislike for each other that often burst into back-page headlines. Gibson claimed that Hartley had something against his Parramatta team and whenever the referee handled an Eels match, drama inevitably followed. The Eels, ironically, won their maiden title in 1981 with Hartley in charge and the controversial whistle-blower switched to a career as a league commentator shortly afterwards. 'Hartley interfered with my life and we had some clashes,' Gibson recalled. 'But I won that battle. He doesn't disturb me now so I don't care about him. If I saw him walking down the street, I'd say "Hello, Greg." But it was a lot different back in '81 when he was causing us so much trouble. He kept threatening to sue me for what I said about him but he never did . . . there was more chance of me suing him for what he did to us.'

Gibson admits he had to make some radical changes when he took the helm at Parramatta in 1981 to whip the club into a premiership contender. 'I got rid of some people in the admin-istration at Parramatta and that was a big step for the club to take. There was one official there on a percentage of the takings and the first thing I had to do was present my team to him and let him cross out the names he didn't like. He learned quick smart he wasn't going to have any luck in that area. The club was very cooperative and we developed an excellent relation-ship.' Although he quit the Eels at the end of 1983 after winning the club a hat-trick of titles, Gibson exploded the myth that he always felt compelled to leave a club after three years. 'I'd heard people say that but it wasn't true,' he said. 'The only time I ever shifted from a club is when they thought my job was easy or someone else could do it as well or better. As soon as I felt that creep in, I walked away. That never happened at Parramatta, though. I was just burned out after three years there and wanted a year off. They were very good to me and it was a hard decision. I regretted very little of what happened at Parramatta and so did they.'

Gibson once described Peter Sterling as the most complete player he had coached, and Wayne Pearce as the one player he never coached who he would have most liked in his team. 'Sterling is number one,' he said. 'This is what Peter Sterling faces every Sunday ... the situation is that every coach whose team is facing up to Parramatta only talks about one player—Sterling. The coach sticks all his defence on one player—Sterling. The message is the same with all coaches: stop Sterling and you've got a chance of winning the football game. I've seen so many games that Parramatta won because they had Sterling ... and the other team didn't.' Of Pearce, Gibson said: 'He had talent but he was also a real professional. I think he could have slotted into any team and done the job.' Gibson actually attempted to sign Pearce during his time at Parramatta, but the then rookie lock declined the offer, preferring to remain at Balmain. 'But it was very flattering to be approached by a man of Gibson's stature,' Pearce said. 'He spoke honourably and wished me well in my future career even though I turned down the approach.'

Pearce was one of the few players to say no to Gibson, and former Roosters pin-up boy Ian Schubert was another. An unknown teenager from Wauchope on the NSW mid-north coast, Schubert trialled with the Roosters in 1974. Gibson immediately saw the youngster's potential and offered Schubert a contract. 'It was one of my hardest decisions, but I opted to turn Jack down and return home for a year and finish school,' Schubert said. 'I came down the following year and it all worked out great. I was still a kid when I arrived and Jack was very protective; he kept me under his wing. But as I became more accustomed to the Sydney lifestyle, I started to have a few late nights. I was boarding with a family that Jack knew and occasionally he'd come up to me and say, "Had a big night out, eh?" He didn't blast me . . . he just let me know in his subtle way that he was aware of what I was up to.' Schubert became a key member of the Roosters' premiership-winning team in his maiden season, inheriting the fullback spot when Russell Fairfax broke his leg mid-year. 'It was a dream come true winning the title in my first year and Jack was such a driving force behind us,' Schubert said. 'He didn't get overly excited after the grand final win; I don't think Jack is that type of guy. But I remember how pleased he was for the older guys in the team like Artie Beetson, Ron Coote, "Bunny" Reilly, John Brass and Bill Mullins. They were all near the end of their careers and I think he knew it was their last chance to win a premiership.'

When Gibson was appointed NSW State of Origin coach in 1989, long-suffering Blues fans rejoiced. After a decade of being dominated by Queensland, the Blues looked to have finally found their man. But those high hopes failed to produce the desired result as a strong Queensland side ravaged the Blues 3–0 to claim yet another series. It was far from plain sailing for the Blues, with Gibson introducing new faces like Laurie Daley and Brad Clyde who struggled with their first taste of big-time football. The critics were quick to jump onto Gibson's back, claiming he had a communication problem with his young side and was well past his best. But, as he has done so often in the past, Gibson enjoyed the last laugh. In his second season in charge, the Blues fought back to win the series 2–1, with the young players Gibson introduced the previous year—under much criticism—coming of age.

'In my first year, we played the absolute best team Queensland could muster,' Gibson reflected. 'If you picked Queensland's strongest ever side, 85 per cent would have come from that side—the likes of Wally Lewis, Gene Miles, Allan Langer, Mal Meninga and Kerrod Walters. They were a great side and had too much class and experience for us. But we beat them the following year in Melbourne to take the title. A major contribution I had in Melbourne was helping to pick the venue after the League's previous experience down there had been ordinary. I suggested to them the main thing they had to do was pick a ground that they could fill—and have all the tickets sold out at least a week before the game. They did that with Olympic Park. Once it became a full house and people couldn't get tickets, the interest was phenomenal. We went down three days before the game and I reckon I must have done 40 to 50 interviews for radio, television and the press. Sports writers came from all over, feature writers from as far as Adelaide and Perth.'

Gibson had to contend with a major drama during that second series in 1990 when a selector leaked to the media that the master coach wanted up-and-coming Glenn Lazarus in his starting line-up ahead of Steve Roach. The selectors had named Roach in the team, with Lazarus on the bench, and the leaking of Gibson's views caused a major and very public scandal in the lead-up to the all-important second game. Gibson once told a radio talk-back caller the biggest problem with Roach was his ears. When the caller asked why, Gibson replied: 'He never takes time out to listen.' Gibson admits that Roach was one of the few players with whom he failed to see eye to eye. 'There weren't many players over the years I could not work with—not many of them bugged me,' he said. 'You ask about Steve Roach, well I was Steve's coach for a very short time. Not long enough to do him any harm. And all but at the end of his career. I'm certainly not suggesting he was short on talent, but time had started to run out. He had started to fade.

He was overweight and looking for short cuts. He made a lot of noise when he played but not much was happening. When the story came out that I was in favour of starting with Lazarus instead of Roach it made Steve a little sour. It didn't help Steve and it just made my job as coach that much harder. But that's in the past. Looking at Steve now—on "The Footy Show", all decked out in pantyhose and lipstick—I can see his career has taken a new direction where I extend my sincere and very best wishes.'

Gibson is convinced his policy of giving youth a go, which has been a trait of his coaching throughout his career, was the turning point for the Blues after being humiliated by Queensland year after year. 'I brought in young blokes like Lazarus, Daley and Clyde and they didn't do that much the first year and we were well beaten,' he said. 'But in the next year, we won the series and those three guys were all prominent. They have all gone on to give great service to New South Wales for several years since.'

The Blues won that Melbourne match 12–6 to clinch the series and Gibson was expected to again take the reins the following year to help NSW attempt to hang onto the prized trophy. But Gibson describes the final stages of the Melbourne game—and the reason he stood down after leading the Blues to victory. 'With five minutes to go when the game was won I went and sat down behind a group of people—they were Melbourne locals and had no idea I was the coach,' he said. 'I just watched the win and the celebrations for the next ten minutes or so from there. Watching from there, it was a very emotional experience. You're going to win . . . you're going to lose, you can coach . . . you can't coach. I thought about it there and then and decided I wasn't interested in doing it again the next year. The pressure was getting to me.'

JACK GIBSON

Gibson recalls how much changed for him in just 12 months following his retirement from active coaching. 'The following year I sat in my study and watched the first State of Origin game on my own and never received a phone call leading up to the match. No-one wanted to know what I thought. That's how long your importance lasts, I came to realise. It wasn't sad or disappointing. I just thought, "Well, that's life and it's good."'

Gibson has spawned something of a coaching empire in his time in the game, with many of his former players and assistant coaches proving fine coaches in their own right. Coaches to emerge from the Gibson stable include Terry Fearnley, Arthur Beetson, John Peard, John Monie, George Piggins, Mark Murray, Ron Hilditch and Mick Cronin. And to a man, they have all agreed that the Gibson influence played a major role in their coaching philosophies. 'I like to think that for them knowing me it never did them any harm,' Gibson reflected. 'They might have gone further without knowing me . . . who knows. But at least I didn't stop them going ahead in the game.'

Easts—or Sydney City—has always been the club Big Jack called home. But when the Roosters dumped Gibson's coach elect in Mark Murray and replaced him with the controversial Phil Gould midway through 1994 for the 1995 season, Gibson came close to walking out on the club that had elected him a life member only months before. 'I'm a lifetime man . . . I've been married for 40 years so far and I spent 21 years at Eastern Suburbs,' he said. 'Yes, the board at Easts was entitled to cut Mark Murray and they did. At the time I disagreed with the appointment of Phil Gould. When he left Canterbury a few years back the club was a little shaky. When he left Penrith, the club was very shaky. Murray had been with Easts for two-and-a-half years and hadn't won that many games, though he improved the club in every other area. His highest paid player was captain Craig Salvatori on $100,000; on today's prices if you got that you could still call yourself an amateur. When Murray got the sack, elements within the club and a so-called player manager put out stories that top players would show no interest in playing for Easts because Murray was coach. That was rubbish. The club had no need to suggest that or believe it. Coach Phil Gould said on presentation evening at the end of 1995, "Easts now has the stature to attract the big-name players." In my 21 years at Easts the club always had the stature—Phil didn't bring it with him—maybe he meant, "Easts now has the bank to attract the big-name players." And he didn't bring that with him either. Being an old Easts fan I'm trying to accept the changes. Maybe if the Mark Murray departure was executed a little differently I could accept the appointment of Phil Gould with a bit more tolerance—who cares anyway? Captain Craig Salvatori out, captain Brad Fittler in. Fittler's pay packet for the 1996 season is more than double what Easts received for the 1995 season through the gate. I can't see how that is going to help the Roosters in the short or long run. Paying out to one player $50,000 to $60,000 a game on a 22 game season is a huge amount and remember that 75 per cent of games is close to what a first grade player will be available to play. While I disagree with some of Easts' decisions, I have maximum respect for 99 per cent of their people from leagues club to football administration. I feel confident the Sydney City Roosters have the talent to win a trophy in the near future and we can all live happily ever after.'

Coaching the national team was the one honour that Gibson never experienced during his lengthy career. His straight-forward 'call-a-spade-a-spade' style is unlikely to have sat well with administrators when they sat down to choose the Test coach, but Gibson insists he never lost any sleep over the position. 'Coaching Australia was a thing that never excited me because whenever there was a vacancy, I had a job,' he said. 'I couldn't see myself being able to combine that with club coaching. My concentration was solely on the club scene and I couldn't have coped—both jobs would have suffered. But having said that, I can understand how others have been able to successfully combine the two.'

Gibson admits he is worried at the course the modern game is taking and has been critical of both sides in the Super League war. 'I'm shattered by the way the game is heading,' he said. 'I don't want to discuss the Super League people . . . as for the ARL, it has spent a lot of money, but not one dollar of it is going back into the game. It's going into individual pockets. They've lost sight of the fact that the regular league fan is an ARL supporter. I wonder if they can survive with all the money they've wasted. If all the money they spent went back to the clubs and to improving facilities for the fans instead of into the players' pockets, it might all eventually be different. It's fair enough that they spent the money, but it's how they distributed it that irks me. They took exactly the same line as the Super League people. Words like "loyalty" are being bandied around disgracefully through all this—by both sides. You can't buy loyalty, dollars are not the currency for loyalty. Any fool will tell you that.'

A highly successful businessman, Jack Gibson is enjoying retirement. He spends his time with wife Judy in his palatial Cronulla waterfront home and combines a leisurely lifestyle of managing his affairs, fishing, playing golf and watching the odd game of footy. 'Sometimes I'd like the opportunity to say yes or no again,' he says of his lack of involvement in the game.

'A lot of people think the older you get, the sillier you get. From my point of view you get smarter as you go through life. But I'm contented on the sidelines just watching it all fall into place . . . or fall apart.'

Perhaps a joke told by John Peard best sums up how Jack Gibson is regarded in the rugby league community. A member of Gibson's crack Easts side of 1974–75, Peard was a fine coach in his own right and is now an entertaining after-dinner speaker and raconteur. 'A footballer died and went to heaven,' Peard tells. '"Who's the big bloke over there in glasses with the clipboard and overcoat smoking a cigarette?" the footballer asked. The reply came: "That's God—he thinks he's Jack Gibson."'

Bush Lore

CHRIS ANDERSON

CLUBS
Halifax (UK) 1984–88,
Canterbury 1990–

PREMIERSHIP RECORD
Games 141, won 89, lost 48, drew 4.
Winning percentage 63.1%.
Semi-finals
1993–95
Grand Finals (2)
1994–95
Premierships (1)
1995

OTHER COACHING ACHIEVEMENTS
Coached Halifax to Challenge Cup victory 1986–87,
First Division championship 1985–86.
Dally M Coach of the Year 1993.

Chris Anderson performed the coaching miracle of the 1990s by steering the Sydney Bulldogs to premiership glory in 1995. In the game's darkest season, no club was more torn apart by the Super League war than the Bulldogs. Mid-season, the club was down and out and looked certain to miss a finals berth. But Anderson somehow managed to hold the Bulldogs together through one crisis to the next. The club fell into the finals and then proceeded to outgun all comers—including raging hot favourites Manly—to win the last Winfield Cup. By winning the premiership, he became only the second coach to win major titles in both hemispheres—with Halifax in England and Canterbury in Australia—emulating the effort of John Monie (Wigan and Parramatta) several years earlier. A classy winger with his beloved Bulldogs in the 1970s and '80s, Anderson broke a series of records and is one of only a handful of wingers to score more than 100 tries in top-grade football.

Anderson was born in Condobolin but spent his high school years at Marist Brothers, Forbes. The move proved a key point in his football career, even at that early age. Anderson was spotted there as a skinny teenager more than 25 years ago by Bulldogs chief executive Peter Moore. Moore vividly recalls the events that led to Anderson joining the Bulldogs in what was to prove one of the most significant signings in the club's history. 'We'd heard good reports about this kid from Forbes so I decided to check him out,' Moore said. 'I was tied up one weekend but our star centre Johnny Greaves was out injured so I asked him if he would go bush to have a look at the kid. Being new to the job of club secretary, I wanted to do everything right and I spent a good half hour preparing this special form for Johnny to fill out. On it I listed a host of categories like "Speed", "Tackling skills", "Discipline",

"Handling ability". I gave it to Johnny before he left and told him to fill it in. Come Monday morning, I opened my office door and there was the form on the floor waiting for me. To my surprise, Johnny hadn't filled in any of the details I asked for. Instead, he wrote in big letters four words right across the form—"WILL PLAY FOR AUSTRALIA". The following week, I went down to have a look myself. I remember it was at a carnival at Yanco, where Marist Brothers were playing the home team from Yanco. It was 15 minutes a half and Forbes won easily, scoring six tries. Of the six, Chris scored four himself and set up the other two. That was good enough for me. I then understood why Johnny had so confidently predicted the kid would go all the way and I signed him virtually on the spot.'

Anderson became the first rugby league player to be awarded a football scholarship, a scheme piloted by Canterbury at the time. The scheme, which has since been copied by most clubs, has produced a host of star players for the Bulldogs including Anderson, Andrew Farrar, Paul Langmack and Michael Hagan. 'It was something that was unheard of in the game prior to that and when Canterbury offered me the scholarship, I grabbed it,' Anderson said. 'They paid for my last three years of school and that was a great help. I did fourth and fifth form at Forbes and then they brought me to Sydney for my final year of school in 1970 at Holy Cross, Ryde. I was playing in the lower grades as well as for the school and it gave me an excellent grounding for what was to come.' But Anderson admits he suffered from something of a culture shock as a kid from the bush in the big city. 'To say it took some getting used to is an understatement,' he said. 'I've always been a country boy and suddenly coming to town all alone was really throwing me in at the deep end. Everything in Sydney was bigger and faster and I just wasn't used to it. I didn't like it much at all and it took me a few years to settle down.' Anderson thought many times of packing it all in and returning to his roots, but was stopped by a greater force than homesickness—true love. 'I stayed with Peter Moore at his house and he had a huge family,' he said. 'Pretty soon after I arrived his eldest—and I've got to say prettiest—daughter Lynne started showing some interest in me and vice versa. She was the one thing that kept me in Sydney. She was, and still is, a very steadying influence on me.'

Moore doesn't remember inviting Anderson to stay at the family house for more than a couple of weeks, however. 'When Chris signed, his parents were worried about the boy coming to the city and being all alone,' Moore said. 'So I told them I'd put him up for the first couple of weeks until he found his feet. He ended up staying for five years and I'm still waiting for him to pay some board. But he tells me he took my daughter off my hands and that should make us even.'

Anderson broke into first grade in his second season with the club in 1971 and quickly established himself as one of the game's brightest young talents. A dashing fullback built low to the ground with the ability to glide past tacklers, Anderson had the happy knack of scoring tries from anywhere on the field. 'It was a bit hard coming into first grade at that time because Canterbury had a fairly old side that was just starting to break up,' he said. 'Guys like Ron Costello, Johnny Greaves, Neville Hornery had been around for a while but were at the stage where they were starting to give it away. They were nearing the end of their careers and a bunch of new young kids, myself included, all came in virtually at the same time to replace them. It was hard to break into the team at first but when I got there, I managed to hold my spot for more than 12 years.'

CHRIS ANDERSON

After early success at fullback and centre, Anderson shifted to the wing and it was there he became a permanent fixture in the Bulldogs' backline. He played on the flank in the 1974 grand final, where the Bulldogs were outclassed 19–4 by a star-studded Easts side. 'It was great getting through to the grand final, but we still had a fairly young side,' Anderson reflected. 'That was a hot Easts team and we did pretty well to hold them for a while. But they were too strong and ran over us with a couple of tries in the second half to finish comfortable winners. It was still a valuable experience for us, though. It was Canterbury's first grand final since 1967 and a lot of the young guys became better players for it.'

In 1975, Anderson enjoyed a dream year—in both hemispheres. 'It started in the summer when Johnny Peek and I went to England to play for Widnes,' he said. 'We had a ball over there and I think the experience in different conditions improved our football as well.' The soft English grounds obviously agreed with Anderson; he scored 18 tries in 19 games. And Widnes spent $2000—a huge sum in those times—to fly Anderson back for the Cup final in May. 'The game was played before a full house at Wembley and we beat Warrington; that's a favourite memory. When I returned, in the space of five weeks I played for City Firsts, New South Wales and Australia. I didn't win a Test spot until a few years later, but the green and gold jumper came in the World Series against New Zealand and I treasured it every bit as much. Then later that year, Lynne and I got married, so it was a fairly eventful time.'

Anderson remained one of league's most dynamic finishers throughout the 1970s. In 1978, he broke Bulldog favourite Eddie Burns' tryscoring record for Canterbury and toured with the Kangaroos, playing all five Tests in England and France. The following year, he helped the Bulldogs into the grand final, but Canterbury again finished the bridesmaid. Ted Glossop's young side made history by becoming the first team to reach the grand final from fifth spot, building momentum week by week in a stirring charge to the big game. 'It was a great effort just to get there, but we probably ran out of gas in doing it,' Anderson reflected. 'St George skipped away to a big lead and even though we came back in the second half, we were never really going to catch them. But the experience we gained again proved a big help. I think that really set us up for the following year.' In 1980, the Bulldogs finally broke through, winning their first premiership in 38 years. Anderson scored the opening try of the grand final against Easts to put the Bulldogs on the way to victory, albeit in controversial circumstances. Rookie centre Chris Mortimer burst away down the right flank and turned the pass inside to Anderson, with the ball appearing to float forward. But referee Greg Hartley, in line with the pass, waved 'play on' and Anderson scooted 30 metres to score between the posts. Steve Gearin's conversion, and an earlier penalty, gave the Bulldogs a 7–0 lead and they never looked back. The enduring memory of that grand final will always be Steve Gearin's sensational try from a towering Greg Brentnall kick which sealed the premiership for Ted Glossop's young side. For Anderson and skipper George Peponis, victory was particularly sweet. The pair were the only two survivors of the team beaten 19–4 by Easts in 1974 and had the satisfaction of seeing the Bulldogs turn it around with an almost identical scoreline, 18–4. 'That was our first premiership in a long time and we won it playing some very attractive football,' Anderson said. 'Ted Glossop was a coach who liked to play an open game and at that time, it worked well. We had the players who could make the ball work and we scored some great tries. In my time at Canterbury, that 1980 side would have to be close to the best. We enjoyed ourselves and played a very exciting style. The critics called us "The Entertainers" and we liked to live up to that tag at every opportunity.'

A severe bout of glandular fever in 1981 put a major dent in Anderson's career. But he still recovered to make the 1982 Kangaroo Invincibles, although he failed to play in any of the major Tests. In 1983, he took over as the Bulldogs' captain, replacing George Peponis, who retired late the previous season. The job fitted easily on Anderson's shoulders; he scored a club-record 19 tries, taking his tally in all grades for the Bulldogs past the century. But after an impressive campaign leading into the big end-of-season games Canterbury fell a hurdle short of the grand final, losing 18–4 to Parramatta in the final. The arrival of Warren Ryan in 1984 saw many changes at Canterbury, with Anderson falling out of favour for the latter stages of his career. Steve Mortimer took over the captaincy, Anderson suffered two broken arms and was eventually dropped to reserve grade by Ryan, with boom youngster Steve O'Brien taking his place. 'It got to the stage where I wasn't enjoying it all that much,' Anderson admits. 'I had a bad run with injury and so at the end of 1984 I decided to get out. I'd been at Canterbury for a long time and I think some of the hunger had probably gone. I thought my life in football was finished but I packed the family up for what was supposed to be 12 months in England just as a sort of holiday. I signed with Hull Kingston Rovers and decided I'd go over there and try playing at five-eighth. I didn't want to play on the wing, I felt I had nothing to prove there any more. I'd done all I needed to do there and wanted a new challenge. Noel Cleal pulled out of a deal there so Hull KR accepted me. It was really a good excuse to get out of Sydney for a while and have a look around Europe. After a couple of months Halifax came in with an offer so I joined up with them. I really enjoyed the final couple of years there. Playing five-eighth gave me a whole new perspective on the game. It's probably a funny time in your career to change positions, particularly such a radical switch from the wing into pivot, which is right in the middle of the action. I also played a bit in the centres and liked the increased workload in both spots.'

Anderson took over as captain-coach of Halifax and enjoyed considerable success in the role, his first as a coach. Boosting the team with Aussie imports Michael Hagan, Martin Bella and Paul Langmack, he steered Halifax to the championship in 1986. For a small league town not used to success, Halifax suddenly found itself the pride of British football, with Anderson becoming a local folk hero. 'The funny thing is I'd never considered coaching as a career. As I said I went over to England with the idea of having a year's holiday and then coming back home and getting a real job,' he said. 'But Halifax gave me the chance and I thought I'd give it a go. There was a lot of control at five-eighth and in a sense I found it easier. It's certainly easier than being non-playing coach up in the grandstand because there you're a long way from the action and find it harder to get your message across to the players during the game. But being out there in the heat of things, you get an immediate feel about what's going right or wrong. Old age eventually caught up with me and I retired in 1987–88 but then I still had another season as coach. The club had a fair bit of success in my time there and one highlight was winning the Challenge Cup at Wembley in 1987. Our fullback was another Aussie veteran in Graham Eadie, who I talked into playing again and he had a couple of fine seasons for us, winning man of the match in the Cup final.' Anderson steered Halifax to Wembley again the following year in his final season in Britain, but his side couldn't repeat its success against another rejuvenated outfit, Wigan. Graham Lowe's men won 38–10 in what was to prove the beginning of Wigan's domination of British football.

Anderson returned to Sydney—and the Bulldogs—in the 1989 season, coaching the President's Cup side. When the first grade side, premiers the previous season, finished well down the ladder, Phil Gould moved on to Penrith and Anderson stepped in. Despite intense criticism that his appointment came through the Bulldogs' well-known family connection, Anderson set about the task of restoring the bite in the Bulldogs. Peter Moore admits that appointing his son-in-law as coach was a move that could have backfired on the club had Anderson not succeeded. 'Looking back, I was probably putting pressure on both Chris and myself, but it wasn't a consideration at the time,' Moore said. 'The position was vacant and I thought Chris was the best man for the job. It has always been a hard situation because of our relationship, but I haven't tried to let it affect business decisions. My attitude has always been that if Chris is good enough, he'll do it. And I know he feels the same way.'

Anderson's first season saw the Bulldogs charge out of the blocks, leading the premiership for much of the first round of 1989. But a form slump and injuries to Terry Lamb, Andrew Farrar, Paul Dunn and Kevin Moore saw the Bulldogs win just one of nine games mid-season. They recovered to finish seventh, with Anderson learning some bitter lessons from his first Winfield Cup campaign. 'We might have bolted out of the blocks a bit early that year,' he said. 'But the injury run was the thing that hit us for six. We lost a lot of good players at the same time and it crippled us. We just didn't have the manpower to replace them.'

It was in Anderson's second season at the helm in 1991 that he really proved his worth as a coach. Over the summer, Warren Ryan and Gould, the club's two previous coaches, declared open season on the Bulldogs. Between them, Ryan's Wests and Gould's Penrith snared star players Paul Dunn, Paul Langmack, Andrew Farrar, David Gillespie and Joe Thomas while another key man, Jason Alchin, was signed by St George. The loss of the six players—all top-quality first graders—suggested the Bulldogs would finish well down the ladder. 'But it ended up being the best thing for us—a blessing in disguise,' Anderson explained. 'If we hadn't lost those blokes at that stage, they would have all grown old together and we would have had more problems down the track. And some of them didn't have the attitude I was looking for. We had to start from scratch and got a lot of kids from the bush and a few more from our local juniors. In the end, we finished better than the previous year despite all the big names going. Young guys like Ewan McGrady, Simon Gillies and Darren Smith came into their own and played some very good football with the extra responsibility. We finished equal fifth with Wests but they just pipped us in a midweek playoff. It was at that time I knew we couldn't afford to rest on our laurels. I told "Bullfrog" (Moore) that we had some fine young players but not much talent coming through. He's always been good at finding young players and it was then we picked up Dean Pay, Jason Smith, Craig Polla-Mounter and Brett Dallas. We won the President's Cup with these kids and they all went on to play significant roles for us in the next few years.'

To the outside observer, Anderson is far from the typical intense 1990s football coach. A laid-back character, Anderson is a man of few words who doesn't seem capable of delivering an inspirational Warren Ryan or Tim Sheens-type pre-game speech. But appearances can be deceiving according to long-serving Bulldog Simon Gillies. 'Chris does appear very low-key and I can understand people thinking that's the way he is,' Gillies said. 'But in reality, he is a very deep thinker and a man who takes a tremendous amount of time to arrive at a decision. He is extremely well organised in everything he does and that's why he seems so laid-back. Everything he does, he has spent a long time thinking about and so he is calm and collected when it comes to decision time. He's never worried before a game, again because his preparation has usually been so good. He knows if we've trained well, chances are we should play accordingly. But the flip side of that is that if we train badly, chances are we won't go so well. In the game itself, he's as intense as any coach. I'd hate to think how much chewing gum he goes through every Sunday and we've lost more than a couple of walkie-talkies every year because they've gone flying into the wall or the floor midway through a match.'

Gillies admits Anderson has been fortunate at Canterbury with the personnel he has had at his disposal. 'Having Terry Lamb and to a lesser extent Martin Bella there made his job on match day a lot easier,' Gillies said. 'They both liked to talk a lot before a game and that took some of the pressure off him in the dressing room. Chris used to tell us that in his day, Steve Mortimer used to rant and rave in the room and the players were happy with that, so he was pleased to let Baa Baa and Marty do the talking. Chris likes to play mind games and tries to have everyone on a similar wavelength for the 80 minutes that counts during a week. It's not an easy thing to do, but he has a way of doing it. He's not a real knockaround type, but he can be one of the boys when he wants to. At training, he sets the mood. If he's relaxed and happy with the way we're going, it's a fairly relaxed session. But if he's not happy, he lets us know it soon enough and the attitude changes.'

Gillies can remember few times that Anderson has blown his cool exterior. 'One was when the Super League thing blew up and our four blokes went back to the ARL,' he said. 'That really shattered him. But as far as games go, I can remember only twice when he's lost it. Once was in 1990 late in the season when Langmack and Dunn were set to quit for rival clubs. They were getting big money elsewhere and Chris thought we weren't performing because we had our minds on other things. He really gave it to us at halftime—by the second half we were certainly more focussed on what we were doing. The only other time was in '95 in the game against the Auckland Warriors. It was a must-win game a few weeks before the finals at home and we were just dreadful. They ran all over us in the first half and Chris knew that mentally, we weren't up to it. I think all the problems we'd been having with the Super League business came out that night. And not even a blast from Chris could save us. They still ended up beating us by 20 points.'

Critics of the Bulldogs and the Peter Moore dynasty are constantly having swipes at the 'family connection' at Belmore. Warren Ryan, in particular, is scathing of the influences that were at work in the club during his time as coach (see separate chapter). But for Moore and his extended family, the proof is on the scoreboard. Canterbury was the most successful club in league in the 1980s and are among the frontrunners in the '90s. 'The criticism has never worried me,' says Anderson, a man who isn't easy to rile. 'I think it has been a source of mirth for writers in the media and critics who have brought it up at my expense at times. I've never found it a problem. It's been hard for my kids at times, probably because of what they copped at school. But they love their football and I don't think it worries them too much. I've got confidence in my own ability and know I can do the job. There's no denying Canterbury is a close club but I see that as one of our strengths.'

If Anderson ever had cause for self-doubt, it would have been at the end of both the 1993 and 1994 seasons. The Bulldogs were the team to beat throughout '93, finishing minor premiers in front of a hot field and winning the club championship for the first time in 54 years. But the wheels fell off the Bulldog machine in the finals. Anderson's men lost 27–12 to St George in the major semi and then crashed 23–16 to Brisbane in the preliminary final. It was an even more heartbreaking story in '94. This time the Bulldogs again won the minor premiership and the club championship, and were determined to make up for their mistakes in the finals the previous season. An epic extra time 19–18 win over Canberra in the major semifinal had the fans convinced that this would indeed be the year of the Bulldog. But Canterbury again fell apart under pressure on the big day, crashing to an embarrassing 36–12 thrashing against Canberra's recharged Green Machine. For Anderson in particular, the dual failures cut deeply. 'They were hard times because we'd done so well right up until the finals in both years. But putting '94 into perspective, there are only two teams that are disappointed with finishing second every year. They're the team that comes second and the team that comes first. With that in mind, we did pretty well. In '93 we learned some valuable lessons and in '94, Canberra were too hot for us on the day. When they play like they did that day, and have a little luck go their way, there's not much you can do to hold them. We didn't have that much big match experience there in '93. I think Terry Lamb was the only player who went into the big games with any finals experience. It was a real learning curve in those two years for the players and 1995 showed they learned the lesson well. We did struggle recovering from that grand final hiding from Canberra, though, I've got to admit. I think it haunted more than a few of our players over the summer and early in '95. We weren't playing all that convincingly early in '95 and that was well before all the Super League rubbish. I think it was a case of still not getting over the grand final in our heads and the fact we played that badly in the most important game of the year.'

But the self-doubts that both Anderson and his team were feeling at the beginning of 1995 were forever erased by the end of September, when the club emerged in triumph from the most turbulent season the game has known. While the Super League war took its toll on every club, it literally tore the heart out of the Bulldogs. Moore was forced to resign his post on the New South Wales Rugby League board early in the year following his switch to the rebel camp in a fore-runner to the trouble ahead. But nothing could prepare the Bulldogs for the turmoil that unfolded one Monday afternoon in May. The Bulldogs had thought, until that day, they were a united camp in the battle for control of the game. While the code had been split down the middle, at least all the Bulldogs were heading in the same direction . . . or so they assumed until that dramatic afternoon. In quick succession, star players Jarrod McCracken, Jim Dymock, Dean Pay and Jason Smith all fronted Anderson, Moore and club president Barry Nelson in the club's offices in the Belmore grandstand. The four declared they had signed massive deals with the ARL and were going to take legal action to get out of their Super League contracts. Anderson admits it was one of the few times he can remember he lost his temper. He berated the four, publicly and privately, sacked McCracken from his team and took a long time to come to terms with the remaining three players. 'I was angry . . . I felt betrayed by them,' he said. 'We were all heading in the one direction and suddenly we weren't. It was a devastating thing to happen mid-season and really shot us down in flames for a while. Everyone was happy to go under the Super League banner at the time we signed. But when the ARL came in with truckloads more money, these guys changed their minds. They sold their loyalty and it was hard to forgive them.'

Simon Gillies reveals the extent to which the four players' about-face affected Anderson. 'It was a huge kick in the guts for the man,' Gillies said. 'It made him question the whole ideology of what he was doing at the club. Chris started to think, "Well, maybe I'm going about it all the wrong way." He brooded over it for a long time and we all knew the pain it was causing him. But at times like that, Chris is an intense guy and there is nothing we could do to help him get over it. Thankfully, in the end, it turned out all right and his ideals and morals came out on top. The club stood tall by the end of the season and Chris Anderson can take the thanks for that more than anyone.'

Moore believed Anderson's firm principles were the one thing that prevented the Bulldogs from selfdestructing in 1995 when the crisis erupted. 'Chris's true strength of character came out through it all,' Moore said. 'He was getting abusive letters and phone calls and was under great pressure from all sides. But he refused to once sacrifice his principles or lower his standards. If he'd done that, he would have lost the respect of all concerned. He dropped the four players who turned their backs on the club and made them earn their spots back. When Jarrod McCracken refused to play reserve grade, he got rid of him. The other three blokes proved themselves and when they did, Chris was only too happy to put them back in the team and that united everyone again.'

Terry Lamb, a loyal on-field general for Anderson, acknowledges the coach was in personal turmoil throughout 1995. 'He tried to keep a lid on it, but we knew he was hurting,' Lamb said. 'Chris was pretty close to most of those four guys, particularly Dean Pay, who he'd brought to the club from Dubbo. When Deano signed with the ARL without even telling Chris, it hurt. If he'd told him beforehand or asked his advice, it would have all been different. He took it hard for a while because he felt so close to the players.' Lamb describes Anderson as a 'man's man'. 'By that I mean he is very down to earth and on a similar wavelength to the players,' he said. 'It's important to him that the boys always get on well. He's happy to go drinking with his players and realises that football is like life—you have your good times and your bad times and you've got to learn to live with that. If a player's a bit thick, Chris will have a bit of a go at him. It's not spiteful or nasty, he just has a bit of fun and often the player concerned will laugh as much as anyone because he knows Chris still cares about him. I'm closer to Chris than the other two coaches I've had at Canterbury, Warren Ryan and Phil Gould. But that's partly because I'm older now and the captain of the team. Chris and I go out and play golf together and are always talking football and how to improve the team. Warren and Phil were good coaches but Chris is right up there with them. He knows how to get the best out of the players and have them in the right frame of mind to play good football.'

Anderson rates the turning point in the Bulldogs' troubled season of 1995 as the final round clash with the last-placed North Queensland Cowboys. The match was little more than a training run for the Bulldogs, who thrashed their rivals 66–4.

But Anderson and his players all felt a special feeling that day. 'It's hard to describe, but that was the afternoon we all knew we could do it,' Anderson said. 'Two special things happened that day—we returned to Belmore, our traditional home, and we farewelled Terry Lamb in his last home game (before his decision to play again in 1996). The emotion of the occasion seemed to bring out the best in us. We suddenly had our confidence high and the motivation of sending Terry out a winner in the finals—everything was in place for the big games.'

The Bulldogs began the finals with a dour 12–8 win over an in-form St George. In a controversial clash played in wet conditions, both sides slogged it out before the Bulldogs scraped home, thanks to a Dean Pay try that appeared to come with the aid of some obstruction. The following week, the Bulldogs built up momentum—and played some of their best football of the year to down Brisbane 24–10. The following week came the game all the Bulldogs had been waiting for—the clash with Canberra. It was payback time and the Bulldogs gained revenge for their grand final hiding 12 months earlier with the sweetest of victories. After clinging shakily to an 11–6 lead midway through the second half, the Bulldogs charged to an emphatic 25–6 win. Anderson isn't the type of man who holds a grudge, but admitted to the media after the game: 'We owed them that one.'

Despite their impressive run of victories, the Bulldogs were still tipped to be cannon fodder for the rampaging Manly machine in the grand final. Everything pointed to a Manly win leading into the game. The Sea Eagles had lost just two games all season—the Bulldogs had lost eight. Manly's attacking record was superior by more than 200 points and their defence better by more than 100 points. The Sea Eagles were at full strength while Canterbury had Brett Dallas out and an injury cloud over game-breaker Jason Smith. And worst of all, the Bulldogs had their preparation for the game thrown into utter chaos by the appearance of the 'gang of four'—McCracken, Pay, Smith and Dymock—in court testifying against the club in their bid to rejoin the ARL and break away from Super League.

'It wasn't what you would call the ideal preparation,' Anderson said with a wry grin. 'But we were fortunate in quite a few areas. The young blokes who came into the side—Robert Relf, Steve Price and Glen Hughes—all rose to the occasion during the finals. The court case kept our minds off the pressure of the game and may have also helped in a funny way. We were that busy trying to hold the place together that we never worried about the pressure. I thought if we could just get through the week intact, we'd be ready for anything. Terry Lamb really held us together through it all—on and off the field—and I doubt we could have done it without him.'

Come grand final day and the script for the game was quickly torn up. Anderson's Bulldogs bustled the classy Manly side from the outset, refusing to allow the Sea Eagles to dictate terms. Any luck on show did go the Bulldogs' way—the first of their three tries came from a forward pass and the second on the seventh tackle—but the better team still won on the day. The Bulldogs triumphed 17–4, holding Manly tryless for the first time all season.

At the end of it all, Anderson could finally afford to put his feet up and look back on the team's achievements. 'We took on a lot of things in 1995,' he said. 'But we met them head-on; we didn't let them just lie around and fester and I'm convinced even though it was hard at the time, it was the best approach. People wrote us off early and all things considered, you couldn't blame them. I just thought if we got to the finals, we could cause some trouble. We had hassles during the year . . .

plenty of them. But everyone knew, even in the worst games, that the effort was still there. Our preparation was ordinary before several games because of the drama, but once they got on the field the players gave their all. Even in a couple of games we lost that we should have won, it wasn't a case of playing badly. It was more the opposition going well and having the ball bounce their way. The most important thing is, they never gave up. When they got to the semis, they began to click. Our senior players like Lamb, Gillies, Dymock, Britt, Pay, Halligan and Polla-Mounter led the way. The young guys—Timu, Hughes, Price and Dallas—responded and they all rose to the occasion. It was very satisfying all round and something we can look back on with pride.'

The last word on Anderson goes to Terry Lamb, the player who has enjoyed so much success under his coaching. 'The man eats, drinks and sleeps Canterbury. He played in the place for over a decade and now is set for a long stay as coach. He believes in the club and what it stands for and it has rubbed off on a lot of players as well.'

The Old Fox

HARRY BATH

CLUBS
Balmain 1961–66,
Newtown 1969–72,
St George 1977–81

PREMIERSHIP RECORD
Games 323, won 169, lost 142, drew 12.
Winning percentage 52.3%.
Semi-finals
1961, 1963–64, 1966, 1977, 1979–80
Grand Finals (4)
1964, 1966, 1977, 1979
Premierships (2)
1977, 1979

OTHER COACHING ACHIEVEMENTS
Coached Australia 1962 and 1968–72. Won World Cup 1968, 1970.
Coached Australia in 3 Tests 1969–71, won 1, lost 2.
12 World Cup matches, won 8, lost 3, drew 1.
6 tour matches, won 4, lost 2.
Coach of the Year 1977.

H arry Bath—The Old Fox—is regarded by many old-timers as the finest coach of forwards Australia has produced. A former star forward himself, Bath learned the trade on the tough battlefields in the north of England. Arguably the greatest player never to represent Australia, Bath brought his ball skills back to Australia for the final years of his career and helped revolutionise the game. After he had hung up his boots, Bath carved out an impressive career at Balmain, Newtown and St George and also coached Australia with great success.

Bath's feat in taking a young St George side—dubbed 'Bath's Babes' by the critics—to the title in 1977 remains one of the best coaching feats of league's modern era. A witty character from the old school, chain smoking Bath, with his trademark huge cauliflower ears, was a familiar face on the sidelines throughout the 1960s and '70s.

Bath grew up in Brisbane in the 1930s, when life was much simpler and choices far less diverse. 'In the summer it was swimming and swimming and in the winter it was football and football,' Bath explained. 'We didn't know anything else or want anything else. That was the way it was and we were happy. We couldn't afford to go to the movies and didn't have surfboards or anything like that. They were tough days and football was the only way to success. I started playing at around six years old as a halfback—they reckoned I wasn't big enough for the forwards,' said the man who went on to become one of the game's most accomplished second-rowers. 'I made up for the lack of weight in those early years with good old-fashioned ticker and after a year or two, I moved into the forwards. At 15, I was playing C grade for Brisbane Souths. I was still there two years later but one day during the war years I went to see the first grade side play. I was sitting quietly in the grandstand when one of the committeemen came up and asked me if I'd play. I couldn't believe it, I was playing first grade and what was even better, we beat Valleys in my debut game. It was a tough baptism and I couldn't get out of bed for three days afterwards. But I didn't care; I cherished every bump and bruise. From that day until I retired in 1959, I was never dropped from first grade. I was lucky really. Football was everything in those days. I worked in a machine shop but straight after closing time, we'd go to training. Then we'd spend hours making the doubles cards for the weekend game and doing other odd jobs. It's very different from how the players are treated nowadays. I thought we were big time because they let us take our jumpers home. I washed mine half a dozen times to make sure it was REALLY clean. In 1945 I made my debut for Queensland as a 20-year-old and I remember we copped a dreadful hiding on the SCG. But I must have done something right because a few Sydney clubs approached me there and then. But I couldn't make up my mind and went home to Brisbane. Balmain persuaded me to tour North Queensland with them over the summer and it was a smart move on their behalf. I got to like the players and signed for the next year, getting 150 quid for the season. Some of the smart arses up north reckoned I wouldn't last five minutes in Sydney so I was pleased to go down and be able to prove them wrong.' Bath helped the Tigers to the premiership in his initial season in 1946 and was well on the way to an Australian jumper the following year when a knee injury, suffered while playing for NSW against Great Britain, brought a sudden end to his season. Balmain won the premiership in Bath's absence and it was while he was recovering that a call came that would change his life. 'A representative of English club Barrow got onto me and offered me a heap of money to go over there.

England was the place to play in those days and plenty of other young Aussies went over there to make their mark. At that time you could pick two or three British sides that would whip the Aussies—now of course it's the other way around. Their players were fitter and stronger than ours for starters. They would work in the mines and if you met them in a twilight game they'd just about kill you after being in the pits all day. They were tough men. Now the machines do all the work for them and the players are professionals so it has all changed. Anyway, some mates in high places told me the ARL was about to bring in a rule banning Aussie players going to England so I acted quickly. I signed and left for England the very day the ban officially came into force.' Playing in a foreign land with many team-mates jealous of Bath's huge sign-on fee, it wasn't long before homesickness set in. He wrote home to a young girl he'd met while working in a Balmain electrical store. The letter so moved the girl she took a six-week boat trip to England and it was there that Harry and Gwen Bath were married.

Barrow failed to live up to some promises it made to the newlywed Baths and Harry asked for a transfer after just one season. Warrington snapped up the burly back-rower and Bath went on to play more than 500 games for the club. He led the club to two Challenge Cup wins, including the 1954 defeat of Halifax before a world record crowd of 102,569 at Odsal Stadium. 'You can't forget a day like that,' Bath said. 'I reckon every bus in Britain must have been there. As well as the 102,000, there were another 20,000 banging on the doors trying to get in.'

It was at Warrington that Bath became team-mates with the player he regards as the most exciting he has seen in 50 years of football—and he was another Aussie. 'Brian Bevan was just a freak,' he said. 'With that bald head and toothless gums, he didn't look like a footballer, but he could score a try out of nothing. They call players tryscoring machines today if they score 15 tries a year—if Bevan bagged twice that many, he'd consider he'd had a lean year.'

After giving over a decade of service to Warrington, Bath finally retired when his knee injury continued to hamper him. He returned to Australia and quickly re-established himself in the other trade he knew best—the pub game. 'But it wasn't long before St George were on the phone and asking me to play one more season,' he said. 'Every other club thought I was over the hill and I wasn't sure they were wrong; my knee was still a worry. I told Gwen I'd give it a go for a few weeks but quit if things didn't work out.' With his English ball skills, Bath was like a breath of fresh air in the bash and barge Australian game. His deft skills, honed from the English ball masters over the previous decade, stamped Bath in a class of his own. He fitted straight into the St George machine and became a key attacking weapon in the Dragons' armour. Bath ended up staying at Saints for three seasons, picking up premierships each year in the midst of the Dragons' amazing 11-year run. 'That team had the ideal mix of youth and experience and a special bond,' he said. 'It was a feeling you don't get today—all for one and one for all—that kind of thing. We were proud of ourselves and of the way we played and I don't think you'll ever see the like of that team again.' Bath finally retired after the 1959 grand final, his career finishing on a sour note. He was sent off in the grand final after a fiery dust-up with Manly knuckleman Rex Mossop. 'We were real rivals in those days, Rex and I, even though we're mates now,' Bath said. 'We got stuck into each other from the start and the ref finally gave us our marching orders. I was retiring anyway, but I went down to the judiciary and they gave me a week's suspension, so I suppose I got the last laugh.'

Keen to use his obvious knowledge of the game, Saints asked Bath to stay with the club and appointed him reserve grade coach in 1960. 'The following year I was offered the Balmain first grade job and jumped at it. It was a bit strange at first, coaching a lot of the guys I'd played with and against, but it didn't take long to get myself on the right track. I'd been around for a long time as a player and knew a lot about the game, so I was confident I'd make it as a coach. I used to tell them to draw the enemy, pinch the wallet from his pocket and leave him standing—without the ball. They were only kids at Balmain; it's not like it is today where clubs buy players from all around the world. I just had a bunch of local lads from Glebe and Balmain. Keith Barnes was fullback and he was a good player and we'd bought Peter Provan over from St George, but that was it as far as experience goes; the rest were barely pups. We won our first game and then lost six in a row. We had some early communication problems. My ideas were very new at the time and strange to the players who took time to adjust. But once I got more used to them and they began to understand me, we started to click. They started to play some good football and got into the finals. We beat Manly in the semis but then went down to Wests the following week in the final 7–5. It would have been good to get into a grand final then, particularly against Saints. But I was satisfied with the progress made in that year and it was a real good beginning for a successful era for Balmain.' The Tigers were competitive throughout Bath's coaching in the '60s and reached the grand final in 1964 against the mighty St George machine. Balmain finished third after the preliminary rounds, but won through to the grand final after impressive wins against Norths and

Parramatta in the semis. But on grand final day the Tigers, as had been the case with the eight teams before and two after them, were powerless to stop the Saints. The young Tigers managed to give Saints an almighty scare, however. Balmain led 4–2 at halftime, courtesy of two Barnes goals. It was the first time the mighty Saints had trailed at the break in the grand final since their run started in 1956, with Bath's tactics of unsettling Saints up front clearly having an effect. It took a brilliant try to grand final specialist Johnny King—created by the dynamic duo of Graeme Langlands and Billy Smith—to put Saints in front. King's touchdown midway through the second half was the only try of the game as the Saints limped to a hard-fought 11–6 win. 'It wasn't easy against Saints; they had so much experience and were so well drilled,' Bath said. 'I knew only too well because I'd been playing with these guys not many years earlier. I could tell my players exactly how they would play the game. It still didn't do any good; they were so good at what they did we couldn't stop them. Under the unlimited tackle rule, they just dominated the game and beat you into submission.'

The Tigers fought their way into the grand final again in 1966—the final year of Saints' remarkable 11 season domination of the code. Balmain was the team to beat for much of the season and were premiership leaders at the halfway mark. But the Tigers staggered badly in the lead-up to the finals, at one stage losing six games out of seven. Balmain still finished in second spot and lost the major semi to Saints 10–2 despite beating the Dragons both times the teams had met earlier in the year. The Tigers earned another crack at Saints a fortnight later in the grand final after accounting for Manly 8–5 in the final. But Bath knew he had problems leading into the big game. 'We had a couple of key players carrying injuries but decided to play them anyway, which was a gamble as there were no replacements in those days,' he said. 'We also weren't in the best form coming into the finals after losing six of those last seven games. We were in the grand final, but confidence was down. They were kids and lost their way at times and I had to keep coming up with ideas to motivate them. Then, to make things worse, my star winger Kevin Yow Yeh went missing in grand final week. I didn't even know where he was or whether he'd play in the game. He ended up flying back into Sydney on the last plane on the Friday night, the night before the game. I still never knew where he'd been. He'd gone bush somewhere mid-week and didn't even tell anyone he was going . . . things were very different in those days and you had to try to keep a tight rein on the players or they would play up on you or just up and leave. Yow Yeh ended up playing in the game but he's dead now, poor bugger.' The Tigers had a formidable side that year with Barnes, although nearing the end of his career, still an inspirational captain and magical goalkicker. The young Tigers pack included goers like Peter Provan, Gary Leo, Dennis Tutty and a raw recruit from Queensland named Arthur Beetson. But there was still no holding Saints, who claimed the final title of their record-breaking era with a 23–4 win.

Bath had six years at Balmain before deciding to return to his other trade, the pub game. 'I bought the White Horse Inn at Parramatta at about that time and decided to concentrate on that,' he said. 'I'd taken Balmain as far as I could take them and knew it was futile going any longer. I was actually still under contract but asked them to let me go; we just weren't going anywhere and it became a frustrating exercise all round. Every time we had a player come off contract, the likes of Manly would buy him straight-away. Even back in the '60s, that was a problem. We were nothing in their eyes. I'd use all my experience to make these kids into good players and then they were gone.'

Bath rejects the popular theory in the game that he was purely a forward's coach. 'Being an old forward, forward play was probably what I knew best,' he said. 'But I could also handle the backs. Look at the 1968 World Cup—our backs had a field day there. And at St George years later, guys like Teddy Goodwin and John Chapman scored plenty of tries as well.' But former Tigers winger Paul Cross, one of the most polished finishers in the '60s who bagged 50 tries for the club, remembers his time under Bath differently. 'Harry was definitely a forwards man and at that time, forwards really did win matches,' Cross said. 'Scrummaging was also important then and he'd work on it. Harry would spend hours with the forwards and the backs, well, we were left to our own devices. It was only in the last stages of a session that we would train as a team. But Harry was fortunate to have an excellent captain in Keith Barnes and he would often supervise the backs at training, so it's not as if we missed out on anything.' Cross enjoyed his time under Bath although he admits some players gave 'The Old Fox' a hard time . . . and none more than Yow Yeh. 'He used to drive Harry mad,' Cross said. 'Kevin was a good player but he just refused to train on Tuesday night. We reckoned he was the bloke who invented shin soreness. Every Tuesday, without fail, his legs would hurt and try as Harry might, he couldn't get him onto the training paddock. Harry was very popular and the thing I'll always remember about the man is that he was a winner. He thought like a winner, walked and talked like a winner and I think that rubbed off on the players he coached.'

After Bath left Balmain, the league hierarchy knew it had a

winner in their midst and didn't want to lose him. Bill Buckley, then boss of the league, approached the former star second-rower in a most unusual way in 1968 to ask him to coach the Australian World Cup team. 'I was driving a taxi in those days and one time I picked Bill up as a fare. He asked me whether I'd be interested in coaching Australia again and we took it from there.' But Bath had to think twice about taking on the job after a brief yet disastrous experience as coach of the Aussies during the 1962 home Test series against Great Britain. Australia lost the series by two Tests to one, but it was the roguish behaviour of the Australian players that upset Bath. 'I had to think long and hard about coaching Australia again because I'd had enough of the players in that bloody 1962 series,' he said. 'That was enough to drive anybody mad. They were a bunch of kids and lairs, not professional footballers like you have today. Looking back, I handled them wrongly, too. I treated them like men and expected them to behave accordingly. But they took advantage of the leeway I gave them and played up something awful, wrecking hotels, throwing food and so on. They'd had a lot of trouble with the Aussie players again on the 1967 Kangaroo tour of Britain when they'd wrecked a few hotels and the like. The manager of that tour, old Jack Drewes, was virtually killed by the bastards and their antics. I really felt sorry for him. So I knew it was going to be no picnic trying to control them. But Bill and I sat down and he insisted that things would change and that I'd have the power to discipline them.' Bath and team manager Clancy Kingston found a simple method of keeping the players in check during the 1968 World Cup campaign on home soil. 'Every time anyone did anything, Clancy and I would just take money out of their pocket to pay for it. It took some time, but after a while they got the message. I don't know how many times we'd have to hand the owner of a pub or hotel a fistful of money and say to him, "Here's the money to fix it, mate, now just forget about it." But I've got to say, the players were a little bit better by then. Most of the players in that '68 squad had been around for a while and had settled down a bit. And I was older and wiser and knew how to handle them so it was a less incident-packed series, although they still kept us on our toes.'

Bath also found more joy on the field in 1968. The Australian team was an all-star line-up and included such outstanding players as Johnny Raper (captain), Graeme Langlands, Ron Coote, Arthur Beetson, Bob Fulton and Johnny King. The home team dominated the Cup, beating all comers before taking on France in the final at the SCG before a crowd of more than 54,000. The Aussies won 20–2, with South Sydney fullback Eric Simms contributing four goals as he scored a record 50 points during the campaign. 'We had a good side, no doubt about it,' Bath said. 'Raper was getting on but was still a force to be reckoned with. And Beetson, Fulton, Dick Thornett and a host of other good players were starting to emerge. We won the Cup easily and I was confident they would dominate the international scene for some time.'

Following the World Cup success, Newtown persuaded Bath to make a return to the club scene in 1969. 'They gave me a call so I thought I'd try my luck there, even though I knew it wasn't going to be easy,' he said. 'Newtown was bankrupt— the club didn't have a zack to its name and so the players were basically a bunch of guys that no-one else wanted. They were a mixture of kids and rejects from other clubs. But we did okay, we held our own. The best result I achieved there was in my final year—in 1972—when we came fifth. That was the year before they introduced the five team semi-finals so I guess you could call us a little bit unlucky. The following year Jack

Gibson came in—I think he could see the potential there as some good kids were coming through the ranks—players like Neil Pringle and Lionel Williamson. They reached the semis in '73 and went as far as the preliminary final. But while Jack got all the credit, a lot of the hard work was done by me in the couple of years before that. I worked harder with the Jets than I did with any team in my life. Hours and hours looking for players and working on the guys we had—it was virtually a fulltime job, which was unheard of in coaching back then.'

Bath coached Australia for the 1970 and '72 World Cup campaigns but the memories of those two tours are not happy ones for him. Australia retained the trophy in 1970 before losing in controversial circumstances in 1972, but it was the clashes with the two team managers that soured Bath's experiences. 'I don't know what it is with officials,' he complained. 'They give you things, you have some success, then they try to take them away from you. Ken Arthurson managed the 1970 team—he wanted to pick the team and just about wanted to coach it as well. And do everything else. I just sat back and watched while he stuffed the team up. We won our first match against New Zealand easily but then lost to both Great Britain and France. We just scraped into the final on points for and against and that's when I took over again. We played the Poms and it was a tough game with a lot of brawling. Our blokes stood up to everything the Poms dished out, though, and we won 12–7 in Leeds. They still talk about that game—that's how hard it was. In '72, we drew the final against the Poms 10–all, but they were awarded the Cup on countback. But that was the game when Graeme Langlands scored that magic try from a kick ahead by Dennis Ward, only to be recalled by the French ref for offside. That try would have got us the money and replays showed it should have been allowed. Anyway, I had problems with officialdom again; Clancy Kingston, the manager, had a host of arguments with Langlands throughout the tour and I was stuck in the middle of it all. They were at each other's throats all tour and disturbing everything—it had an effect on the whole team. You've got no idea how bloody hard it is, being coach of a team in France where you don't speak the language, without all this going on as well. You're trying to just coach the team while the captain and the manager are at war. In the end, I had to get the two of them into a room, shut the door and sort it out. One would say one thing, the other would say something totally different. It was a mess and a situation I didn't enjoy. The team harmony was shot to pieces, so I threw it in—I never coached Australia again.'

But Bath's greatest coaching triumph was yet to come—at the famous St George club. 'I went back to the pub business for a while and had the Cauliflower Hotel down at Waterloo and was happy doing that,' he said. 'I had a couple of years back in Brisbane, coaching my old club Souths, before coming back to Sydney again. One day Alan Clarkson, a league journalist who I'd known for some years, rang and asked me if I'd be interested in getting back into coaching again. By that stage, football wasn't my top priority any more and I didn't fancy all the hard work of getting a team of battlers again. I said to Clarko "Probably not", but asked which club just out of curiosity. When he told me it was St George and (secretary) Frank Facer told him to ring and see if I was interested, my attitude changed. I'd enjoyed my time at Saints as a player and fancied their playing strength. They had a good young side of goers with the potential to improve. In '75 they'd copped a mother of a hiding from Easts in the grand final but this was going to be two years later. Langlands was stepping down as coach and there was a fair side there. I went to see Facer but he was a hard man when it came to negotiating. He told me the amount Langlands was on—it was peanuts really—and I told him it wouldn't have been worth my while for that much. I still had the pub and it was doing all right; coaching would have meant spending a lot of time away from the business. I told Frank I'd think about it but as soon as I walked out the door, I'd made up my mind not to do it. A couple of weeks later, Saints official Laurie Doust called and asked why I hadn't got back to them. I told them Facer's offer wasn't worth considering. So Laurie sweetened the pot a little and I signed what was a fair incentive contract. But I wish when I was talking to them I knew I was going to win the comp in my first year there—I would have charged them a lot more than I did.' Bath's Babes were given little chance of taking out the premiership when the 1977 season kicked off. 'But that didn't worry me. I quite liked coaching kids who would listen and learn,' Bath said. 'Everyone talks of that Saints side as "Bath's Babes" but really you could have applied that title to every team I coached. First at Balmain, then at Newtown and finally at Saints, I mainly had kids to work with, but I wasn't complaining. Early that year, Frank Facer asked me to go on a drive with him down to Wollongong and we looked at a young front-rower called Craig Young. Frank asked me what I thought and I replied, "I'm not sure if the bastard can play football, but he looks the part." He was still a teenager but he had a huge neck and hulky shoulders even at that age. So we signed him up and brought him to town. Craig, Jon Jansen and Robert Stone all had potential then but were like wild bulls. I had to work on them and teach them the finer points of the game.' With Graeme Langlands retiring and Billy Smith dropped to reserve grade mid-season, the last link with St George's golden era of 1956–66 was severed that season. Yet

HARRY BATH

Bath's young side brought the Dragons their first title since the golden 11-year run, albeit in dramatic circumstances in 1977. Beaten grand finalists the previous year, Parramatta were widely tipped as the side to beat for much of that winter. Boosted by the signing of pointscoring wizard Mick Cronin from the country and a tougher team following their grand final loss to Manly 12 months earlier, the Eels looked to have too many big guns for Saints on grand final day. But Bath, whose match plans always revolved around making maximum use of his forwards, had willing workers up front in rookies Young, Jansen and Stone and experienced campaigners Rod Reddy, Bruce Starkey and skipper Steve Edge. The grand final was a 9–all draw—the first in the game's history—with the teams forced to slug it out again for the title of premiers seven days later. Saints romped home 22–0 in the replay in a spiteful affair in which their tactics have often been questioned. Saints' enforcer Rod Reddy received caution after caution as he battered the Parramatta pack. Bath just gives a wry smile when asked about Saints' tactics that day, but Reddy was more enlightening. 'Harry got us to intimidate the opposition and it worked perfectly in the grand final,' Reddy said. 'He'd pin-point one player in their side and we'd all rile him up. One bloke would pick on him, then another and then another. So in effect it was the whole pack against the one opposition player and it worked very well. We knew we'd win the replay after the first draw—we were younger and hungrier than them. I remember all week in the lead-up to the replay we were so relaxed and in control. We didn't even train that much. We were as fit as we had to be and knew what to do. We'd sit in the middle of Kogarah and listen to Harry's words of wisdom. We stretched the rules to the limit in the replay, but we overwhelmed them and finished convincing winners.'

When told of Reddy's comments, the old fox in Bath quickly came out. He immediately shifted the blame for the roughhouse tactics squarely back on the lanky second-rower. 'Pig's arse it was my idea,' Bath said with a hearty laugh. 'That was all Rocket's doing—he never needed any encouragement in that area. He just didn't like Ray Price and every time he saw him, he wanted to belt the crap out of him. There were a lot of incidents in that game but Parramatta weren't angels either. A couple of our blokes were king-hit. Leading up to the replay, some comments of the Parramatta players got back to our blokes. They were all cocksure and saying how they were going to run over the top of us and it was the worst thing they could have said. My blokes were breathing fire after that and couldn't wait to get out there and make them eat their words.'

The one thing that upsets Bath when he recalls Saints' memorable run to premiership glory in 1977 was that the players could have won themselves a fortune—and didn't. 'We won our last 12 games to take the title but I remember at the start of the run telling the blokes they could win the whole thing. Well, they nearly fell over. I even rang a bookie to see what odds he'd give us and he quoted us at 12–1, which I thought was pretty fair. I tried to get them to back themselves but the silly buggers wouldn't do it. They didn't believe they could win it.'

Steve Edge, captain of Saints' '77 side and a key man in the '79 triumph, didn't blink when asked what he remembered most about Bath. 'It was those ears,' Edge grinned. 'They were just massive. The funniest thing I ever saw in my life was after one of those grand final wins—I think it was in 1977—Harry put on one of those huge 10-gallon hats as we celebrated. And his ears STILL stuck out! I'll never forget the first time we met Harry at the start of 1977, he got us all together for a team meeting and most of us had never seen him before. He spoke to us for an hour or more about coaching, life, what he expected of us and the like. It was a serious talk and finally, when he finished, he asked if there were any questions or comments. Brian Wood, a young second-rower who was with us at the time, got up and said, "All right, coach, the joke's over . . . you can take off the fake ears now." The whole place broke up—it was a classic moment.'

Edge described Bath as a coach who gave his players free rein to express their attacking instincts. 'It wasn't often that he would haul a bloke over the coals for doing something wrong,' Edge said. 'So long as you were trying something that had a chance of coming off, that was good enough for him. Harry wasn't super technical and liked to play an open game. The bloke loved to talk and could really inspire a team before a big game. He did a great job with us in 1977 and really moulded a side that had no right to win the premiership into champions. I think Harry really enjoyed the "Bath's Babes" image of us, even though it was largely created by the media. He liked being the underdog and played that up to the hilt.'

Bath finally quit Saints at the end of 1981 after an indifferent season. 'I announced at the start of the year I was quitting and looking back, that may have been a mistake,' he said. 'I was hoping it would bring out the best in the players, but some of them let me down.' Bath's half-century association with the game came to a sad, anti-climactic end before a paltry crowd at Kogarah on a chilly August afternoon in 1981. The Dragons were humiliated 20–11 by a team of Newtown reserve graders, with Jets coach Warren Ryan resting all his star players for the upcoming semi-finals. When asked by reporters after the match for his choice of man of the match, the old Bath humour still emerged. 'It should have been me,' Bath quipped 'I did it toughest.'

Like many league men of his generation, Bath has little time for the modern game. 'I'd had enough by 1981 and was glad to get out,' he said. 'I watch it on television occasionally now and have missed it on the odd occasion over the years but I've been away from it so long, it doesn't concern me any more. To be honest, the game doesn't appeal to me the way it's played now. There's no skill in it—the players are like robots. It's like American football now. The players are programmed to run so many times, then kick the ball downfield and it all starts again. The ball does move a lot, but mainly because they're kicking it from one end to the other. I haven't seen a good game for some time, although the 1995 grand final wasn't bad. Arthur Clues, another Aussie who played in England and still lives over there, wrote to me a while ago and said exactly the same thing about the way the game is going. If I tried getting back into it now they'd all say, "Look at that silly bugger, what does he know?"'

Bath, now owner-manager of the Horse and Jockey Motel in Warwick just over the Queensland border, has been suffering from ill heath in recent years. 'I've had two strokes—at one stage they put me on life support and thought I was going to die. But I've still got some fight in me—I pulled through.' Although he has now lost contact with many of his team-mates and the players he coached, Bath remains an authentic league legend and one of the best loved characters of the sport's post-war era.

Bookie Bob's Winning Ways

BOB BAX

CLUBS
Goondiwindi 1949 (captain-coach),
Rockhampton Fitzroys 1952 (captain-coach),
Mitchell 1953–54 (captain-coach),
Brothers Brisbane 1955–59,
Norths Brisbane 1960–70, 1977–78

BRISBANE PREMIERSHIP RECORD
Games 401, won 279, lost 112, drew 10.
Winning percentage 69.6%.
Semi-finals
1955–70, 1977
Grand finals (14)
1955–64, 1966–67, 1969–70
Premierships (9)
1956, 1958, 1960–64, 1966, 1969

OTHER COACHING ACHIEVEMENTS
Won premierships as captain-coach with Goondiwindi
and Rockhampton Fitzroys.
Coached Queensland 1971–72. 7 matches, 0 wins.

Bob Bax is the coach with the Midas touch. His results make him the most successful coach Queensland rugby league has ever known. North of the border, Bax is Jack Gibson, Tim Sheens and Warren Ryan all rolled into one. In 18 years of first grade coaching in the Brisbane competition, Bax steered his teams to the grand final 14 times, winning nine premierships. The Bax magic began with Brothers in the mid 1950s. He led the club to the grand final in his maiden season as a coach in 1955, leaving the field early in the reserve grade grand final to address his players for the big game. Brothers lost that premiership decider, but it was to prove one of the few big match defeats in Bax's long career. After five successful years at Brothers, he switched to Norths, leading the Devils to the most successful era the club has known. Norths won the title in each of Bax's first five years, missed out for a year in 1965 and then claimed another two premierships in 1966 and 1969. A cheeky character who now earns a living at the racetrack, Bax retains close ties with the game he loves. Now in his seventies, he is still on several committees at Norths and is an adviser and close confidant to Brisbane Broncos coach Wayne Bennett.

Bax was born in 1925 at Mannum, a small town on the Murray River in South Australia. 'My mother was my father's second wife; his first wife had died,' he explained. 'But I think my father wanted to get away from family and the like, so in 1929 we all went overland and finished at a place called Dajarra, near Mount Isa. And it really is the end of the world. On the 50th Mt Isa jubilee celebration a few years back, I decided to go back to Dajarra to find out just why my father brought my mother there. I was none the wiser, though. It merely confirmed my view that the place is the arsehole of the earth. The white population when I returned was 12, and I ended up having to shout beer for the lot of them. I started playing footy at halfback in Mount Isa when I was just a lad at the local convent school. There wasn't a whole lot else to do, frankly. The coach was a bloke named Frank Hogg, who'd played in the 1929 Brisbane grand final for Brothers. He was a great coach; we beat all the state schools and I immediately developed a love of the game. That kept on right through school and when I finished, I began an apprenticeship as an electrician in Mount Isa. I was there for five years—from 1941 to 1946. A mate of mine, Pat McMahon, who ended up playing for Australia a couple of years later, was also from Mount Isa. He moved to Toowoomba and asked me to go along with him. I went down and had one game but I didn't like it and was all set to return home. But then I ran into Jack Reardon, who'd played for Australia in the '30s. I knew him a bit and he invited me to go and watch a trial match involving his club, Brisbane Brothers, the next day. I got there and he asked me if I wanted a game. But I didn't have any gear. That didn't worry Jack. He got me some boots and shorts and I had one of those good trials where I came on 10 minutes before halftime when the opposition was tired and was able to do a bit of damage. The team had two halfbacks, but one ended up as coach the next year, Les Ridgewell, and the other transferred to Wests. So the opening was there and that's how I started playing footy in Brisbane.'

Bax played for Brothers in 1947–48 but suffered a bad ankle injury early the second season. 'No-one had any money in those days and I got an offer to go to Goondiwindi to coach. I wasn't able to do anything because of my injured leg so I thought "Why not?" The telegram I received said I'd get 17 pounds 10 shillings a week plus free accommodation—to me that was a small fortune. I arrived with a five-pound note to my name and that's where I started my coaching career. We won the south-west premiership that year and I left with 200 pounds in my pocket, so everyone was happy. We played against local teams in the area as well as a couple across the NSW border like Boggabilla. Years later I coached former Queensland player Fonda Metassa, who was a great mate. We used to have these good natured slanging matches. I'd bag him over something, but he always thought he had the upper hand because he had worn the maroon jersey and I hadn't. "When did you ever play interstate football?" he'd ask. And I'd answer that I played for Goondiwindi against Boggabilla in 1948. It was five miles over the New South Wales border, so in my opinion I qualified.'

Bax then returned as a player to Brothers, before a stint in Rockhampton as captain-coach of the Fitzroy club in 1952. 'We won the premiership and then I also had a stint with Mitchell up there. I didn't have much success at Mitchell, but I learned an important lesson—it's harder to win than to lose. I returned to Brothers in 1955 as coach. I was reluctant to take the job on because the incumbent coach, Les Ridgewell, was a mate of mine. He brought me into grade at Brothers almost a decade earlier. When they offered me the job, my first instinct was to tell them to go and shove it. But then the committee came to me and said, "Listen, you're mad if you don't put in for it. Because even if you don't we can guarantee you Les won't be getting the job." When they put it like that, I signed. And Les and I remained the best of mates—he realised that was just the way the world turns.'

Bax found himself in an amazing position on grand final day in his maiden season as coach in 1955. 'I was playing in reserve grade at halfback because even though I'd had a few injuries during the season, I was basically all right. On grand final day we were there in both first and reserve grades and what a funny day it turned out to be. The reserve grade coach was a lovely bloke, Percy Berrigan, but the sort of coach who only knew one way. As soon as he got into the dressing room, he'd yell, scream and swear his head off. At halftime we were a few points down and I knew what Percy would do. He'd go off his brain and we didn't need that. So as soon as the players all got back into the dressing room, I ordered one bloke to lock the door and keep Perce out. I just told the players calmly what we had to do to win, but Perce was fuming. I don't think he ever forgave me. We were winning well by late in the second half so seven minutes from fulltime, I came off and went into the dressing room to give the A-graders their last-minute instructions. But I was no good; I was out of breath and couldn't put all my energy into it. We got beaten in first grade by Valleys, but they were unbeaten all season and were the best team that year by far. In retrospect, I couldn't complain.'

Bax-coached teams—first at Brothers and then Norths—made the Brisbane grand final for the next 10 years in a remarkable run that other coaches, both in Sydney and Brisbane, could only marvel at. 'We had a good side at Brothers and won two titles, a reserve grade premiership and finished runners-up on the other three occasions,' he said. 'In 1957, it was only my inexperience in coaching that cost us when Valleys won a thriller 18–17. In '59, we led Norths 8–0 and should have gone on to win it. But looking back, we lost that game long before we took the field and it was no surprise they ended up beating us. The preparation wasn't right and the final result showed. They were hard lessons I learned in those early years, but I think they helped me become a better coach as time went by. Brothers appointed a new president in 1960 and he was filthy on me for leaving the club a few years earlier. This bloke knew how to hold a grudge and it was obvious

he didn't want me to coach the side. They gave the job to someone else. I was living at the time—and still am now—around
100 yards from Norths' oval. I got a call one day from them and
they said, "It's a funny thing . . . we're a club without a coach
and you're a coach without a club." Clive Churchill had
coached them but left when he got a better offer. They asked
me what I wanted and I had no idea. My pay arrangement at
Brothers was loose to say the least. They usually whipped
around the hat for me at the end of the season and I'd pocket
around 50 quid if I was lucky. So I quickly set my conditions—
100 pounds to sign on, 150 to make the top four, 175 to make
the grand final and 200 to take out the premiership. We won
the lot and I finished with 206 quid for the year—which was a
pretty sum in those days.' Norths experienced their greatest
ever winning run under Bax's heady guidance. The club won
the premiership for six straight years from 1959, the year
before he arrived, until 1964. And Bax added further titles in
1966 and 1969 for good measure. Norths were hardly a big
name team, which made Bax's success all the more impressive.
'We didn't have too many stars, but there were players around
then who I just found and brought to the club and had success
with,' he said. 'There was a heap of them—you just had to go
looking. In the '70s, Steve Calder and Tony Trent were just
bumming around in Sydney so I told them to come up. They
both played some great footy for us and Steve is still in the
Broncos' coaching ranks now. Joe Kilroy . . . someone tipped
me off he could play when he was just a kid so I drove a couple of hundred miles to watch him play. He was in hot demand
and I remember bumping into an official from another club.
He said to me, "We've got Joe Kilroy playing with us this year."
I replied, "That will be news to my mum; Joe is living with her
and he'll be playing for Norths." That quietened him down

quick smart. A couple of years later a coach from a rival club told me he'd signed Joe up for the following season. I fronted Joe and asked him what was going on. He said it was true— he'd signed with the other club because he thought it was a good offer. I asked him if I could see the contract so he went and got it. I just tore it up there and then, in front of him. I gave him a contract to stay with us for the same amount and said, "Here, sign this and be on your way" and he did. Those were the type of things you could do in those days . . . you probably wouldn't get away with it now.'

Bax quit Norths at the end of the 1970 season but responded to the call to arms from the Devils to make a comeback in 1977. 'I never really wanted to give it away in the first place,' he explained. 'But my wife was driving me mad. She wanted me to give it away because it was taking up so much of my time. She wouldn't see me for days and weeks on end, so I relented. But I made a deal with her. I said that if Norths ever came last, I'd come back. Well, sure enough, they finished with the wooden spoon in 1976, so I returned the following year. I came back but it was probably the worst thing I ever did. We did okay that first year in '77; we made the finals and finished third. The next year was a disaster, though. There's an old saying you only get out of life what you put into it. And I found out just how true that was in 1978. I started a couple of new businesses connected with the racing industry that year and devoted most of my time and energy into them. I always believed in training my players three times during the week and once on Sunday morning. That probably sounds crazy now but I firmly believed in giving the players a last run on the day of the game just to sharpen them up. Anyway, the team barely saw me in 1978. We ran last—by far the worst result in my career. The only consolation was that Easts won the premiership and we played them three times during the year. They beat us 12–7 in the first round, we beat them 16–13 in the second and beat them again 12–7 in the third. So whenever anyone mentions that we came last that year, I can at least say, "Ah, yes, but we beat the premiers two times out of three." It doesn't mean a thing, I know, but at least it shows we had the team to do it . . . we just couldn't aim up consistently in '78 and it was a disappointing way to finish my career. I would have liked another year to try to make amends but I could see it was going to be no good. With my work commitments, I just didn't have the time. It wouldn't have been fair on the players and it wouldn't have been fair on me. I kept an involvement, though. Norths elected me president in the early '60s and I kept that job until 1994. Even now I'm still on three committees and am constantly in and out of the place. I've always got my own opinion of things and am happy to express it.'

Bax believes his unashamed passion for rugby league played a large part in his success. 'Unfortunately for my poor wife, football has been my life,' he said. 'It has always come first . . . I knew nothing else. In Mount Isa in fifth grade it took over my life and has had a hold of it ever since. As I said before, you get out of things what you put into them and I gave rugby league everything I had. A lot of people wouldn't understand devoting all that time to it, but I never hesitated because I loved the game more than I loved anything.'

Long-serving coach Paul Broughton regards Bax as a ground-breaking coach in the Brisbane League. Broughton, who now holds a senior management position with the Australian Rugby League, coached opposite Bax in the Brisbane competition in the 1970s. 'There's no doubt that Bob Bax was among the smartest coaches ever to come out of Queensland,' Broughton said. 'He had his players using a highly disciplined brand of football and was very keen on them offloading as they hit the line, a type of play that few clubs thought to employ at that stage. He carried so much in his head and had the ability to impart his great knowledge to his players. If you had to compare him to someone in the modern era, it would probably be Phil Gould. Off the field, Bob was highly popular and a person you'd always go out of your way to have a chat to. He knew so much about football and was never backward in coming forward with his views.'

Bax admits he had an uncompromising approach to coaching that may not be quite so successful in the current era. 'I called a spade a spade and if you didn't like it, too bloody bad,' he said. 'I have to admit, I did some terrible things to players over the years. I never took them behind the shithouse and belted them like some coaches I knew . . . I was never big enough to do that. I was only 10 stone 7, so if I tried that, they probably would have belted me straight back. When I was angry with them, I refused to talk to them. Or worse, I would humiliate them in front of the whole team. Looking back, it's probably not very nice. But it worked for me and ultimately the player benefited. I would yell at them and insult them so much that they felt they just had to respond. I got them angry and they had to go out and redeem themselves in the eyes of me and their mates. And in their own eyes, probably, too. One year when we won the comp at Norths we played the winners of the Ipswich competition, Brothers, at Lang Park in a challenge match. I'd gone to the races and got back to the ground five minutes before kickoff. At halftime, we found ourselves down 16–5. We had six players from our reserve grade side who were supposed to get a run in the second half. So a few of the guys, including Fonda Metassa, were taking their gear off. I exploded. I yelled at Fonda, "What do you think you're doing, you Greek so and so. Put that jumper back on. I want you to go out there in the second half and stop pussy footing around and show me how you can really bloody play." I told the six reserves to piss off. "Sorry, but these blokes got us into this trouble and there's no easy way out for them. They're staying until the bitter end." I just paced up and down the dressing room without saying another word, I was that angry, because they weren't having a go. Then the hooter went to go back on and they got up. "Sit down, you pack of bastards, I haven't finished with you yet," I said. "If we don't win this game, I'll never talk to any of you useless pricks again. Now get out there and do it." A lot of blokes probably couldn't, but I could talk to them like that. And it worked, we turned it around and won 26–16. You probably couldn't do that these days, but I was so close to them that I could get away with it. And more often than not, it did the trick. I don't want to sound like a lair . . . but these things really happened. It wasn't so much anything about my coaching that got me success, it was my relationship with the players. They knew me and what I wanted and they were willing to work with me to get it. They trained hard and I knew how to push the right buttons with them. And most important of all, we remained friends through it all. We were all very close. On the Saturday night before a Sunday grand final, I'd have them all over at my place. We'd have a blackboard lecture . . . I'd put all our guys' names down and then the other team opposite them on the blackboard. They'd have two or three beers, no more. I'd start the lecture by highlighting the strengths of the opposition fullback, and the weaknesses in our fullback. I'd go through the team one by one and it would be fairly demoralising for our guys. By the time I'd finished, you would think we couldn't have beaten anyone the next day. But that got them in the right frame of mind. It got rid of any over-confidence that may have been there and got them determined to beat the opposition. After I'd finished my lecture, they were ready to run through a brick wall to win. It was little things like that I did. They worked for me ... I was no bloody genius, but I knew how to wind the players up. Because they were all mates of mine and we were so close, I knew exactly how to get the best out of them.'

Bax admits he was harder on talented players than those with little ability. 'I was tough on the guys with the ability because nothing upset me more than seeing a great talent wasted,' he said. 'I've seen so many players with real ability who have just coasted through their careers. Often they don't realise how they wasted their talent until it's too late. If they cruised along without really trying their hardest, it made me mad. I used to really get up them because lazy players needed that sort of prodding. Believe it or not, I actually mothered the players without ability. If they tried hard, that was good enough for me. I was realistic enough to believe you couldn't turn a draughthorse into a Melbourne Cup winner. But I really respected the guys who kept plugging away. Every team needs that sort of player and I was proud to have them in my team.'

The only area in which Bax failed to take success was inter-state football for Queensland against New South Wales. Bax had control of the Maroons in 1971 and '72 but failed to win either series, although he did extend the star-studded NSW side. But in an era when the Blues dominated the annual clashes, Bax agrees Queensland faced a near impossible task. 'The really annoying thing about those days was that half the New South Wales team were Queenslanders,' Bax recalled. 'It was before State of Origin football and guys like Arthur Beetson were in the NSW side even though they were born and bred in Queensland. Somehow, it didn't seem fair—especially if you happened to be coaching Queensland at the time! I was very friendly with QRL boss Ron McAuliffe at the time and he devised this scheme to try to even the odds. We picked a special training squad of 20 of the state's best players and they trained full-time under my control for a couple of months. They ate, drank and slept football and we got some good footballers out of that. But the benefits were more long term, after I had gone. In 1971 they thrashed us 30–2 in the opening game. It was a fiery affair in which four players—three of ours and one of theirs—got marched. In the second match, we improved 100 per cent and only went down 17–15. It was a game we should have won but their extra experience got them home. Considering we were up against the likes of Beetson, Langlands, Fulton and Billy Smith—a virtual Test team—it was a guts effort. The following year, they won the first two games to clinch the series, but our guys fought back to win the final game 11–10 in Sydney. I was very proud of them for that. We really had nothing to play for and were on enemy territory but still came up with a great win. Admittedly, New South Wales did rest a few of their stars because the series was over, but my reaction to that is too bloody bad—it was their fault for not playing the buggers. They obviously thought they could beat us with their B team but we gave them a rude shock.'

The Maroons' win was their first in 24 matches but despite the result, Bax found himself on the outer with McAuliffe. 'When I took the job on we both agreed it was going to be a tough grind,' Bax said. 'I told McAuliffe it would take a while to get the results he wanted. He said that was fair enough and gave me three years. But they replaced me after that second year with Barry Muir. That series after I got punted was the one in which Queensland failed to score a point in the three games. I can be a mean bastard at times . . . I remember a mate asked me what I thought of the series after it was over. "Well," I told him, "I liked the scores." He was a Queenslander through and through and didn't share the joke. You couldn't blame me, could you? I think most blokes would have done the same after they had been sacked.'

Like most successful coaches, Bax didn't mind trying the unorthodox. 'I remember on one Queensland tour to New Zealand, I had all sorts of trouble with a couple of officials who accompanied us,' he said. 'I always hated officials; they never stopped trying to put their nose in the coach's business. If they weren't trying to pick the team for you, they were telling you what to do with the players at training and how to play the game. On this particular tour there was plenty of interference, so I got fed up. I called the team together—I think there were 24 players—before the biggest match against Auckland. I said to them, "I'm not going to pick a team—you blokes can do it." I handed them each a pen and paper and told them to name their own starting side. Whoever got the most votes was in. Funnily enough, one big forward who I didn't particularly want in the side got up and said, "I don't need a pen and paper—here's my team." And he reeled off 13 names. And would you believe it, that was the 13 players who ended up getting the nod from their team-mates. Seems this bloke wasn't such a bad judge after all. And we beat Auckland, even though they were favourites. Everyone was happy with the team— they could hardly bitch seeing they picked it themselves—and they went out and played some great football. It was some-thing different, but it worked for us on that particular day. I don't know if I'd try it again, though.'

Bax was also willing to give players who had been wiped by other coaches a clean slate. 'I always checked out players myself. I didn't rely on hearsay or what other coaches did,' he said. 'When I took over Norths in 1960 there was this big young forward doing the rounds called Lloyd Weier. Everyone at the club told me to steer clear of him. They said the previous coach, Clive Churchill, didn't want him. I asked, "Why not?" and nobody could answer me. I told a couple of committeemen, "Just find out where he lives and bring him to me . . . all I know is that he is six feet three and 17 stone. Anyone built like that has got a fair chance of making it." They tracked him down and he played some good footy for us before moving down to Norths in Sydney. And he played a few Tests for Australia. So I was a good judge that time. An Australian rules player called Barry Spring turned up at training one day. He'd barely played league in his life but he was big and strong and could kick the ball a mile. I gave him a go and he developed into a very good fullback. One year he kicked 14 field goals and played in a winning grand final team for us.'

Bax has been an aide and confidant to Brisbane Broncos coach Wayne Bennett for many years. He coached Bennett as a young winger with Brisbane Souths and remains a member of the Broncos' coaching panel. 'It hasn't been easy because I've tried to combine helping out at the Broncos with the work I do at Norths,' he said. 'But Wayne and I go way back and I like to play a part in things with the Broncos, however small. I keep some statistics for them and do it just to stay active. At the end of 1995, I spoke to Wayne and he said, "There's some money for you up at the club for the work you've done all year." That really surprised me—I would have done it for nothing. As I keep saying, the football has always been my life and I just love to stay involved.'

Bax doesn't attempt to hide his disenchantment with rugby league in the 1990s. 'The game now gives me the shits,' he says. 'The money has just rooted it all and a lot of other people feel the same. It's crazy the way both the Australian Rugby League and Super League have gone on. Splashing money around like it's a game of Monopoly gone haywire. I don't know who to blame ... both sides are probably equally at fault. Ken Arthurson and the ARL had to wait for those impostors to come in and change things. Otherwise they would have kept paying the players a pittance for the rest of their lives. Everyone is blaming the Super League people and they have a lot to answer for, no question. But I'm just as dirty with the ARL. They were happy to give the players next to nothing and as soon as the competition arrived, they suddenly started splashing around heaps of dough. The game itself is great, though. The players are real athletes and the ball movement can still take your breath away. It's just a pity that all this crap off the field is ruining it for the fans.'

Bax remains one of Queensland football's most enduring characters. On match days, he can still be seen serving hot dogs in the Norths canteen, in which he has a share. Formerly a part-time SP bookmaker, he gave evidence to the Fitzgerald report into police corruption in Queensland but was never charged. 'I've got a million stories from my life and the game, some are boring, some not so,' he said. 'As a matter of fact, I started to write my own life story in 1968. I did about 60 pages and then lost interest. If I started to name names and incidents, it would probably be a best-seller. Plenty of heads would roll, let me tell you. But a lot of things from the past are best left alone. I've still got the manuscript somewhere, though.'

The Quiet Man

WAYNE BENNETT

CLUBS
Souths (Brisbane) 1977–79, 1984–85,
Brothers (Brisbane) 1980–82,
Canberra 1987,
Brisbane Broncos 1988–

BRISBANE PREMIERSHIP RECORD
Games 170, won 86, lost 81, drew 3.
Winning percentage 50.6%.
Semi-finals
1979–80, 1984–85
Grand finals (3)
1979, 1984–85
Premierships (1)
1985

ARL PREMIERSHIP RECORD
Games 218, won 146, lost 70, drew 2.
Winning percentage 67.0%.
Semi-finals
1987, 1990, 1992–95
Grand finals (3)
1987, 1992–93
Premierships (2)
1992–93

OTHER COACHING ACHIEVEMENTS
Coached Queensland 1986–88. Won State of Origin series 1987–88.
Games 10, won 5, lost 5. Dally M Coach of the Year 1987.

Wayne Bennett has been the man at the heart and soul of the spectacular success of the Brisbane Broncos. The club's coach since its inaugural year in 1988, Bennett has guided the Broncos with single-minded determination and strength. A rangy fullback-winger, Bennett was a star in the Brisbane domestic competition in the early 1970s and played one Test for his country. After an impressive start to his coaching career with Brothers and Souths, he was given a chance in the big time at Canberra in 1987, joining Don Furner in an unusual co-coaching set-up. Bennett responded to the challenge, being a strong factor in guiding the Raiders to their first grand final (against Manly) before returning to Brisbane the following year to fulfil his destiny. Under Bennett's steady hand, the Broncos have developed into one of league's all-time great club sides, finishing streets ahead of the field in 1992–93, winning back-to-back titles. A quiet, somewhat brooding type, Bennett is an intensely private individual who gives little away to the media or public. But his players reveal another side to him, a strong-willed man who shares a special relationship with his teams.

Bennett played his early football in Toowoomba before moving to Brisbane to further his career. He made a sensational debut for Queensland on the wing as an unknown in 1971. Although stationed just down the road from Lang Park at the police barracks as a young cadet, he was totally taken aback by the big match atmosphere on the night. A quiet 20-year-old, he found himself up against one of the game's most seasoned campaigners in veteran Newtown winger Lionel Williamson. But Bennett's problems began well before he took the field. 'When I came over the top of the hill down Milton Road all I could see was a mass of people and I became so nervous,' Bennett recalled in Steve Ricketts' book *Lang Park—the*

First 36 Years. 'By the time I got to the ground I didn't want to be there. But within three minutes I scored. I vaguely remember putting the ball down. I think it was pure instinct at the time. But I remember the crowd went out of control. They went absolutely crazy at the spectacle of a Queenslander scoring a try so early in a match against New South Wales. It was a very, very special moment in my football career.'

But if Bennett thought he was in for a pat on the back from coach Bob Bax, he received a rude shock at halftime. 'I was furious and told him so first chance I got,' Bax recalled. 'The kid had done well to get to the line but then dived over in the corner with nobody within cooee of him. I yelled, "Why didn't you go under the posts?" but he had no answer. He was still a young kid and probably the nerves and the noise of the crowd got to him—it happens to the best of them. As it was, those three points were our only points of the night; New South Wales beat us 12–3. Had he scored under the posts and made it 5–0 with the conversion, we might have gone on with it . . . but who knows.'

Despite that blast, Bax took Bennett under his wing. As the two most influential coaches Queensland has produced, the pair still share a special friendship. 'I knew Wayne from a very early age when my Norths team used to come up against Souths,' Bax said. 'He was always a man we'd have to watch. Then I took a Queensland side to New Zealand and Wayne was on the wing. We won our first game, somewhere down the bottom of the North Island, fairly easily. But then we went to the South Island and came up against a mob that supposedly couldn't play. The only problem was, they could play. They had us down by a big score at halftime—I think it was 17–4. I gave one of my famous halftime speeches . . . I abused them from one end of the dressing room to the other. I was annoyed because I knew what they could do and that they weren't showing it. My words must have been some help because we turned it around and won 18–17. Then in the final game, we met Auckland and were warned by everyone—you won't beat Auckland. They reckoned they hadn't been beaten at home by a touring side since the 1920s. The game started and they scored an early try—down Wayne's wing. He missed the tackle on some big Maori bloke badly and when they came in at halftime, I got stuck into him. "You'll never play for me again, you big cat," I told him. I was severe on him because I knew he was a good player. I was harder on the blokes with talent than the battlers. But he responded and I don't think he made another mistake while I was coaching him.'

Bax believes he left an important legacy with Bennett. 'I reckon I was the one who taught him how to swear,' he said. 'He has this image of being quiet and reserved, but he has surprised me a couple of times at halftime in the Broncos' dressing room with the way he's gone off. He's been so bad on occasion, he even reminds me of myself. Dropping "f" and "s" words every couple of seconds and getting stuck into the players for their mistakes. If things are going bad, Wayne can go off as well as the best of them. He's not the Mister Nice Guy the public thinks he is. He's a serious bloke—it's not often you'll see him smile. But I found Wayne very dedicated and astute. Even now, I keep statistics for him . . . how long they have the ball, error rates . . . that sort of thing. I always used to have a bloke keep those stats for me when I was coaching. I don't know what he does with them; maybe he throws them away when I give them to him for all I know. But I enjoy keeping them and helping out with the Broncos in some small way.'

Veteran league official Paul Broughton coached Bennett at Brothers in 1974 and was quickly taken by the youngster's appreciation of the finer points of the game. 'Wayne was a fairly quiet type, just as he is now, but it was at team meetings that I really came to understand just how much he knew about the game,' Broughton said. 'He always had his say then and when he did, everyone would listen. He read people and the game so well. I thought more than once that this guy was going to have a major influence on rugby league. At that time, Wayne was working as an instructor at the police academy and from that, he gained an insight into people and how to control them. They are two priceless attributes for a coach and Wayne picked them up relatively early. We had a good side in those days at Brothers; Wayne was a top class fullback and we had a couple of other experienced players in Ian Dauth and Graham Quinn. We reached the grand final in 1974, but in a tryless game, Valleys beat us 9–2. Wayne got into coaching a few years later in Brisbane and it didn't surprise me that he had some success. He copied drills from basketball, which was still only a relatively small sport in Australia back then, but huge in the United States. And he worked out sophisticated game plans long before most coaches ever thought of using them. He was well and truly ahead of his time and I rate him among the most astute coaches the game has seen.'

Bennett served his coaching apprenticeship in the Brisbane domestic competition, beginning with a stint as captain-coach of Souths in 1977. Bennett took over the reins mid-season following an in-house crisis and remained with the club another two seasons. After a period of financial trouble in the mid '70s, Souths enjoyed a revival under Bennett. The club finished just outside the finals in 1978 and in 1979 made the grand final for the first time in 16 years. But Ross Strudwick's Valleys side ended Bennett's hopes of premiership success, taking the grand final in convincing style 26–0. Bennett then moved to

Brothers, leading the club to the semi-finals in his first season. It was a rare successful season for the struggling Brothers club, but Bennett couldn't maintain the standard in his two following years there in 1981 and '82, with the club finishing well down the ladder. It was a frustrating time for Bennett at a club with meagre finances and little playing talent.

The 1983 season saw Bennett return to Souths, but in the role of coaching director. He regained the job of head coach in 1984, steering Souths to the grand final, only to again taste defeat, this time at the hands of Wynnum-Manly by a crushing 42–8 scoreline. But the following season, Bennett finally broke through, winning Souths only their second title in 30 years. After the heavy loss the previous year, victory was never sweeter. 'That win was so special for me because the '84 loss was the worst moment of my career,' Bennett said years later. 'To be able to bounce back 12 months later and take the title was a great achievement by the players.' In Bennett's premiership-winning team of 1985 were rookie fullback Gary Belcher and centres Mal Meninga and Peter Jackson, three players who were to enjoy future success with him with both Canberra and the Queensland State of Origin side.

Jackson rates Bennett's performance in getting Souths the trophy against Wynnum as one of the best coaching feats of recent times. 'That Wynnum team would have beaten the Canterbury team that won the 1995 Winfield Cup by 20 points,' said Jackson, now an assistant coach with the Bulldogs. 'They had Wally Lewis, Gene Miles, Greg Dowling and a heap of other stars. They thrashed us in '84 and I think that was a turning point in Wayne's career. He inherited a team that played contract football, an old-fashioned style pioneered by Duncan Thompson with a host of set moves. After the thrashing by Wynnum, he was forced to re-evaluate himself.

And the next year he was a totally different coach. He dumped the old style and let the players use their own skills. We responded and beat Wynnum for the title even though they were hot favourites. And Wayne has stuck with that style throughout his time at Canberra and with the Broncos. He lets you play as an individual in the context of the team and good players appreciate that latitude.' Jackson feels well credentialled to comment on Bennett's coaching, having been associated with him for many years at three different clubs, 'It was even my misfortune as a young police cadet to have Wayne as my coach and instructor at the academy in Brisbane,' he said. 'He was a real drill sergeant there and gave us a tough time. But I came to like the bloke and followed him to Souths, then Canberra and back to Brisbane. He's been something of a father figure to me. The impressive thing about Wayne Bennett is that the man has no ego; he's not interested in what the papers or TV commentators say about him. Wayne is in it for personal satisfaction and to help the players reach their potential—nothing more. He is a very disciplined individual who practises what he preaches. He's a great believer in routine; he trains at the same time every day, catches the same plane on match day and has the players room with the same blokes every time. He believes that routine helps bring out the best in them, particularly on the road. We had some disagreements, particularly once when he dropped me to reserve grade at the Broncos and I didn't cop it all that well. But we smoothed it over and are very close now.'

Bennett's credentials in the Brisbane competition were highly impressive, but it was his deeds with the Canberra Raiders in 1987 that really made the league world sit up and take notice. Veteran coach Don Furner, who had been with Canberra since the club's inception in 1982, saw the need to bring some new ideas to the Raiders. Furner brought Bennett to Canberra to take charge of a young club that was on the verge of realising its potential. With the pair as co-coaches, and Bennett handling most of the day-to-day running of the team, Canberra quickly blossomed. The Furner–Bennett combination was dubbed 'The Odd Couple' and coaching may never have seen two more different men working together in charge of a football team. Furner's open, smiling personality was a sharp contrast to Bennett's quiet, brooding manner. But Furner insists the partnership was harmonious and efficient from start to finish. 'I checked Wayne out very thoroughly before I invited him down to join us,' Furner said. 'I knew he was different to me, but that was never a problem. I asked a lot of people about him and never heard a bad word. And now that I've got to know him, I don't think you'll find a man with better qualities. He's loyal, studious and honest. He gets the respect from his players and his man management skills are excellent, which is one of the strengths of his coaching. There were times we had our differences, but we kept them between ourselves. We always presented a united front, for the sake of the club, and what happened in the selection room stayed there. I had absolute confidence in Wayne's integrity—it was the only way a set-up like ours could have worked. I was the one who presented our public face by talking to the media because that's one aspect of the job Wayne never fancied. But he didn't care who got the credit, so long as the job got done. Wayne came in with plenty of new ideas and the players immediately warmed to him. Looking back, I don't think there's any doubt the arrival of Wayne, Gary Belcher and Mal Meninga proved the turning point in the Canberra story. They transformed us from an out-of-town team with potential to a real power in the game.'

WAYNE BENNETT

Those in the know reveal that although Bennett and Furner were listed as co-coaches, it was Bennett who did all the technical work with the team. 'Wayne was the one and only coach,' Peter Jackson said. 'Don Furner stood back and let him take over. He'd get out there occasionally when the television cameras were at training and spoke to the media after matches. But that was about the limit of his involvement with the team.' Bennett's arrival didn't go down so smoothly with everyone at Canberra. 'Gary Belcher, Mal Meninga and I had played under him in Brisbane and knew what he was like,' Jackson said. 'But he had a few run-ins with blokes who didn't like his style, particularly Chris O'Sullivan. Chris was a brilliant individual but a selfish player on the field who didn't fit into Wayne's plans. He'd been at the club since it started and felt entitled to run the show at halfback. But Wayne wanted Ivan Henjak at half and that got Chris's nose out of joint. They had a running battle which Benny won—he doesn't lose many. In the end, O'Sullivan went to five-eighth and played some good football there.'

With Bennett structuring Canberra's game to make full use of the team's undoubted potential, the Raiders quickly developed into an excitement machine. The Raiders reached the finals for the first time in 1987, but quickly had their momentum halted by Easts in the opening weekend of the big matches at the SCG, losing 25–16. Bennett and his men learned the lesson of finals football quickly, however. The following week, they totally demoralised South Sydney 46–12 to re-emerge as a title contender. That match became infamous as 'Steve Mavin's game', with the Raiders constantly pressuring the rookie winger in the opening 20 minutes. After a couple of glaring errors—and a couple of unfortunate bounces—Mavin was hauled from the field by coach George Piggins midway through the first half. But the horse had already bolted—the Raiders were well on their way to the biggest finals win for many years.

Their confidence renewed, Canberra faced Easts the following weekend, with an ace up their sleeve—Mal Meninga. The inspirational centre was back on deck after breaking his arm for the second time in the season. Meninga scored a powerhouse try as the ACT rejoiced, with the Raiders reaching their first grand final, winning 32–24. It was the first time in the game's long history a team from outside the Sydney metropolitan area had reached the grand final, and a clear indication of the changing demographics of the rugby league world. Bennett and Furner tried in vain to keep the lid on the celebrations during the following week as the Raiders faced a formidable grand final opponent—Bob Fulton's Manly Sea Eagles. 'We were desperate to keep everyone's feet on the ground, but it wasn't easy,' recalled Furner. 'Here we were, a bunch of battlers from the bush, playing in the biggest game of the year. Queanbeyan went wild and even the people in Canberra city got behind us. The support was great, but it was probably a bit too much for the boys in hindsight.'

Come grand final day, the Raiders' worst fears were realised. The Canberra attacking machine failed to hit top gear, appearing to suffer from an attack of stage fright. And in defence, the Raiders were bamboozled by Manly's ball-playing wizard Cliff Lyons. It was Lyons who produced the only try of the first half, stepping past his opposite O'Sullivan to plunge over beside the posts, giving Manly a 6–0 lead at the break. Michael O'Connor added a couple of penalty goals and a try early in the second half as Manly charged to a 16–2 lead. O'Sullivan replied with a late try for the gallant Raiders, but it only proved a consolation effort as Manly took the last grand final at the SCG by 18–8. After the match, a bitter Bennett complained about his rival Bob Fulton's use of the head bin. Fulton made several key replacements at vital stages of the match, with Sea Eagle stars allegedly concussed. It was not long after that match that the rules regarding head bin replacements were changed by the league, but this came as little comfort for Bennett. Soon after the defeat, he found himself facing a new challenge . . . back where it all began for him in Brisbane.

Wayne Bennett can thank Jack Gibson for getting him one of rugby league's prize jobs—the post of head coach of the Brisbane Broncos. It was Gibson who, late in 1987, insisted to Broncos chairman Paul 'Porky' Morgan that Bennett was his man. Bennett was given the job and has been there ever since in one of the longest associations between coach and club that league has known. That initial recommendation wasn't the first favour Gibson did for Bennett, a coach very much in the Jack Gibson mould. In 1979, when Bennett's Brisbane Souths side faced a tough semi-final against the fancied Easts team, Souths president Jack Astill asked Bennett what could be done to improve the team's chances. Bennett's answer was simple—get Jack Gibson up here. Gibson accepted Bennett's invitation and spoke to the players at training, as well as showing a couple of motivational videos. 'His presence had a great impact on the players,' Bennett said later. 'For me it was the start of a friendship and a relationship which I value today as much as I ever did.'

Several years later, when Bennett was coach of the Queensland team that played in an exhibition State of Origin match in Los Angeles, Gibson was also there as a commentator for Channel Nine. A couple of days before the game, Gibson took Bennett to the Dallas Cowboys' pre-season training camp. The visit provided Bennett with a fascinating insight into the world of professional football. Just as Gibson has done over many years, Bennett picked up a host of ideas in that brief visit that he has used to his advantage on the local scene. As an added bonus, Gibson introduced Bennett to legendary American coaches Tom Landry and Dick Nolan. 'For a boy from Queensland, it was something, I can tell you,' Bennett said.

Paul Morgan confirms Gibson's recommendation went a long way towards ensuring Bennett fulfilling his destiny with the Broncos. 'We actually spoke with Bennett before asking Jack for his advice,' Morgan said. 'But Wayne was under contract to Canberra and knocked us back. We accepted his decision at the time but soon realised our mistake. Jack told us we had to get a Queenslander for the job and Wayne was the best man. Arthur Beetson said the same thing. So we approached Wayne again and moved mountains and finally got him to come up here . . . thank God. I'd hate to think where the Broncos would be now if we hadn't.' But there was a problem getting Bennett back to Brisbane—Canberra didn't want to release him. 'Wayne was under contract to us and there's no way we wanted to let him go,' Don Furner explained. 'When we signed him, the idea was for him to take over from me when I stepped down. And he made such an impression on us in that one short year that we were desperate to keep him. There's no way someone like Wayne Bennett wears out his welcome. But Brisbane was home. I think his family missed the place and so after a lot of agonising, we let him go.'

The Bennett–Morgan relationship, such a key factor in the success of the Broncos, actually had its roots many years earlier. 'Not many people know it, but Wayne and I played together in Toowoomba for All Whites more years ago than I'd care to remember,' Morgan said. 'Back then, we all knew he was destined for big things and it didn't surprise me when he went on to play for Australia. I was just a hard-working back-rower but Wayne was a fullback-winger with real class. When he flashed into the backline, you always knew something exciting was about to happen. I wouldn't say that we were close mates back then, but we were on the same team and certainly got on well.' The pair then went their separate ways for more than a decade, before Morgan approached Bennett about renewing the association.

'It wasn't easy to get Wayne out of Canberra, but we did it,' he said. 'And we let him know from the start that he would be in charge. We guaranteed him a free hand when it came to running his football team and I knew Wayne would never have it any other way. The board has always been happy to leave him in total control, because we know he's the best man for the job. He never signed a contract, but with Wayne Bennett that is not a problem. His word is good enough and I didn't see the need to get any terms down on paper.' Morgan admits that Bennett's role with the Broncos is much more than just a football coach. 'He is a major contributor at board level,' Morgan said. 'Any major decision that affects the club, we want Wayne's input. As for his future, he will stay with the club as long as he wants to. Personally, I hope it's still a few years. I would find it hard to imagine him coaching anywhere else.'

Morgan acknowledges that Bennett does have a weakness as a coach. 'He tends to be too loyal to his players, particularly those who have done the right thing by him over a number of years,' Morgan said. 'He will give a player who probably should be dropped another chance or two to redeem himself. But I think the players respect him for that. The coach who drops half a dozen players every time he hits a rough patch soon loses the respect of the team. With young kids, Wayne gives them four years to come good and then if they don't make the grade, he cuts them loose. That may seem a bit harsh, but most coaches would be hard pressed to give a youngster more than a season or two, at the most, to prove his worth. Wayne believes that all players develop differently and is prepared to give the kid with talent time to show what he's got. Through this player loyalty, he has built up a tremendous spirit within the club. They all talk about Canterbury being the family club. I can assure you, with Wayne Bennett at the helm, the Broncos are just as close and just as strong as any club.'

The Broncos, with Bennett in the driving seat, started life in the big league in spectacular fashion. On Sunday, 6 March 1988, in a match few Queenslanders will forget, the Brisbane Broncos made their premiership debut against then premiers Manly at Lang Park. It took just 80 minutes to show all and sundry a new force had arrived on the premiership scene. The fulltime score read Brisbane 44, Manly 10. It was an awesome performance, the biggest ever win by a club in its premiership debut. But the one man in the capacity crowd at Lang Park that day not totally convinced of the Broncos' worth was Wayne Bennett himself. Wally Lewis takes up the story. 'We had been building up to this game for months and it meant so much to us,' Lewis said. 'When we got out on the field, we just smashed Manly from one end of the park to the other. The crowd loved every minute of it and when we got back into the dressing room, we were on the highest of highs. There were blokes jumping up and down, yelling and screaming and carrying on. If you didn't know any better, you'd think we'd just won the grand final. But then Wayne came into the room and quickly brought us back down to earth. Suddenly there was complete silence in the room. "You blokes are kidding yourselves if you think you've got it made," he said in a stern voice. "This was the easiest game you'll play all year—you were always going to win the first one. The test is going to come later on and you can't let this win get to your heads." We were all left chewing on his words and then he walked past me, winked and gave an ever-so-slight smile as he whispered so only I could hear, "We've got one hell of a football team here, son".'

The Broncos kept up the momentum for the opening six rounds before 'hitting the wall', as if Bennett's prediction came back to haunt them. With a team chock full of internationals and State of Origin stars, they proved themselves capable of beating the best of them. But the Broncos clearly had troubles adapting to the weekly grind of life in the fast lane, losing several games they should have won and ultimately missing a finals berth. Bennett's men learned some harsh lessons in that maiden winter and appeared a far more mature outfit in 1989. But the team again suffered the staggers, this time mid-season when the likes of Lewis, Allan Langer, Kerrod Walters, Gene Miles, Sam Backo and Tony Currie were on State of Origin duty. Brisbane finished equal fifth with the Gavin Miller-inspired Cronulla side and were hotly tipped to reach their maiden finals via a mid-week playoff. But the Sharks totally outplayed the Broncos on the Tuesday night at Parramatta Stadium, knocking Bennett's men out of business with a convincing 38–14 win.

Paul Morgan admits these were trying times for the Broncos, with Bennett the man well and truly in the hot seat. 'We had the hopes of all of Queensland riding on us and it was a heavy burden at times,' he said. 'It was hard for the people to be patient; they wanted success there and then. The pub talk at the time—and we all heard it—was that the only thing wrong with the Broncos was Wayne Bennett. My answer to that, and it was something I told everyone who I found spouting that line, was that the only thing RIGHT about the Broncos was Wayne Bennett. He never lost his cool and knew the club was on the right track and it was only a matter of time.'

Morgan believes that although the Broncos didn't taste success in those early days, Bennett laid important ground-work for the years ahead. 'I suppose it was proof of the old saying that Rome wasn't built in a day,' Morgan said. 'We were competing against teams that had been around for half a century or more and we were the new kids on the block. We had a great start with players like Lewis, Langer and Miles, but that obviously wasn't enough. That's where Wayne proved so valuable. He saw the talent in young guys like Steve Renouf, Andrew Gee, Michael Hancock, Terry Matterson and Chris Johns. All of those players will readily admit how much they owe to Wayne. And even Alfie Langer, champion player that he is, probably wouldn't have risen to such heights without Wayne there; it was Wayne who really made Alfie what he is today. In those early years he worked on giving the players confidence and making them believe in both themselves and the coach. The later results show how successful he was.'

Morgan concedes it hasn't been all smooth sailing for Bennett, with the crowd and media baying for his blood at different times. 'It took us five years to win the premiership and there were some lean times over those seasons,' Morgan said. 'There were those who didn't like his style and I believe Wayne himself may have had doubts about his ability at certain stages. But the key was that in the bad years, we all stuck together and there were no cracks in the wall. Everyone wanted the same thing and there were no petty jealousies or rivalries that could have torn us apart.'

Brian Canavan, a member of the Broncos' coaching staff in the club's early days who has since had stints at Cronulla and

Sydney City, wasn't surprised that Brisbane struggled in the formation years. 'There were such high expectations placed on both the players and Wayne and that created pressure,' Canavan said. 'But the bottom line is the players were used to running around in the Brisbane domestic competition where consistency wasn't demanded. Even guys like Wally Lewis and Gene Miles knew they only had to produce a good game once a month or so and at State of Origin time. All of a sudden they were faced with 22 high-pressure games a year and a lot of travelling and they couldn't handle it. Also, a lot of these blokes were rivals for years and suddenly thrown together into the same team. There were some lingering feuds there that Wayne had to contend with. Despite it all, Wayne handled it well and it was due to him, more than anyone else, that the club was able to turn itself around.'

Bennett has also played an integral part in Queensland State of Origin folklore. As coach of the Maroons for three seasons between 1986 and 1988, he was a key figure in some of Origin's most memorable moments. His first campaign in 1986 was nothing short of disastrous, with Wayne Pearce's Blues recording their first clean sweep against a Queensland side accustomed to dominating the Origin series. Peter Jackson believes Bennett had troubles in that initial season adapting to the step up in class. 'It was his first experience coaching the likes of Wally Lewis and Gene Miles and I think he felt a little intimidated by them,' Jackson said. 'He didn't know how to handle them. He was also shocked by the Origin tradition of getting out on the town and hitting the piss for the first three nights of camp. I remember we had a team meeting and he demanded to know how many of us went out three times in the one week on the drink. Only Wally and I put our hands up—and I wasn't sure whether we were brave, or stupid, or just honest. But the upshot was we were allowed to go out and get drunk as sailors, while all the other blokes had to stay in the hotel and go to bed.'

Bennett's hopes of erasing the Blues' State or Origin whitewash suffered a devastating blow in the first match of the 1987 series. In one of State of Origin's most dramatic games, a late try by NSW centre Mark McGaw gave the Blues a last minute 20–16 win at Lang Park. The defeat was Bennett's fourth in as many Origin matches, but the turnaround proved swift and decisive. It came in the mud at the SCG in the second game, where the Maroons won an arm-wrestle encounter 12–6. Their pride and confidence restored, the Maroons won the decider 10–8, ending a two-year Origin drought. Bennett's revenge was complete when, in his final year as coach in 1988, he piloted the Maroons to a 3–0 win, reversing the result of his maiden season. The Brisbane *Courier-Mail* hailed Bennett as 'undoubtedly the best coach in the world' after the series, which now extended Bennett's winning run to five straight Origin games. But quietly and without fanfare, Bennett stepped down at the end of the series, deciding to put all his energy into the Broncos' bid for the premiership they so desperately craved.

Wayne Bennett's moment of truth with the Broncos came at the end of 1990 when he decided to take on the most powerful player in the game—Wally Lewis. From the start, there was poor chemistry in the Bennett–Lewis relationship. Bennett, the quiet, almost introverted coach, and Lewis, his outspoken, controversial on-field leader, never seemed at ease. The pair clashed behind closed doors more than once, with Bennett relieving Lewis of the club captaincy in a major rebuke. But worse was to follow. Soon after Lewis controversially missed out on the 1990 Kangaroos because of injury, Bennett made the decision to release the man known as 'The King' to thousands of adoring fans north of the border. The move was bold, brazen, and but for Bennett's strength and personality, could have proved his downfall. Several prominent critics in Brisbane have described the Broncos' sacking of Lewis among the most courageous ever taken by a sporting administration in Australia.

Moves to remove Lewis came out of Bennett's annual post season interviews with his players. At the end of each playing season, Bennett has sat players down individually and talked to them at length about their perception of the team's strengths and weaknesses. When several senior players said they did not feel comfortable playing under Lewis, who they described as a dictatorial captain, Bennett felt obliged to act. Further black marks against the captain's name were that he was late to training more than once and failed to mingle with the club's younger players. But like most arguments, there were two sides to the Lewis–Bennett feud. Those on Lewis's side claimed Bennett could not handle The King's high profile and popularity. Bennett supporters believed Lewis's dominant personality and clashes with officialdom were harming the team as a unit. To Paul Morgan, Lewis's demise became official the day Bennett said The King had to go. 'That was a difficult time, without doubt,' Morgan said. 'But again, we were 100 per cent behind Wayne. Once the decision was made, it was signed, sealed and delivered as far as the club was concerned. There were plenty of people who wanted to scalp us over the issue, I won't deny. But looking back, it made us stronger and helped the club as a whole.'

Peter Jackson said Lewis's downfall in Bennett's eyes was that he failed to set a good example to the younger players in the club. 'He was a poor trainer and sneered at the blokes who really worked hard at training,' Jackson said. 'That was one of his biggest sins in the eyes of Wayne and the club. We all knew there was going to be drama after we lost that mid-week play-off to Cronulla in 1989. Porky Morgan got pissed and bagged everyone and there were clearly going to be changes. But we had no idea Wally was going to be the one to go until it happened. It came as a shock to us all.'

Brian Canavan saw the departure of Lewis as inevitable. 'The question Wayne would have asked before making his decision was whether Wally was going to contribute to the overall success of the organisation,' Canavan said. 'When he decided the answer was no, he made the decision that the bloke had to go. Never mind that Wally was known as "Mr Queensland Rugby League". Wayne Bennett is a strong-willed individual and when he makes a decision, that's it. If he'd got hold of Wally a couple of years earlier, he might have been able to turn him around and thrash out a compromise. But Wally had been used to running his own race for too long.'

Before the Lewis drama the Broncos finally made the play-offs in 1990, but that historic achievement quickly degenerated into a disappointment for Bennett. In a major upset, the Broncos were out-muscled 26–16 by Penrith in their first finals appearance. The following week, they regrouped to down Manly 12–4. After that match, Bennett fired an uncharacteristic and bitter broadside at the media for their coverage of the loss to Penrith. In a tirade that lasted all of five minutes outside the Broncos' dressing room at the SFS, Bennett declared to a gathering of over 20 pressmen his anger over the way they blasted the Broncos for losing to Penrith. 'You should all be ashamed of yourselves,' he said. 'The things you wrote about these players in here were disgusting.' The following week, after the preliminary final, Bennett was very much lost for words as the

Broncos were ingloriously thrashed 32–4 by Tim Sheens' Canberra Green Machine. With Lewis no longer in their ranks and Gene Miles hampered by injury, the Broncos struggled again in 1991, failing to make the finals. Miles quit the club at the end of the year, opting to finish his career in Britain. While many critics predicted the Broncos would have problems in 1992 without their two old stagers, Bennett and Morgan saw things very differently. 'We saw '92 as the first "clean" side at the Broncos since the club began,' Morgan said. 'By that I meant that the old guard was gone, replaced by the young kids Wayne had groomed. Don't get me wrong, guys like Wally and Gene gave us great service and were champion players. But now Wayne had the team he hand-picked with exactly the players he wanted. The "Bennettisation" of the team, as I like to call it, was complete.'

There was no holding back the Broncos in 1992–93 as they beat all comers to claim back-to-back titles in impressive style. In both grand finals, they outgunned a plucky, but clearly inferior St George to take the Winfield Cup trophy north of the border. In 1992, as the Broncos carved up Saints in the second half en route to a crushing 28–8 win, a Sydney Football Stadium member tells of Bennett sitting stony-faced high in the grandstand. 'He showed no emotion, even as they ran in try after try and the title was clearly theirs,' the member said. 'Everyone up there was watching him and finally, one bloke couldn't stand it any longer. With a couple of minutes to go, he yelled out, "Come on, Wayne, you've won the bloody thing . . . give us a bit of a smile!" He never acknowledged the bloke, but on Bennett's lips, we could all just notice the faintest trace of a grin.'

Classy five-eighth Kevin Walters, a key man in the Broncos' on-field make-up, sees Bennett as something of a father figure to his players. 'You know that he is always there for you,'

Walters said. 'If you ever have a problem, to do with football or anything else, Wayne is only too glad to listen. And nine times out of ten, he'll give you the right advice. He is a wise man and plenty of the players, myself included, have gone to him when we've needed guidance. The key thing is probably respect. All the players respect Wayne, both as a football coach and as a man.' Walters says the image of Bennett as a dour, intense character is largely created by the media. 'He'll mix with the players and still enjoy a good time when he feels like it, but he knows when to keep his distance as well. Wayne smiles as much as the next bloke. He has had a few bad experiences with the media over the years and as a result of that, he's always a bit wary of them. But on a day-to-day basis with his team, he's fine.' Walters admits Bennett uses a less structured approach than most modern coaches. 'Wayne is high on the discipline because he realises how important it is in the game,' he said. 'But the skill level in our team is fairly high and Wayne is happy to give us a free rein, within reason of course. You'd be crazy to try to get the likes of Steve Renouf, Willie Carne and Michael Hancock to play within a tight game plan. But we always have to take responsibility for our actions; if a player does something out of line, Wayne will pull him back into order fairly quickly. He keeps us on our toes and I think the reason he's been able to stay with the one club for so long is that he always has new ideas and approaches. Wayne is forever on the lookout for something fresh to motivate both himself and the team.'

Peter Jackson sums Bennett up as one-third of the ideal coach. 'The perfect coach would be a combination of Bennett, Chris Anderson and Bob Fulton,' Jackson said. 'Bozo would provide the tactics, Chris would ensure the club was happy and motivated and Wayne would ensure the mental preparation every week was nothing short of perfect.'

The Little Master

CLIVE CHURCHILL

CLUBS
Souths 1958 (captain-coach), 1967–75,
Norths (Brisbane) 1959 (captain-coach),
Moree 1961 (captain-coach),
Canterbury 1963–64

SYDNEY PREMIERSHIP RECORD
Games 260, won 148, lost 107, drew 5.
Winning percentage 57%.
Semi-finals
1967–72, 1974
Grand Finals (5)
1967–71
Premierships (4)
1967–68, 1970–71

BRISBANE PREMIERSHIP RECORD
Games 22, won 15, lost 7. Winning percentage 68%.
Semi-finals
1959
Grand finals (1)
1959
Premierships (1)
1959

OTHER COACHING ACHIEVEMENTS
Coached Queensland 1961. Games 4, won 3, lost 1.
Coached Australia 1959–60. Tests 9, won 5, lost 3, drew 1.
Tour matches 31, won 22, lost 9.

Clive Churchill—The Little Master—was the heart and soul of the South Sydney machine that ruled rugby league in the late 1960s and early '70s. While not a brilliant coach in the tactical sense, Churchill was a shrewd motivator and wily campaigner, who learned many tricks during his illustrious playing career that he successfully applied as coach. A highly popular coach, Churchill was a man of integrity who knew how to get the best out of his players. He moulded a star-studded Souths outfit into one of rugby league's all-time great teams, capturing four premierships in five years and narrowly missing a fifth. He was one of the few truly great players to also make a significant mark in the game as a coach.

Long-serving league official 'Jersey' Flegg once described Churchill as 'the best all-round champion that rugby league has known' and few who saw Churchill in his heyday would dare to argue. Legend has it that Flegg spotted Churchill playing at five-eighth in a schoolboy representative match at the SCG and predicted, 'One day that lad will become an international and captain Australia in Test football.' Churchill did that and more, to become the most famous Rabbitoh of them all—the man destined to be remembered as 'The Little Master'.

Churchill was born at Merewether, a Newcastle suburb, in 1927 and began his league career as a tiny youngster playing for the local church school. When told by his coach to play centre, young Clive knew so little about the game, he charged up to the scrumbase and attempted to pack down with the forwards. But he quickly picked up the tricks of the trade, developing into a whiz kid at Marist Brothers, Hamilton. The school's coach, Brother Lucien, moved him to five-eighth and in his final year at school, Churchill topped 200 points. By the age of 18, he was playing fullback in first grade for Central

Newcastle. Churchill played for Country Seconds against Sydney in 1947 and it was after that match his career took a major step forward. The young fullback received an urgent telegram from long-serving Souths official Dave Spring, requesting a meeting. Churchill took little convincing to join the club, receiving a sign-on fee of 12 pounds per match.

Churchill played his first match for Souths late in 1947— and wanted to immediately go home. He played so poorly, in his opinion, that he felt he didn't belong in the big time. Churchill hurt an ankle early in the match but chose to play on, eager to make an impression, and was well short of his best. He told the Rabbitohs he wanted to go back to Newcastle, but was persuaded to stay for a 28-day trial period. Just a handful of games later, he found form and confidence. The fleet-footed youngster was an instant sensation, but there was a price to his new-found fame. The slightly built Churchill was a marked man in virtually every game he played, with opposition teams determined to unsettle him. In an infamous early clash with Newtown, former Bluebag toughman Frank 'Bumper' Farrell came face to face with Churchill for the first time. Farrell crash-tackled Churchill and as the youngster got to his feet, greeted him warmly with a big smile and the words 'Hello, son'. Farrell then grabbed Churchill's head with his two massive hands and twisted it as if he intended to pop it off his shoulders. The incident left Churchill with a cauliflower ear and began a long-running feud between the pair. But Churchill survived everything opposition teams could throw at him and by the end of his maiden season in 1948, was selected to tour with the Kangaroos.

Souths almost lost Churchill the following year when English club Workington Town made a massive offer of 10,000 pounds for his services. It was an offer Souths, or any other

Sydney club at the time, could never come close to matching. Churchill, earning 4 pounds 10 shillings per week as a sporting goods salesman, accepted the deal and prepared to begin a new life in England. But the Australian Rugby League refused to allow him to go, applying a poaching ban they had introduced the previous year to stop the flood of Australian talent to England.

By 1950, Churchill was Australian captain and enjoyed what he later described as one of his proudest moments in the Third Test against Great Britain in Sydney. With the Test series tied at 1–1, Churchill led the home side into the historic decider on a mudheap at the SCG. Winger Ron Roberts scored the only try of the game as Australia won a tight clash 5–2. The win earned Australia the Ashes for the first time in 30 years, with delighted fans invading the pitch and mobbing Churchill and his team-mates.

A cheeky sense of humour was an integral part of Churchill's make-up—both as a player and later as coach. Before a tense clash between New South Wales and Great Britain at the SCG in 1950, Lions skipper Ernest Ward approached Churchill in the middle of the field for the coin toss. Instead of shaking hands, Churchill slipped a small bar of soap into the Englishman's open palm. A stunned crowd of more than 50,000 watched as Ward threw the soap into the mud, snarling, 'You'll pay for that, you black bastard.' Churchill had a simple explanation for the ploy. 'I liked English people, but hated English footballers,' he said later. 'On the field they kept referring to the Australians as convicts. They threw in the dirt and really turned my dislike into hate.'

Churchill excelled on the representative arena, playing a record 99 consecutive matches. One critic said he played 'with the devil in his heart and an angel on his shoulder'. His smart running game revolutionised attacking play, with Churchill proving the prototype of the modern attacking fullback. Great Australian running fullbacks like Graeme Langlands, Graham Eadie and Garry Jack have all followed the Little Master's lead.

Courage was Churchill's trademark. In a famous club match against Manly in 1955, he broke his left wrist in the first half while making a typically fearless tackle on a man much bigger than himself. The little fullback refused to leave the field, playing on valiantly with the wrist taped up flimsily with the cover of an old exercise book. Churchill booted the winning goal late in the match to keep Souths' finals hopes alive with a 9–7 triumph. The injury put Churchill out for the year, but Souths went on to take the title with a memorable eight-match winning streak. The Rabbitohs dominated the Sydney premiership for much of Churchill's time at the club. They won five titles in six years from 1950 to 1955, with the star fullback forming a devastating combination with speedy winger Ian Moir. Time and again, Churchill would dazzle defenders with his quick footwork and acceleration, before sending the speedy Moir into the clear.

The brilliant fullback ended his illustrious career at Souths on a sad note, quitting the club over a pay dispute in 1958 to go to Brisbane. But Churchill put his 12-month stint in Queensland to good use, kicking off his impressive coaching career. He coached Northern Suburbs to their first premiership win in 19 years and coached the Maroons in the interstate series. Up against many of the Blues stars he had played alongside for years, Churchill steered the Maroons to an impressive 3–1 series win. In 1959, with only his brief experience in Brisbane and two years as captain-coach of Souths, Churchill was handed the rare honour of coaching the Kangaroos to Britain and France. Captained by Keith Barnes, the Roos were a formidable line-up which included a young Reg Gasnier, who took Britain and France by storm. A coach who always wore his heart on his sleeve, Churchill was in trouble early in the tour. In only the second match in Britain, the former full-back great earned the ire of the crowd during a fiery encounter at Oldham. Sections of a capacity crowd of more than 17,000 pelted Churchill with rubbish and orange peel. The coach responded by spraying the mob with water. It took the intervention of manager Jack Argent and several policemen to prevent the incident developing into a major row. The Kangaroos won the First Test at Swinton 22–14, thanks to three razzle-dazzle tries from the unstoppable Gasnier. Churchill wrote in his biography that only days later, he had a strange conversation with a local official. The official congratulated him on winning the Test, but predicted he would not win the second. When Churchill asked why, the official replied, 'Because thee won't be ALLOWED to win.' The words proved prophetic as the Kangaroos faced a determined British side in the Second Test at Headingley a fortnight later. A series of controversial decisions from referee Ron Gelder went against the Aussies, with Britain winning 11–10. Churchill could only think back to the words of the official as his team went down in highly contentious circumstances. Their confidence boosted, the Englishmen won the deciding Test at Wigan 18–12, to retain the Ashes. Again the Australians had several close calls go against them, this time under the notorious referee Eric 'Sergeant Major' Clay. Clay's performance prompted an extraordinary outburst by the normally diplomatic Argent at the post match reception. 'Gentlemen, it is easy to understand why an Australian side has never won the Ashes in England when you have such biased referees,' Argent told a stunned gathering of officials and dignitaries. League's most prized trophy had once again eluded the Aussies, with Churchill completing his fourth and last Roo tour without realising his ambition of bringing home the Ashes.

After the tour, Churchill made limited appearances in the bush, playing his last game at Moree in 1960. He also had a two-year stint as coach of Canterbury in the early '60s. It was while coaching Canterbury that Churchill found himself in an unlikely situation—thrown out of the Souths dressing room. 'I'd played at Souths for 11 years and never thought anything like that would ever happen to me,' Churchill revealed in a serialisation of his life story, written in the now defunct *Sun* newspaper when he retired from coaching in 1975. 'The bloke who ordered me out is dead now, but he grabbed me as soon as I walked into the room after the game. He said: "Hey, you, get out of here . . . you're not welcome." I couldn't believe it. All I wanted to do was say hello to a few of my mates. I said to the official: "Look at you . . . you're a great example." Then I turned and walked out of the room. Some of the players could see what was happening and called me back, but I wasn't hanging around. As it was, I met with a few of the boys afterwards and had a few beers with them. I guess the official hadn't forgiven me for leaving in 1958, but that was on a principle and I still think I was entitled to leave when I did. Souths hadn't paid me for coaching for the season and I thought I had a right to challenge them.'

After several lean years for the club in the early '60s, Souths welcomed Churchill back like a long lost son in 1967—as coach. The Rabbitohs were moulding a fine young team which included Ron Coote, Mike Cleary, Bob McCarthy, Jim Lisle, Gary Stevens and John Sattler, but were looking for the man to mould them all together. In Churchill, the Rabbitohs made a wise choice.

The 1967 season was the start of a new era for league;

St George's mighty 11-year run was poised to come to an end, the four tackle rule was introduced and newcomers Penrith and Cronulla joined the premiership. Souths' young team, playing with plenty of attacking bravado and spirit under Churchill's guidance, shaped as contenders from the outset. Grand finalists in 1965, the Rabbitohs slumped to sixth in '66, culminating in the sacking of loyal Souths man Bernie Purcell as coach. Under a new coach in Churchill, the Rabbitohs had it all to prove the following year. Churchill was to make one of his shrewdest moves long before a ball was kicked that season. In Souths' pack was a wild bull of a young forward who had already established a reputation as a troublemaker after only a couple of seasons in Sydney football. But Churchill, a former inspirational captain in his day, saw something in the fearsome John Sattler that others didn't. Churchill approached Sattler and offered him the captaincy in a move slammed by the critics as football lunacy. 'No-one was more surprised than me when Clive and (club president) Denis Donoghue approached me and asked me to do the job,' Sattler recalled. 'It was a risk, without doubt. I had a reputation as a wild man and to say the referees didn't like me was an understatement. My first reaction was to shit myself. I was still fairly young and we had a couple of experienced internationals in the side in Jimmy Lisle and Mike Cleary. But neither of them wanted the job and promised they'd help me out. So I took it on and after finding my way, grew to really like the job. The players responded and the rest is history.'

Sattler recalls Churchill as a happy-go-lucky character who had the respect of all his players. 'He was very different from Bernie Purcell, who coached us until then,' Sattler said. 'Bernie was more technical whereas Clive concentrated on keeping morale up. He wanted to keep us all laughing and happy and we played good football as a result. There were times we'd be in big trouble at halftime and he'd come into the room and tell a joke. But in one match, after we'd played poorly in the first half, Clive walked in at halftime and yelled: "I don't want to talk to youse after that. Youse work it out." With that he walked out again. And it worked; we knew he was dirty and really lifted our effort in the second half.'

Churchill gave the Rabbitohs a free rein in attack and players like Coote, McCarthy, Cleary, O'Neill and Sattler needed little encouragement to do just that. Churchill saw McCarthy and Coote as lethal weapons in attack and stationed them out wide on either side of the field rather than close to the ruck. This break from tradition led to both players scoring a heap of tries as they were given the ball with room to move against smaller opponents out wide. In the grand final of 1967, McCarthy's positioning out wide proved decisive. In a tight, hard-fought encounter against Canterbury, the Bulldogs led 8–5 and were on the attack minutes from halftime. But a long pass from Berries hooker Col Brown was swooped upon by McCarthy, who was lurking out among the centres. McCarthy charged through to intercept the ball and raced 80 metres to score in the turning point of the match. Souths hung on to win 12–10, with Churchill bringing the club its first premiership in 12 years.

McCarthy said Churchill developed the ploy of using both himself and Coote out wide from his own experience playing against the all-star French line-up of 1951. The Frenchmen came to Australia and gave the locals a football lesson in the Test series. More than 20 years later, Churchill still raved about their skills. 'The French were brilliant, strong, tough, fast and unorthodox,' Churchill wrote in the *Sun*. 'Their standard will probably never be equalled. Not even the great English sides or the all-conquering St George or South Sydney club sides could match them. They had two magnificent second-rowers in Ponsinet and Brousse who were as big as houses and ran like three-quarters.' And it was on Ponsinet and Brousse that Churchill attempted to model McCarthy and Coote. 'I was too young to remember them, but Clive never stopped talking about that French side,' McCarthy recalls. 'They obviously made a huge impression on him with the way the big blokes ran amok out wide because that's what he kept impressing on Ronnie Coote and myself. Forwards always used to hang around the ruck in those days so it took a bit of convincing to get us to stay out near the flanks. But we quickly saw what an effective ploy it was and enjoyed the extra room to move. The four tackle rule came into the game in 1967 and that persuaded Clive to put us out among the backs. He used to say we were wasting our time in tight and he was right.'

McCarthy saw Churchill as the perfect coach to succeed Bernie Purcell with the Rabbitohs. 'Bernie sowed the seed for that great Souths side and deserves plenty of credit,' McCarthy said. 'You couldn't say Clive was a technical coach but he knew how to keep everyone's mind on the job and he kept us happy. We all respected him and a prime motivation for playing well was not to let Clive down. He didn't believe in ranting and raving, even though there were many times he could have had a go at us. I remember one big game against Manly at the SCG, we were leading with a few minutes to go and I had a brain explosion. I kicked the ball over the top but it was regathered by their little halfback Graham Williams and he sent Ken Irvine on his way. I thought Kenny would score for sure but somehow we pulled him down just short of the corner. My relief didn't last long—Ken played the ball, they passed it along the backline and John McDonald scored on the other wing. I'd lost us the game and had my head down when I got back to the dressing room. I expected a blast and fully deserved one. If I'd done that nowadays, I could have expected to be in reserve grade the following week. But all Clive did was glance my way, frown for a second and give his shirt a little pull, as if to say, "You won't do that again, will you, son?" He got his message across. I never tried anything stupid like that again.'

The Rabbitohs began their title defence slowly in 1968, losing five of their eleven first round games. But Churchill and his men were a big match team, and as the scent of the finals hit their nostrils, they found peak form. The Rabbitohs won their last nine games to capture the minor premiership from Manly. But the Sea Eagles shocked Souths with an impressive 23–15 win in the major semi-final, winning a grand final spot as a result. Souths had to make the big game the hard way, by beating St George, now captain-coached by Johnny Raper, 20–8 in the final. Churchill fine-tuned his team on grand final day, moving Sattler to the second row alongside former centre Bob Moses. That gave Souths a powerhouse front row of Jim Morgan, Elwyn Walters and John O'Neill and it was up front that the Rabbitohs asserted their superiority. Again, an intercept try turned the match in Souths' favour. This time it was the speedy Mike Cleary who scooped up a loose Manly pass and raced away for his team's lone try. The try gave Souths the impetus for a 13–9 win—and back-to-back titles for coach Churchill.

The Rabbitohs were raging hot favourites to make it three in a row in 1969, with Churchill's young side maturing into a superb all-round team. Souths won the minor premiership and on grand final day, most experts had the big game against a brash young Balmain side done and won well before the 3pm kickoff. Captain Sattler agrees the Rabbitohs took the Tigers too lightly. 'We were 100–1 on,' Sattler recalls. 'Everyone thought we were going to romp home. Before the game we were up in the grandstand, looking down at the Giltinan Shield. I was sitting next to John "Lurch" O'Neill and he just shook his head and growled: "It's a bloody joke, playing this mob of cats. We're going to murder them. We should just pick up that shield and take it down to the Cauliflower Hotel and have a beer."

'Anyway, it's history now that they were too good for us in the game. I'll never forget the stunned look on Lurch's face with about five minutes to go. "You know something," he muttered to me. "This mob of cats is going to beat us".'

But Churchill, a coach who enjoyed great popularity because he always put his players first, took full responsibility for the team's shock 11–2 loss. In the *Sun*'s serialisation of his career, Churchill blamed no-one but himself for the defeat, still regarded today among the biggest upsets in league history. 'It was my fault,' Churchill wrote. 'I blame myself because the tactics were wrong. When the players came off at halftime, I should have told them to kick to make Balmain back-pedal. We were getting nowhere against their defence but I didn't think they could tackle so well for so long. I looked around the dressing room at the players sitting in front of me and I thought what a great side . . . we won't get beaten. I had too much faith in them and I under-estimated Balmain. It was going to be a matter of time. Move the ball about and stand deeper, I told them.' Churchill saw his dream of a hat-trick of titles vanish when little-known winger Sid Williams plunged over in the corner midway through the second half to extend Balmain's lead to 9–0. 'When Williams went for that line, I knew we had lost,' Churchill wrote. 'Again, even though I give instructions, I thought the captain could have changed them if the tactics weren't working. Perhaps he could have ordered them to start kicking. But it was my fault and I accept that.'

CLIVE CHURCHILL

The Rabbitohs didn't take long to get back on track after that heartbreaking setback. Souths made amends in the best possible way in 1970, winning the title they lost 12 months earlier. The men from Redfern again finished minor premiers, but this time there were no slip-ups in the big end-of-season games as they beat Manly 23–12 on grand final day. It was in that match that Churchill witnessed the bravest act he ever saw on a football field. John Sattler's effort in leading the Rabbitohs to victory despite a badly broken jaw, suffered in a sickening off-the-ball incident in the opening minutes, has gone down in league folklore. 'When I walked out to greet the players after we had won, tears came to my eyes; I had a lump in my throat,' Churchill wrote in the *Sun*. 'Just to see and know what this man had been through . . . you just can't measure that. I don't think I've ever been more proud to say I was from South Sydney. Satts' face was covered in blood, but he didn't complain once.' Early in the match, Churchill was oblivious to the drama, despite seeing Sattler king-hit by a Manly forward. 'It never dawned on me that Satts had broken his jaw,' Churchill wrote. 'When the side came off at halftime, his mouth seemed to gape open. I asked him what was wrong and he said, "Nothing. I'm okay." As they started filing out for the second half, Bobby McCarthy said to me "Satts has a broken jaw . . . he shouldn't be going back."

'I rushed out of the dressing room to pull him back, but I was too late. Sattler was already running out of the gate and onto the field. He really didn't want to give me a chance. The way he played that second half, you can't believe a man would go through so much. When my wife Joyce saw him in hospital that night she just cried. He looked an awful mess; it was the bravest thing I have ever seen in all my years of football.'

Economic forces began to eat away at the Souths empire in 1971. Classy young forward Jim Morgan crossed Anzac Parade to join Eastern Suburbs, while Bob Moses went to big spenders Manly. Ron Coote, who was destined to become a Rooster 12 months later, sat out the opening rounds after a contract dispute with the club. But Churchill had enough petrol in the tank to steer the Rabbitohs to yet another minor premiership. Manly, buoyed by the signing of crafty Englishman Mal Reilly, finished second on the ladder and along with Jack Gibson's St George presented formidable opposition to Souths' quest of a fourth title in five years. Souths downed the Sea Eagles 19–13 in the major semi, advancing straight to the grand final. Manly gambled on Reilly's suspect knee in the final and paid a heavy penalty, bowing out 15–12 to Saints. Gibson had reached his first grand final and fielded a formidable side that included Graeme Langlands, Billy Smith, Ken Maddison and Barry Beath. Souths held the narrowest of leads at halftime—1–0—courtesy of an Eric Simms field goal. But when Ray Branighan crossed in the corner just 60 seconds into the second half, the title was again on its way to Redfern. After a tough struggle, Souths emerged 16–10 winners. As Churchill and his players did their lap of honour to the tune of 'Glory Glory to South Sydney' on the SCG's scratchy public address system, few in the capacity crowd could have realised they were witnessing the end of an era. The wolves began to pick at the bones of the financially strapped Rabbitohs in the following seasons, with John O'Neill and Branighan both joining Manly and Coote and Elwyn Walters signing rich deals at Easts. Souths haven't won a title since—and realistically are unlikely to again.

Churchill continued to coach the Rabbitohs despite the setbacks, although even he must surely have seen the writing on the wall. The Rabbitohs scraped into the finals in 1972, before finishing seventh in 1973, fifth in 1974 and at the bottom of the ladder in Churchill's last season in 1975. Angry with club officials and the way they failed to retain star players or develop new ones, Churchill became more and more disillusioned. In the end, he resigned before the club had the chance to axe him midway through the 1975 season. Club management took offence at a series of typically straight-talking Churchill columns in the *Sun*. Churchill met with club officials one July night midway through 1975 and handed in his resignation when grilled over his actions. 'It was like being in a courtroom . . . I wasn't going to be cross-examined and that's why I quit,' Churchill told the media the next day. 'I didn't go in there intending to quit and they said they didn't intend sacking me. But when they brought up all the things of the past, I thought what's the use of talking. They were armed with all sorts of stories . . . they were conducting a courtroom drama. "Did you say this . . . did you say that?"'

Churchill then fired a boots-and-all farewell blast at the club in the *Sun* the following day. Clearly the rapport and respect The Little Master had cultivated with his players over the past nine seasons had been eroded away. 'There's no loyalty at Souths,' he wrote. 'No spirit. Too much backchat from players who think they know best. I don't think the players want to listen to me. I've watched them in the dressing room before matches and at halftime. Some stand in the corners talking to each other while I'm giving an address. Others are fiddling with their boots. I know they're not listening and I've seen them disobey my orders so many times on the field. I even had a player backchat me. He virtually told me to mind my own business. Things like that hurt me. I've been part of Souths too long to cop it. I love the club, I love the atmosphere, but I can't stay on any longer.'

Journalist Gary Lester, who was the ghost writer for Churchill's columns, says the former Test star could no longer contain his frustration at club officials. 'Clive was dirty and wasn't afraid to say so,' Lester said. 'In the end, it was a series of columns we wrote detailing what was wrong in the place that upset the club officials and that's why they decided to force him to quit. I think he saw what was happening at Souths as the beginning of the end for the club and he was certainly proved right—they have had lean times over the past 20 years. I remember it surprised me that he was prepared to say what he did and he never backed down despite the strife his comments caused for him.' Lester remembers Churchill as one of league's most durable characters. 'Clive was friendly, cheeky and got on with everyone,' he said. 'One night after a training session in the wet at Redfern, all the players picked him up and threw him in the biggest heap of mud they could find. They all laughed their heads off, and none more so than Clive. That was before the rot set in and I really felt sorry that his parting from the club was so bitter.'

Bobby McCarthy had the unenviable task of succeeding Churchill, captain-coaching Souths for the last five rounds of the premiership. 'It was hard taking over from him, particularly as I liked the little bloke so much,' McCarthy said. 'The club had been decimated by the likes of Easts and Manly and I understood why Clive wanted out. He was sick and tired of it all. The officials really were pretty ordinary at Souths back then and would have frustrated anyone. They told me I was too old at the end of that season so I went to Canterbury for a couple of years. Then they re-signed me in 1977. Work that out . . . they must have thought I'd found the fountain of youth.'

After retiring, Churchill continued his close association

with league. He was a regular fixture at many games, was a judge for the *Daily Mirror*'s Dally M awards and ran a bottle shop in Sydney's eastern suburbs. In 1982, he made front page news when two thieves bashed him with a shotgun while attempting to rob his store. Even in such a time of trauma, Churchill could see the humour. 'They broke the shotgun over me head,' he told reporters from his hospital bed only hours later. 'So I knew they couldn't shoot me.'

The league world was stunned to learn early in 1985 that Churchill was suffering from cancer. In typical fashion, he vowed to fight with all his strength. 'I'll give the battle everything I've got,' he told reporters. In June of that year, a crowd of more than 500 guests at a special dinner at Randwick Racecourse paid tribute to The Little Master. Keynote speaker Alan Jones declared: 'Clive Churchill is a man not of his time ... but beyond his time. We all feel for the greatness that is Churchill—he's the Carl Lewis, the Don Bradman, the Walter Lindrum of league.' In his last public appearance the following week, Churchill kicked off a Monday Night Football clash at the SCG, the ground where he enjoyed so many triumphs both as player and coach. Clearly weak and many kilos below his usual weight, Churchill was given a standing ovation all the way back to the grandstand. Less than two months later, The Little Master died.

Sydney afforded one of its favourite sons a massive funeral, with thousands of mourners lining the streets around St Mary's Cathedral. Former team-mates carried the coffin, draped in Souths and Australian jumpers, as sportsmen, politicians and many everyday Australians paid their final respects.

Seven years after his death, Churchill was paid the ultimate accolade. The respected magazine *Rugby League Week* polled a host of experts from many different eras to find the best league player of all time. Churchill came out at the head of a who's who of the code down the years. The award reinforced the view that The Little Master will always hold a special place in league history.

Bozo

BOB FULTON

CLUBS
Easts 1979 (captain-coach), 1980–82,
Manly 1983–88, 1993–

PREMIERSHIP RECORD
Games 323, won 210, lost 104, drew 9.
Winning percentage 65%.
Semi-finals
1980, 1981–84, 1986–88, 1993–95
Grand finals (4)
1980, 1983, 1987, 1995
Premierships (1)
1987

OTHER COACHING ACHIEVEMENTS
Coached Australia 1989–. Has never lost a Test series. Tests 35.
Won 29, lost 5, drew 1.
Coached Australia to 1992, 1995 World Cup victories.
Tour matches 36, won 35, lost 1.
Dally M Coach of the Year 1981, 1983.

I
t is one of rugby league's greatest ironies that Bob Fulton was born in England. British league fans have spent much of the past three decades rueing the decision of Fulton's parents to migrate to Australia while young Robert was still a baby. For Fulton became the scourge of the Englishmen, first as a player in the heated Ashes battles of the 1970s and in more recent times as coach of Australia's all-conquering Kangaroos.

Bob Fulton can rightly claim to be the most dominant figure in Australian league in the past 30 years as both a player and coach. A controversial character, Fulton was a 'love him or hate him' player in his heyday with the Manly club. And two decades on, little has changed. As coach of Manly and Australia, he has many critics, but just as many who admire and support him. Fulton's influence in the game cannot be denied. When the code was in crisis early in 1995 in the Super League war, Fulton was one of the first to get the call to arms. The ARL enlisted the astute Fulton to do its player negotiations in the wake of a mass buying spree by Super League. And while some critics again attacked him for taking on the role, declaring it a conflict of interests with his job as Manly coach, his success could not be denied. Fulton persuaded a host of league's biggest names to remain loyal to the ARL at a time when further defections could have seen the game's governing body collapse. For Bob Fulton, it was all part of a day's work and the former glamour boy is happy to thumb his nose at his detractors and get on with business.

'Bozo' Fulton was the complete player. Rare talent, hard work and a ruthless professionalism combined to make him one of the game's greats. In a 14-year career, Fulton bagged 147 tries—third on league's all-time list behind fellow legends Ken Irvine and Harold Horder. A classy five-eighth and centre,

Fulton was a classic opportunist, a brilliant individual who could turn a game in the blink of an eye.

He was brought to Manly from his home town of Wollongong as a teenager by Ken Arthurson in 1966. The move proved a significant one in league history, and the beginning of a relationship between the two that was to play a major role in the future direction of the code for years to come. A mature youngster with great skills, Fulton quickly made his mark. By 1967, he was in the New South Wales side and a shock omission from the Kangaroo touring party. Australian honours came 12 months later in 1968—as did his first grand final berth, as captain of the losing Manly team against the then mighty Souths. He became an integral part of the Australian team in the early '70s and went on to play 20 Tests for his country, including two Kangaroo tours. When Fulton was at his peak, Manly won their first three premierships—in 1972, 1973 and 1976. His performance in the 1973 premiership decider remains one of league's great grand final displays. In a brutal match that featured several all-in brawls, Fulton's class shone through. The flying Sea Eagle scored two grand solo tries—one in each half—to edge Manly ahead of a brash Cronulla side 10–7. After captaining Manly to victory in 1976, Fulton stunned the league world by switching to Eastern Suburbs. After 11 years as a Sea Eagle, he opted to move to the Roosters, with media magnate Kerry Packer playing a key role in his switch. Fulton finished his career with three seasons at Easts and it was there he began his coaching apprenticeship.

But Fulton has dreadful memories of his first season in coaching in 1979. 'It's something I'd prefer to forget,' he admits. 'And when I talk about my coaching career, I like to think it really only started the following year in 1980. I say that because I was captain-coach in '79 and the job was very hard.

I was the last of the "c-c", except for Wally Lewis when he tried the job at Gold Coast a few years back. That was a real transition time for Easts. Senior players like Arthur Beetson, who I took over from as captain-coach, and Bob O'Reilly left; Ron Coote and Bill Mullins both retired. We went with a youth program, similar to what we've been doing at Manly for the past few years. We bought "Crusher" Cleal as an unknown from the bush and guys like Marty Gurr, John Tobin and Gary Warnecke came through the juniors. Ken Wright came from rugby union. We finished well down the ladder in '79 but things improved the following year. I decided to retire and concentrate on the coaching. I could have played for another couple of years but found I couldn't do both jobs properly. Videos had come in then and the coach's role was getting busier and more complex. As soon as I retired, the job became so much simpler for me . . . I didn't have to worry about training, getting myself fit, my own form, injuries and the like. As a club, we were really fit; we had George Daldry as our trainer and he knew how to get the best out of the boys. Every player in the team bar one worked at the leagues club, so few people realise it, but we were virtually full-time professionals then in 1980. We'd have a training run at lunchtime and another in the afternoon and were in great condition. Up front we were tough with a couple of strong and experienced front-rowers in John Harvey and Royce Ayliffe. But really, we were basically a young side with guys like Gurr, Warnecke, David Michael, Steve McFarlane and Des O'Reilly. We finished minor premiers and those blokes busted their guts to get there. In the grand final, Canterbury were too good for us; they had a fairly young side too but had been in the grand final the year before and obviously learned some lessons from that. They played better under pressure whereas we probably let the occasion get to us.

That's one reason it annoys me that the smarties say I've always had the best sides at Manly and Easts. We have gone through transition periods like any other club and the critics just don't look at the facts. In the mid '70s when Easts won two straight titles they had 11 current internationals; years later, I had a side that we'd basically put together at short notice. Coaching is all about players . . . if you haven't got them, you may as well forget it. No coach has ever won a title without brilliant players . . . I don't care who he is.'

The Roosters also won the minor premiership under Fulton the following year in 1981, but missed the grand final, falling a step short to Warren Ryan's exciting young Newtown side. In '82, they finished third, again narrowly missing the grand final. The following year, Fulton received the call home to Manly, where he was greeted as the prodigal son. Despite leading the club to the grand final the previous year, coach Ray Ritchie was dumped to make way for Fulton. 'Leaving Easts after six years wasn't an easy decision,' Fulton said. 'They were a close-knit bunch of blokes and I had a lot of time for the officials there. They had men like Nick Politis, Ron Jones and John Quayle at Easts in those days. The club was very well run, but the lure to return to Manly was also strong. Ken Arthurson, who was like a second father to me, called and offered me the job and after a few years at Easts, it seemed a good time to move on. Coaching Manly, the club where I played for most of my career, was always a dream. We made the grand final in my first year but ran into the Parramatta side that beat everyone in that era. They were a great team and won three comps in a row . . . how many clubs have done that in the modern era? They had six or seven of the best players in the world in their positions in their team. Guys like Cronin, Ella, Sterling, Price, Kenny and Grothe. It's pretty hard to beat a team with that sort of personnel.'

Manly came close to the money for the next few years but Fulton finally removed the 'monkey' from his back in 1987. After coming so close in previous seasons, he broke through to savour premiership glory. It was early that season that Fulton came up with his infamous 'cement truck' line after a controversial loss at Cronulla. When his side was beaten 18–13 in a match which featured several contentious decisions, Fulton declared: 'I hope he (Harrigan) gets hit by a cement truck.' The fallout from that off-the-cuff comment was remarkable. He was fined by the NSW Rugby League but Manly produced an amazing turnaround after a slow start to the season. The Sea Eagles won 12 straight games—finishing ahead in the penalties on each occasion. The Sea Eagles roared home to win the minor premiership before beating grand final newcomers Canberra 18–8 to take the trophy. 'We had the right mix that year and reaped the rewards for a rebuilding program that we began after my first year there in 1983,' Fulton said. 'Winning that grand final was the culmination of several years' hard work. That was a very versatile team that could play any one of a number of styles. There were guys like Paul Vautin, Kevin Ward and Ronnie Gibbs who did the hard work up front and could mix it with the best of them. Ward's performance up front in the finals was outstanding and he was a real asset when he joined us from England. Des Hasler was a great worker and there was brilliance in attack in players like Cliff Lyons, Noel Cleal, Dale Shearer and Michael O'Connor. Vautin was a fine captain and has shown in more recent times that if he wanted to coach Manly—or any other team for that matter—he'd be a success.'

The prospect of coaching Australia saw Fulton step down as Manly coach at the end of the 1988 season. 'That's not a position you apply for, it's one you're appointed to,' Fulton said. 'Like going back to coach Manly, coaching Australia was a dream I'd had for some time. When it was offered to me, I didn't think I could really knock it back. I was approached by John Brennan of Radio 2UE at around the same time to be on the radio and working in the media was something that was pretty hard when you're involved in the weekly grind of coaching. So I had two new challenges in 1989 and went about them very happily. The Manly board wanted me to remain at the club and I gave it some thought, but I needed a change and in the end, it was a good move for me all round. I didn't lose touch with Manly; I stayed involved in the junior development side, helping bring young kids to the club. That was very satisfying and an important area and the Manly club is now reaping the rewards of the time we put in finding and developing those kids. Gone are the days where you've got a first grade coach and two lower grade coaches. The head coach now has to look at getting the best of the players under his control, he has to supervise junior development and recruitment programs. It's a very satisfying part of the job, particularly for me, seeing the young guys like Nik Kosef, John Hopoate and Steve Menzies progress through the ranks and achieve the ultimate honour of playing for Australia.'

Fulton's emergence as Australian coach coincided with a bold new breed of young players breaking into the green and gold. The likes of Brad Clyde, Laurie Daley, Greg Alexander, Michael Hancock, Brad Fittler, Mark Geyer and Kevin and Kerrod Walters all made their Australian debuts in Fulton's first two years as coach. All were to make a significant impact on the scene as Australia maintained its lofty standing on the game's international stage. But old Fulton favourites like Steve Roach, Paul Sironen and Dale Shearer weren't forgotten either. The critics were up in arms more than once in 1989–90–91 when the trio somehow made Test selection despite either missing or failing to perform in State of Origin football. Fulton's influence in the selection room has been undoubted, with his critics again claiming he wields too much power.

A man who isn't afraid to speak his mind, Fulton has had to contend with 'Bozo bashers' since he first appeared in Sydney football as a snowy-haired teenager in the 1960s. At the end of Australia's successful World Cup campaign in 1995, a national sporting magazine named Fulton as the most unpopular personality in the game. In the year when Super League split the game and created many bitter feuds, this was no mean feat. In his early, more fiery days as a coach, Fulton would often ring journalists who had been critical of him to return serve. But the Fulton, 1990s model, is a more mature and mellow version of the original. 'I see and hear the criticism and it doesn't really worry me all that much these days,' he shrugged. 'Because I've been involved with two clubs that aren't always all that popular in Manly and Easts, I think I've copped a bit. And because Ken Arthurson is like a second father to me, and also happens to be a powerful figure in the game, people make snide remarks. If my relationship with Arko is a problem for other people, so be it. It's certainly not a problem for me. I'm also straightforward in my opinions. If a journalist asks me a question, I'll answer it. I don't try to hide anything and will usually give a direct answer. Now that sometimes offends people. But if that's not what they want to hear, it's their bad luck and they can go and suck. There are too many soft-cocks in rugby league who only say what people want to hear. I don't give a damn about what people think. If I was to crap around and answer questions like other people in the game, I might be more accepted. But that's not my style. I'm not saying I'm right all the time; I've been wrong on plenty of occasions. But at least I've said what I think and haven't tried to hide my views. In 1995, I copped heaps for criticising a referee (Kiwi Phil Houston) after a Test match against New Zealand. In the three years I've been back at Manly, I haven't criticised one referee at club level. The guy I bagged was dropped straight after that match by the same organisation that appointed him to reserve grade. In England after the '95 World Cup I didn't abuse (English referees director Greg) McCallum. I made a valid point to him about the way the penalties and some crucial decisions went in our semi against New Zealand. I told him he went over there to clean up the game and open up the 10 metres, yet we never saw that in a game refereed by one of his English referees. I don't want to be a politician or a diplomat; it's not the way I operate. What some of these people forget is that coaching a football team isn't a popularity contest. As for my ability as a coach, all I can do is point to my record. Every year I've coached. I've got my teams to the finals except one, in 1984 when we lost a midweek playoff to Penrith. I've been criticised for how we've gone on occasion in the finals but in most of those years, we've come in fourth or fifth and had key players missing through injury. But we've still got there and finished ahead of plenty of teams.'

Although his finals record is poor by his own admission, Fulton's coaching statistics still make impressive reading. He was the game's 'winningest' coach in the '80s, winning more than 64 per cent of the games he contested at club level. When one considers the likes of Jack Gibson, Warren Ryan and Tim Sheens were also coaching—and winning premierships—in the '80s, Fulton's figures are impressive indeed.

His representative coaching career is even more imposing. On the 1990 and 1994 Kangaroo tours, Fulton brought home the Ashes, but not without his share of anxious moments. In 1990, the Roos' magnificent winning run from the previous two undefeated tours finally came to an end. In a memorable First Test at Wembley Stadium, Great Britain outclassed the Aussies 19–12 before an emotional crowd of more than 52,000. The match brought about a crisis of confidence for Fulton. He was forced to cast aside player loyalties and go for the in-form men to rescue the series. Out went Allan Langer, Martin Bella and Kerrod Walters, replaced by Ricky Stuart, Glenn Lazarus and Ben Elias. All three were to play key roles in the remainder of the series. In the Second Test, Australia was staring at Ashes defeat for the first time in almost 20 years. But a late Mal Meninga try, after a length-of-the-field Ricky Stuart break, gave the Kangaroos a last-gasp 14–10 win. Their spirit bruised and broken, the Englishmen capitulated in the deciding Test, losing 14–0. It was a remarkably similar story in 1994, with the Lions again drawing first blood—and again at Wembley. This time a gallant British side, reduced to 12 men following the first-half dismissal of skipper Shaun Edwards, held on to score a fine 8–4 win. And again, Fulton had hard decisions to make. He again dropped Langer, bringing in Stuart to call the shots at halfback. And winger Rod Wishart, second-rower Dean Pay and prop Lazarus were all brought in to add starch to the Aussies' performance. The result was a devastating 38–8 trouncing of the Lions, with all the new men again playing key roles. The Third Test, again, was a mere formality as the Aussies romped home 23–4. Bob Fulton, the lad born in Lancashire, had again frustrated England's bid for Ashes glory.

After a four-year lay-off from the club scene, Fulton found himself back in charge of Manly in remarkable circumstances just weeks before the 1993 kickoff. 'I was in the country on business when I got an urgent phone call from (Manly chief executive) Frank Stanton. Frank's first words to me were, "Are you available?" I had no idea what he was talking about. I asked, "For what?" Then he explained that Graham Lowe was very ill and couldn't coach the team any more. It came right from nowhere; I had no intention of coaching at club level again and had already made up my mind I'd never coach anywhere apart from Manly. I told Frank I'd have to check it with my wife Anne first and the family and also 2UE and my business. I sorted it out over the next two days and accepted the job, only a couple of weeks before the season began. So I was back in the hurly-burly of it all, but I'd had a good break from the weekly pressure and was fresh and keen again. It was a fairly hectic time, though. Manly had just lost Marty Bella to Canterbury, Kevin Iro went back to England and Michael O'Connor had retired. We didn't replace them with anyone. It looked like being a hard year for us and that's the way it turned out. Everyone was tipping us to come in eleventh or twelfth but we made the finals and finished fourth when a very good Brisbane side knocked us out.'

It was very much a similar situation in 1994, when the Sea Eagles again came in at the bottom end of the finals before being eliminated by the Broncos. But Manly finally looked on target to repeat their success of 1987 in 1995, when the club led the premiership from go to whoa. The Sea Eagles were the outstanding team throughout the year, winning an incredible 16 games straight to start the season. Bozo's boys won the minor premiership, boasted the game's best attacking and best defensive records. They produced the year's top pointscorer (Matthew Ridge) and top tryscorer (Steve Menzies) and shattered a host of records with their pointscoring prowess. In the finals, they won their way through to the grand final with impressive wins over Cronulla and Newcastle. But on the big day, everything suddenly went wrong for the hottest grand final favourites in years. Bustled by a Sydney Bulldogs side that made the most of several contentious decisions that went their way, the Sea Eagles crashed 17–4 in a grand final nightmare. Fulton could only lament on the unfairness of the new eight-team finals series in reviewing his team's heartache. 'We didn't get what we deserved out of the season, and neither did Canberra for that matter,' Fulton said. 'Over the 22 rounds, we were the two outstanding teams in the premiership. We both won 20 of our 22 games and finished six points clear of the field. But we didn't get the second bite of the cherry that I believe we were entitled to because of the new finals system. There's nothing we can do about it now, and I don't want to sound like a whinger. As minor premiers, we got no more advantage than the team that came in fourth and that is a weakness in the system that has to be looked at. It all came down to one game where we didn't play particularly well and the other team got some doubtful decisions. Canterbury played great on the day and played better than us. But the video shows they scored three tries—one from a pass that was a metre forward and another on the seventh tackle. That really kicked us in the guts, particularly the seventh tackle try as our guys knew they'd had their last tackle and didn't get back in the defensive line. You've got to play the whistle, but that was cruel. I'm fairly certain that even though we didn't play well, we could have still got out with a win if those decisions hadn't gone against us. They say you make your own luck in this game, but to me, that's bullshit.'

In recent years, Fulton has combined coaching both Manly and Australia with considerable success. He steered the Kangaroos to impressive results on the 1994 Kangaroo tour, as well as the 1995 World Cup. Unlike many coaches, including the maestro Jack Gibson, who said he could never mix club and representative coaching, Fulton sees no problem with the dual roles. 'It probably helped going through it all as a player. I'm not saying it's a criteria, but it is a bit of an advantage. When I was playing, I learned to deal with a hectic schedule that comes up from time to time during a season. I think that as long as your club role, which has to come first and foremost, doesn't suffer, then you should feel comfortable about handling the two jobs. I can only judge my performance by how Manly has gone since I returned to the club and had both the club and Australian jobs. And we've had three excellent years. It hasn't affected us adversely, but it's not something I can take the credit for. We've got a good staff at Manly, an astute chief executive and a supportive board. And Australia has also gone well. I know people say that me being Australian coach gives me some sort of advantage, but I don't know what it is. I don't go sounding out players every time they come into the Test team about playing for Manly. In the three years that I've been back at the club, we've only signed four "name" players—Mark Carroll, Terry Hill, David Gillespie and Jim Serdaris for '96—and we needed them to replace players who have gone elsewhere. These guys have made us tougher up front and have been a major factor in our success.'

Fulton's critics—and Super League supporters who had long been upset at his perceived power in the game—had a field day midway through 1995 when Australia lost hooker Wayne Bartrim through injury days before the Third Test against the Kiwis. Test selector Arthur Beetson slammed Fulton in the media, claiming that the selectors had voted to bring in Cronulla's Aaron Raper as the replacement. But Fulton overruled the selectors, bringing in Wests' Jim Serdaris, who had already agreed to play with Fulton's Manly team the following year. Mention of the affair, which was blown into back page headlines for several days afterwards, makes Fulton see red. 'For God's sake, that was a storm over nothing,' he said. 'Beetson was outvoted by the other selectors 5–1. Even Aaron Raper's father Johnny agreed with my assessment of the situation, which was that only days before the match, we needed to bring in an experienced replacement. Aaron Raper is a great kid but it would have been unfair to anyone to bring in a rookie so close to a big match against tough opposition. All it was with Arthur is that he spat out his dummy. And I remember when he coached Australia, he was dirty because he didn't get the team he wanted and he resigned over it! That's the ridiculous part about it. I was put in a position where a player pulled out and late in the week I wanted a particular replacement. If a coach can't get that, there is something wrong. And I make no apologies for having a shot at Arthur at the time. I mean who's coaching the team—him or me? He jumped up and down and said he was going to quit the selection panel—they're still waiting for his resignation in Phillip Street. They should have sacked him and ended it all.'

Fulton's assistant at Manly, Marty Gurr, is better qualified than most to assess the Sea Eagles' mentor. Gurr, who has the makings of a fine first grade coach in his own right, was a rookie fullback at Easts in 1980 when Fulton made his first grand final. He played under Fulton at Manly years later before accepting a job on the club's coaching staff. 'The thing about Bob is that he backs his convictions,' Gurr said. 'He doesn't beat around the bush and while that doesn't make him a great politician, I think it helps him as a football coach. The players always know where they stand. He is loyal to his players and lets them back their own skills. While Bob wants to play the game a particular way, he's not about to shackle the

likes of Cliff Lyons or Steve Menzies. The guy has probably
mellowed a bit, but basically because he has become more
comfortable in what he is doing. He has been coaching a long
time and has become better as he's gone along. The secret of
his success is that he has always been willing and able to
change with the times. As the game has changed, Bob hasn't
been too proud to change with it. Some coaches with bigger
egos have resisted change and paid the penalty, but Bob has
been flexible and hence his longevity in such a tough job.'

Fulton rates the performance of the young Australian side
at the 1995 World Cup as the pinnacle of his coaching career.
With the game Down Under ravaged by the Super League war,
Australia sent a squad variously described as 'also-rans' and
'third raters' to defend the Cup in Britain. After an early loss to
England in the opening game, the young Aussies came of age.
They romped through the other preliminary games, downed
New Zealand in a tough semi-final and then gained their
revenge over England in the final at Wembley to snare the trophy. 'From a personal point of view, I can't say enough about
the effort those young blokes put in,' Fulton said. 'I was so
proud of them. They were behind the eight ball early after that
loss to England and could have caved in under pressure. But
they showed real character to fight back. We scored more
points than anyone in the competition and played some very
entertaining football. It showed the Super League people that
no-one is indispensable. People over here and in England said
we'd go out the back door and that made us only more determined. It was some of the best A grade death riding I'd ever
seen. We stuck it up quite a few critics who wanted to see us
get beaten. As a coach, I'd have to say winning that tourna-
ment was my proudest moment. Like a player, as a coach you
want to perform for your country. And what we did over there,

against supreme adversity, was just magic. The feeling of elation and pride we all felt was very special. I was also over the moon after the clean sweep of New Zealand mid-year. Before the series, everyone rated the Kiwis as the best team their country had produced in over a decade. And on paper, I had to agree with them. The Super League battle was at its height when the series was played. A lot of these kids were tossed jumpers but they handled themselves superbly and showed real character. That was a real confidence boost for us all and helped build the team for the testing time we were to have months later in the World Cup.'

Fulton admits he has picked up excellent coaching tips from several of the game's best judges over the years. 'Frank Stanton coached me for a long time at Manly and I learned some very valuable things from him. And when I went to Easts in 1977, the Jack Gibson influence was still there even though Jack had left 12 months earlier. The place was run very much along the guidelines Jack had laid down. I consider them two of the most important coaches of the modern era. Jack set the foundations for us all at club level with his deeds over a number of years. And Frank Stanton was just as big an influence on the Test scene. He brought a new professionalism to the game at that level and was a key figure in Australia's rise to the dominant world power. I was lucky enough to play under Frank at club and international level and he was a big influence. There have been some excellent coaches in the time I've been involved in it . . . Phil Gould, Tim Sheens and Wayne Bennett for example. There are others as well but those three are probably the pick of the bunch. Sheens and Bennett have won a few comps between them but having said that, they've also had great material to work with. Again, it doesn't matter how good a coach you are, you've got to have the raw material. Look at

Canberra when Glenn Lazarus left the place a few years back. It took them a good couple of years to recover. And as soon as he went to Brisbane, they won two comps in a row. I remember the year Ricky Stuart injured himself just before the finals and Canberra bombed out. It just proves you've got to have the class players to do the job. The players are more important than any coach. If you've got the better players than your opposition, you should win 99.9 per cent of the time.'

Fulton sees coaching in modern rugby league as a complex task. 'Leaving aside the tactical side of the game and man management, getting the best out of the players under your control is arguably your most important task. On a week-to-week basis, it's your job to make sure they are consistent in both attack and defence. You've got to also have a solid match plan in both those areas. Then there's the opposition, you have to be able to understand their strengths and weaknesses and convey them to your own players. There's a lot of juggling of personalities and that's where man management comes in. And it's not just your first grade team. It's all through the grades and includes the coaching staff and officials. You've got to make sure you appoint the right staff and have the right lines of communication with the players and officials. That's where a good chief executive is important. The players need to be confident that the club is solid at the top and the relationship between the coach and chief executive is strong. You've got to work at the grass roots on junior development. You have to work with your junior coaches and make sure they are on the same wavelength. I put a lot of time into that and I know Tim Sheens does the same in Canberra. Gone are the days when you can buy a premiership. Every club needs to nurture and develop its own talent. At the end of any given year, hopefully you can look back and say, "We started the year with these guys and they have become better players. And we achieved the best we could with the talent under our control." If you can say that truthfully, then you've done a good job. From an overall point of view, the coach oversees the whole club, handling the half dozen or more areas I've just outlined, and makes sure the place runs smoothly. You've got to have the finger on the pulse everywhere and if you don't you risk losing touch. It's a very hands-on job, but not as hands-on as it used to be. Now it's a more varied position where you've got to watch a whole variety of areas. You've got to have discipline and I think coaches even need to train a bit themselves to keep mentally alert. And lastly, you've got to look the part. People may tell you differenty, but appearances are still important. It's a job with a lot of pressure but plenty of rewards. As I said, when I quit Manly originally I never intended to get back into it. But it has been very satisfying and I feel it is in my blood—it would probably be hard to stop.'

Fulton is destined to remain a key figure in rugby league well past the year 2000 and after his coaching days are over, it's not hard to imagine him accepting a job at the game's highest level in administration. Again, he'll have his critics, but Fulton won't let them worry him one bit as he goes about doing the job in his own style . . . just as he has for the past 30 years with considerable success.

The Man From Otahuhu

GRAHAM LOWE

CLUBS
Otahuhu (New Zealand) 1977–78, Norths (Brisbane) 1980–82,
Wigan (UK) 1986–89, Manly 1990–92, North Queensland 1996–

BRISBANE PREMIERSHIP RECORD
Games 59, won, 29, lost 30. Winning percentage 49.1%.
Semi-finals
1980
Grand finals (1)
1980
Premierships (1)
1980

ENGLISH CHAMPIONSHIP RECORD
Games 82, won 64, lost 16, drew 2. Winning percentage 78.0%.

ARL PREMIERSHIP RECORD
Games 70, won 40, lost 27, drew 3. Winning percentage 57.1%.
Semi finals
1990–91

OTHER COACHING ACHIEVEMENTS
Won Auckland premiership 1977–78, English Challenge Cup
1987–88, 1988–89, Lancashire Cup 1986–87, 1987–88, 1988–89,
John Player Cup 1986–87, 1988–89, English First Division
championship 1986–87, English premiership 1986–87,
World Cup championship 1987, Australian State of Origin title
1991. Coached New Zealand in 19 Tests. Won 10, lost 8, drew 1.
Coached Queensland in 6 State of Origin matches,
3 wins, 3 losses.

C oaching journeyman Graham Lowe has tasted phenomenal success in rugby league's three strongest
nations—New Zealand, Great Britain and Australia—
over the past 20 years. A popular character with great support
among the media and public, Lowe is a talented coach with the
ability to get the best out of the players. His wholehearted
approach has seen him develop a tremendous rapport with his
players and he has had the happy knack of winning titles, and
doing it in style. Articulate and intelligent, Lowe has fought a
constant battle with illness over the past decade.

A great ambassador for his homeland, Lowe is owed a massive debt by rugby league in New Zealand. Former Prime
Minister David Lange once said of Lowe: 'Graham Lowe's
greatest score has been the impact he made on the New
Zealand public. He has transformed the image of rugby league
from underdog sport to a captivating spectator game.'

Graham Lowe was a run-of-the-mill player with Otahuhu,
one of the leading clubs in New Zealand, for much of his
teenage years. 'Actually, I had some ability,' he joked. 'It's the
selectors who didn't—they never picked me. I was just a
player but I was a trier. I filled in at centre, five-eighth or back-
row ... wherever I could get a game really. I badly damaged
both my shoulders in 1969 when I was 23 and that was in the
time before they did total reconstructions, which are so routine
nowadays. The doctors operated on both shoulders but it
wasn't a success; I lost some of the movement and had to give
it away. For the next few years I drifted away from football and
began my own auto-electrical business. The coaching side of it
just started out of the blue. The coach of Otahuhu under-18s
was going overseas and couldn't find anyone to take his place.
He was running out of time and was desperate so he asked me.
I won the comp in that first year, again the next year and then

finished second in reserve grade. That was good enough to give me a start in first grade and we won two comps in a row.'

After four premierships in five years at Otahuhu, Lowe was forced to pack up his family and move to Brisbane. 'My eldest daughter was an asthmatic and the doctors thought the cold, wet New Zealand climate was making her problem worse,' he said. 'They suggested we shift to somewhere warmer and Brisbane seemed the best alternative at the time. It ended up a very significant move in my football career, although football certainly wasn't the major consideration at the time.' Lowe was appointed coach of struggling Norths in the Brisbane domestic competition soon after his arrival and was faced with a mammoth task to make the club competitive. 'Norths had finished bottom of the ladder the previous year and were in pretty poor shape,' he said. 'They had lost most of their players and it was going to be a struggle. But I brought Mark Graham to the club with me from New Zealand and he made a big difference. We finished in fifth spot in my first year and I was pretty happy with that considering the state the club had been in. The following year, Mark Murray and Greg Conescu, who both went on to play for Australia, became regular first graders. We won the comp and it was the club's first premiership in more than a decade so everyone in the place was pretty stoked.'

Lowe then received an offer to return home as director of coaching in New Zealand, incorporating national coach. 'That was a senior role and one I felt comfortable in taking at the time,' he said. 'By that stage I'd managed to form my own views on coaching and I knew where I was heading. In those early coaching days, I saw a lot of myself and my mates in the players I was coaching. I was still young enough to identify with them and understand them. I remember forming much of my early coaching philosophy at school. That was probably one of the few things school taught me because I couldn't wait to leave the place. And the reason behind that was that they never knew or cared what made Graham Lowe tick. To them, I was just a number in the place. They didn't know me or want to help me. I feel, after looking at that, that the key to getting through to an individual, whether a schoolboy or a football player, is to work with him one on one. That's when you really get to know them, find out their likes and dislikes, and get to establish a relationship. You get them to trust you and confide in you and you also find it easier to help them improve. Because I wasn't treated like that, I think the way I do now. I realise the importance of someone taking the time and effort to try to help you as a person. You can train a football team as a unit and a lot of coaches probably do, but to me, treating them as 13 individuals is the way to go. I always try to make players feel that they are special—that they're not just there to make up the numbers.'

Lowe's first series coaching New Zealand against Australia came in 1983, with the Kiwi stocks close to an all-time low. New Zealand hadn't won a Test against 'big brother' for more than a decade, let alone a series. The First Test went very much to script, with the Aussies beating a determined, but outclassed Kiwi outfit 16–4 in Auckland. But the Second Test at Brisbane's Lang Park produced one of the biggest boilovers on the international scene for decades. The Kiwis turned the tables to record a splendid 19–12 win to square the two-match series. 'The Kiwis had been used to getting flogged for years and so a drawn series was treated like a win back home,' Lowe recalled. 'I always felt when I took over the team that the New Zealanders suffered from an inferiority complex when they played Australia. I think the players were torn between tackling the Aussies and asking them for their autographs. They were in awe of the big name Aussie players and it showed on the field. So I worked hard on changing that attitude. And even though we lost the First Test by 16–4, I was happy. I could see the players changing their ways and from memory, I think we broke Australia's line more often than they broke ours. Our finishing let us down, but I knew it was something I could work on. Our confidence improved in the Second Test in Brisbane and that was all we needed. It was a great effort because our best player, Mark Graham, missed the Second Test through injury. We had unsung heroes like James Leuluai, Fred Ah Kuoi, Howie Tamati and Nick Wright who weren't thought of highly by the Aussies, but they did the job. In fact, we should have beaten them by more than seven points. In the years that followed, players like Olsen Filipaina and Joe Ropati came along. They might not have been all that consistent at club level in Sydney, but every time they pulled on the Kiwi jumper, they were a force to be reckoned with.'

Lowe set about changing the way New Zealanders thought about their rugby league as he made the Kiwis a force on the international scene after years of poor performances. 'The key, in my opinion, was to look at the Aussies and learn from their success,' he said. 'I have always had the highest respect for Australian football and felt we had plenty to learn from what was going on over here. They spent millions of dollars on junior development and the results were there for everyone to see. So I tried to improve our junior development in a similar vein. I also found that over the years in New Zealand, a lot of players with ability had managed to get offside with the establishment. They were square pegs trying to fit into round holes. But often, they had only small problems and just needed to be looked after. Often they were great talents who couldn't get a look in, but all they needed was someone to look after them. I tried to bring those guys to the forefront and a lot of them gave good value, which surprised a fair few people in New Zealand. But I had faith in them . . . and I knew that if someone gave them the chance, they would produce the goods.'

Lowe coached the Kiwis for four years from 1983 to 1986 and the campaigns with the national team are among his fondest memories. 'They were great times and we achieved some fine results, given our poor track record prior to that,' he said. 'We held our own against most countries and always rose to the occasion against Australia. In my final series against the Aussies in 1986, they beat us 3–0 but even though it was a clean sweep, it was still a contest. We pushed them in every game and it was only that little extra class and experience that got them home. In 1985, I consider that we morally won the series. We had a French referee and he absolutely shafted us. They won the First Test 26–20 in a game that was a real toss-up. Then we were leading the Second Test all the way before a try in the last minute by John Ribot got them home. We made a mistake and Wally Lewis, great player that he was, punished us for it. Wally was the difference between the teams. But even so the try came from a forward pass—Ribot himself has admitted to me since then that the try should never have been awarded. Then in the Third Test, we beat them 18–0; it was the first time an Australian team had ever been held scoreless against New Zealand so that was a satisfying way to finish a frustrating series.'

Lowe ended his stint as Kiwi coach on a sour note and still has bitter memories of the experience. 'I retired as Kiwi coach at the beginning of 1986, accepting the job to coach Wigan soon afterwards. But the New Zealand Rugby League asked me to stay involved with the national team and return from Wigan to coach them in the World Cup that year, which I agreed to do. I never had a contract. In fact I've never had a contract in all the time I've been coaching. We went to Papua New Guinea that year and we lost the final Test. I was about to head off to Wigan when the NZRL officials called me in for a meeting. They asked me how I was going to handle both the Wigan and New Zealand jobs. I could tell by their tone that their attitude had suddenly changed and they didn't want me to do the job any more. The penny suddenly dropped. I said to them, "Are you people giving me the sack?" and they replied, "No . . . we're just giving you an offer you can't refuse." So I just walked out and that was it. To this day all those at the meeting can say what they like, but they know and I know that they breached the verbal contract we had agreed on. I still had a couple of years to go and the financial terms were very good. But I never got a cent out of them. I was more ashamed of the fools that they had made of themselves than I felt hurt or wounded myself. They looked like absolute dickheads in the public's eyes . . . the people knew what was going on. Why did they dump me? All I can assume happened is that they decided I was too outspoken for them. I have this habit of saying what is on my mind; I never bullshit. I think that was too much for them and they decided I had to go. But they could have found a more honourable way to do it than they did. It was a low act.'

Fortunately for Lowe, he had bigger fish to fry—at Wigan. 'I went over to watch the British Challenge Cup final the previous year and was approached by a couple of clubs while I was just sitting in the Wembley grandstand,' he said. 'Wigan wasn't one of them, but then they got onto me the following day. I can only guess they saw me there but decided on a more subtle form of attack. I went over and had lunch with them and was immediately swept away by their vision and drive, particularly chairman Maurice Lindsay. At that time, Wigan wasn't the highly successful club people now know. The team enjoyed great support but hadn't won the championship for around 25 years. They were probably the sleeping giant of the game over there. They were always up there and won the odd trophy, but were a long way from the dominant force they are today. But I could see the ambition of the directors. They wanted to make Wigan the league equivalent of Liverpool in soccer. Listening to them just inspired me. Their forward thinking was great and I took to them immediately because they had the courage to really try to change the way things were. They were prepared, on the spot, to put me on and give me absolute and complete control of the team and everything to do with running it. As far as I can see, a coach can ask for no more. And that was probably the thing that clinched it for me; I didn't need any time to think it over. I got up from the table, shook their hands and said to them, "I'll see you in August".'

Lowe's first target when he went to Wigan was his old friend Mark Graham. 'I would have loved to get Mark over there, but we couldn't get him away from North Sydney,' Lowe said. 'So I got Dean Bell from New Zealand and he gave great service over a number of years. Maurice had also heard that Ian Roberts, who was then just a young kid with potential at Souths, was born in England and had a British passport. He asked me about him and I knew virtually nothing about the guy. But I asked Mark Graham his opinion and he said the kid was a champion in the making. So Maurice went out and bought him and he gave us great value in a guest stint. Adrian Shelford from New Zealand was another player who joined us and went well. We signed Kevin Iro, who was then an established Test star for the Kiwis, but he put a condition on signing. He said he'd come, but only if we also took his brother

Tony. I'd never heard of Tony, so it was a fairly unusual request. I said to Kevin, "Who is he and what's he like?" Kevin replied, "I think he's a better player than I am." It was only when he arrived that Kevin told me the full story—that Tony had only played two games of league in his life. He was playing social rugby union in New Zealand at the time. Kevin had conned me, but it turned out great. Tony developed into a great strike weapon and of course Kevin was also an excellent buy. In that first year, the only thing we didn't win was Wembley. We got knocked out in the first round by one of the lesser teams and that was a bit of a disappointment. But we won the championship by the length of the straight and played some great football along the way. The fans wanted Wembley, though. So we made up for it the next year. We went there, which was an experience in itself, and beat Halifax in the final. People say Wembley is unforgettable and it's true. It's such a wonderful arena with so much atmosphere. I don't think there's anywhere in the world to match it.'

Like John Monie, who has also coached in both hemispheres, Lowe has noted major differences between British and Australian and New Zealand fans. 'People over here are far more reserved than in Britain,' Lowe said. 'For instance, no-one over here will start singing at a game because they'll be concerned that the bloke next to them will think they're a dickhead. But in England, they all get into it. They love singing as it shows their passion for the game. They're not worried about what someone might think. But at the same time, they're not sheep. The fans over there are really well educated on football and know what they're talking about. The rivalry between some clubs has to be seen to be believed. I learned very quickly that the feeling between St Helens and Wigan is every bit as fierce as that between New South Wales and Queensland.

Every time they play, it's like State of Origin rivalry. I remember the first day I arrived at Wigan, bumping into this old bloke who'd been a fan of the club all his life. And he said to me, "Listen, there's only two things you have to do here . . . get us to Wembley and beat St Helens. If you do that, you'll have no worries".'

Lowe stayed at Wigan for three years and won just about every trophy on offer. 'We had a lot of success and I feel much of that happened because the club was strong at the top. I was so lucky to have a guy like Maurice Lindsay in charge. I learned so much from him in those three years, I wouldn't know where to start describing it. His man management skills are tremendous, he's tough and he's the original iron fist in a silk glove. He had this way of getting things done with a minimum of fuss that other people would have found too difficult. And even though he was so strong and influential, he never tried to interfere with my coaching or handling of the team. He was always supportive and there to boost my confidence if it was down. At a couple of crucial times when I had disputes with some of the club's big name players, he always backed me. If he hadn't, I don't know what would have happened. There were probably times he didn't think I was right, but he still backed me and that great loyalty will always be appreciated.'

Lowe admits that he had problems with star players Ellery Hanley, Shaun Edwards and Andy Gregory in his time at Wigan. 'We had some disagreements, but there are always two sides to every story,' he said. 'In fairness to the players, they are treated like gods by the fans over there and that is a difficult situation for them at times. And perhaps it makes them lose a bit of their perspective. It's not easy for them to keep their feet on the ground. I must say that Ellery Hanley is the most professional footballer I've had anything to do with. No-one even comes close to him, that's how good he was in every aspect of his life, on and off the field. We had a major confrontation once where I dropped him from the team for four or five weeks. He didn't like it at all, and neither did I for that matter. And now that I look back on it a few years later, I believe we were both wrong. We were too hard-nosed and unwilling to compromise. Now, with that little extra experience behind me, I wouldn't have allowed it to go as far as it did. I would have sat him down and talked it out, rather than had us both sulking and angry. Eventually we worked it out, but it should have happened sooner. In the end, though, I've got nothing but admiration for Ellery. He will go down as one of the game's greats and there isn't much about the game he doesn't know. Shaun Edwards . . . well a lot of people aren't keen on him and in Australia, in particular, he's copped plenty of bagging. We also had our moments, but the guy has rugby league in his veins and he's a winner. He was a very valuable part of the team. He's been there, done that so many times that you just have to respect him. Shaun continually proves people wrong. Andy Gregory and I also had confrontations. But, as I said with Ellery, I think I was as much to blame as the players were. We were all being stubborn and caught up in the heat of the moment . . . we should have worked it out.'

Maurice Lindsay offered Lowe an unprecedented life contract at Wigan, such was the success of the former New Zealand coach in his new home. But after three years with the club, Lowe began to feel the urge to return home. 'The lifetime offer was very flattering and something I'd never heard of for a coach in league before,' he said. 'I was just missing my kids too much, though, and knew I had to come back. They were on the other side of the world and I felt like I was losing touch with them. Maurice tried everything he knew to keep me but my mind was made up. When news that I'd quit Wigan and was retiring to return Down Under broke, a heap of offers came from Aussie clubs. I was approached by Easts, Norths, Gold Coast, Cronulla and a couple more I can't even remember. But then Ken Arthurson rang me up and asked me if I'd consider taking the Manly job. I'd never thought of coaching Manly but had a lot of respect for Arko and what he'd done for the game. So I listened to what he had to say. And then I met Manly chief executive Doug Daley and immediately liked the man. I'd say he was one of the unsung heroes of rugby league. He had a great love of the game and devoted much of his life to it. He was a real gentleman and I knew if he gave me his word, I could trust it. It was because of those two men— Arthurson and Daley—that I decided to go to Manly.'

But Lowe arrived in Sydney in 1990 to find Manly a club in turmoil following the controversial decision by the Sea Eagles' board to sack one of the club's favourite sons. Manly's move to axe Paul Vautin, the popular second-rower who had given a decade's service, created a storm. 'And I walked right into the middle of it,' Lowe recalled. 'I thought to myself, "What have I struck here?" The media was having a field day, angry fans were letting their feelings be known and both sides were having plenty to say. I admired Paul as a player and wouldn't have minded coaching him. But I could see keeping him would have been asking for trouble. There was so much ill feeling between him and Doug and other people at the club that I don't think it could have ever been repaired. It would have been buying into too big a problem, particularly for a new coach still feeling his way. So I stayed right out of that. I just left it up to the board to handle it. They were the ones who made the decision to cut Paul well before I got there and I didn't want it to be my problem.

'When we started the 1990 season, things settled down, as they often do. I was made to feel very welcome at Manly and had no trouble fitting in. I gave a second lease of life to a couple of guys who everyone thought were washed up in David Liddiard and David Hosking. They wanted a chance and got it and really made the most of the opportunity. We also brought in young guys like Matt Dunford, John Jones, Frank Stokes and Craig Hancock and they also rose to the occasion. They were full of enthusiasm and that probably rubbed off on some of the older members of the team. Manly was a very talented side with players like Michael O'Connor, Des Hasler and Cliff Lyons and I enjoyed coaching them. We made the semis in both my first two years without making a huge impact. In 1990 we beat Balmain but were then unlucky to meet the powerful Brisbane side next up and they knocked us out. Considering we were 12th the year before I arrived, though, it was a big improvement and I was satisfied. In 1991, we finished in the top three but were beaten by Norths first up and then lost 34–26 to another great side in Canberra. Even though we lost that game, it sticks in my mind as one of the best performances of any team I coached. I remember in the week leading up to the game, we were in a hell of a state. We didn't even have a training run, we had so many players out injured. I remember that distinctly because we got to training and I could see trying to run the players was going to be no use. So I asked the club to send us down 10 dozen eggs and we had an egg throwing contest. That was our lead-up to the biggest game of the year. I knew they couldn't train and the only chance we had was to go in with the right mental approach. So the egg throwing took their minds off the tense match coming up and helped to relax them. Then the game started and we lost a couple more players early on. Despite that, we pushed

Canberra all the way. They were a great side and were shooting for three titles in a row. They came out on top, but we gave them one hell of a fright. It may not have been a victory, but I felt so proud of the effort put in by the players. To me, there are some things that are more important than winning or losing and I don't just analyse a season by where my team finishes on the table. I believe that if the coach and the players can maintain the same enthusiasm at the end of the season as they did at the beginning, then they have succeeded. As a coach, while everyone judges you by wins and losses, I have my own standards. There have been times when we've had a good winning year and I've been disappointed. And others when we've finished down the ladder but I have been very happy. Coaching isn't a black or white business in my eyes, even though I know it is in most people's.'

Those who know Lowe best describe him as a shrewd motivator. Former Australian captain Wally Lewis, after just one week under Lowe's wing before an Oceania v Europe promotional match, described Lowe as the best coach he'd ever played under. In the foreword to Lowe's biography *Lowe and Behold*, written by Richard Becht, the well-travelled Mark Graham describes Lowe as the complete coach. 'Graham Lowe is a great motivator, but it doesn't end there,' Graham wrote. 'He has it all. He doesn't fit into one category of football coaching. Nothing is left to chance ... players have confidence in him to deal with every aspect of coaching.' Graham relates a story from the pair's days together at Brisbane Norths in 1980 that he felt best sums up Lowe's approach to the game. 'We lost to a team we should have flogged so Lowie ordered punishment training the next night. He wouldn't even talk to us and handed a note to our captain, Mark Murray, telling us what to do. Four hours later we finished. The following

Sunday we lost again so Graham ordered another Monday night practice. We were all ready to go at 6pm expecting the worst but Graham told us all to go back into the changing room, get dressed again and then get in our cars and follow him. He took us straight to the pub, we all got rotten drunk and we didn't lose another game all season as we went on to win the grand final.'

Lowe created history in 1991 by becoming the first non-Queenslander to be appointed coach of the Maroons State of Origin team. For the fiercely parochial Queenslanders to select an 'outsider' as coach represented a major break with tradition and the significance was not lost on Lowe. 'It was a great honour for me,' he said. 'I'd spent a fair bit of time in Queensland and always liked the people, but I was still a foreigner. Winning Test matches with New Zealand was a career high, as you'd expect. But I rate just being invited to coach Queensland in a series like the State of Origin right up there with it. We won that first series and it has gone down on record as one of the best Origin series ever played. It was very special to me because it was Wally Lewis's last series and it meant so much to all of us to send him out a winner. Those emotional scenes at Lang Park after the final game were just so moving—everyone felt so happy for the bloke.'

Back on the club scene, the Sea Eagles missed the finals in 1992 in heartbreaking circumstances. Manly only needed to win their last round home clash against Illawarra at Brookvale to qualify and looked on course when Michael O'Connor, playing what was to be his last game for the club, snapped up a 50 metre intercept to score. But the Steelers fought back, scoring a late try to knock the Sea Eagles out of contention and reach the finals for the first time themselves. That disappointment was nothing, however, compared to what was to come for Lowe over the off season. 'I was really looking forward to the start of 1993 because I'd had a rough trot leading into just about every previous season in Sydney,' he said. 'I seemed to go from one life-threatening illness to another. But in the lead-up to '93, I felt on top of the world. In the early trials, I started getting bad headaches. And when I did that, my speech was starting to slur. Then I passed out a couple of times. I went and saw the doctor and he thought it was just a matter of altering the medication I was on to get me back on the right track. But it didn't seem right. I remember going from the doctor and sitting by myself on the local beach and thinking it over. My body had been telling me for the past three years that something was wrong. I'd survived what they told me I wasn't going to survive. But I still wasn't out of the woods. Maybe I was going to end up with some terrible permanent disability . . . I could lose my speech or have a stroke or whatever. I jumped straight back into my car and drove down to the club and told them I was going to retire. They asked when, and I replied, "Now". I was sorry to leave them in the lurch so close to the start of the season, but I really didn't see myself as having any alternative.'

Lowe's instincts proved correct. Not long after his dramatic announcement, he entered hospital for brain surgery on a life-threatening haemorrhage. He has fought a constant battle against illness since then, but contends the high-stress life of a football coach did not contribute to his problems. 'There is a lot of stress involved in coaching, but I don't see it as a major problem. I love the game and am involved because I want to be there. I think some people make the pressures sound worse than they really are. You have to put it all in perspective. To me, the stress on a coach is nothing compared to the stress on a single mother with a mortgage trying to bring up three or four kids. Now that's stress. I needed a triple bypass soon after quitting Manly, but I don't believe that had anything to do with coaching. It's just something that happened to my body and needed to be corrected.'

On doctor's advice, Lowe completely retired from active work in 1993 but took on some part-time commentary duties later that year with TV New Zealand. 'That was like a lifeline to me for a couple of reasons,' he said. 'Firstly because it allowed me to get back involved with the game I love so much. And secondly because it gave me the opportunity to work with (commentator) Graeme Hughes. He really turned my life around. He helped me more than anyone. He seemed to understand what I'd gone through and provided me with the chance to do something with my life again. Getting involved with TVNZ and getting to know Graeme really kicked me on again. He showed me a lot about life in general and I owe him so much. He's a great mate and I don't know where I would have ended up if I hadn't met him.'

Hughes, a former NSW representative at both rugby league and cricket, sees Lowe as one of the few nice guys left in the coaching business. 'There is a saying that nice guys run last and a lot of coaches seem to believe this because they go out of their way to be tough on people,' Hughes said. 'The only two genuinely nice blokes who I've known in 20 years' association with the game are Lowie and (former Canterbury and Cronulla coach) Ted Glossop. They are living proof that you can be a good bloke and still be successful. When Lowie came to TV, we clicked instantly and had a lot of fun together. I'd like to think I taught him a bit about presenting himself on air and he became very comfortable in the job. At a time when he was very hurt about having to give up coaching because of his health, TV gave him a new interest and he revelled in it. He began to view things differently from this new perspective. As he became more comfortable, he started to slow down and have more fun. Although he came into TV cold, he had an advantage because he always knew how to get on with the media and that's one of the reasons we hired him. There are plenty of great coaches who are dreadful with the media. But Graham had a rapport with the journos, because he is a genuine bloke who will always tell you what he thinks. It's that sincerity that made me confident he would appeal to the viewers on television.'

Since he left Manly, Lowe has found his good name has been blackened in the Sea Eagles' nest. The Super League war, in which Lowe and Manly find themselves on opposite sides, has caused antagonism. 'That sort of thing has happened and it is regrettable,' Lowe said. 'Most of the time, I just try to ignore it. Paul Vautin is one of Manly's all-time greats and in 1995 we got ourselves involved in a public slanging match. It really happened out of the blue. A journalist asked me how he would go as Queensland State of Origin coach and I answered by saying I knew little about him as a coach. Then the journo asked my opinion of him as a person and I told him I don't respect anyone who'd call a player a spastic in public. Vautin then had a pot shot at me on television and seems to have used every excuse to have digs at other times too. Not everyone has such a powerful position from which to vent a personal attack on someone. He tries to make things difficult for me with his comments, but they don't worry me in the slightest. Life goes on.'

Graeme Hughes believes Manly's anger towards Lowe comes from the image change he brought about at the club in his short time there. 'It's well known that Manly is the most hated club in the game,' Hughes said. 'But when Lowie went there, he changed all that simply by the way he acted and treated people. If you like, he took the prick out of Manly. And when he left, the club was again disliked. Probably the people at the club resent him for that.'

Lowe was thrown another lifeline back into rugby league by the North Queensland Cowboys. With Tim Sheens already signed to coach the club in 1997, the Cowboys were looking for a short-term man to fill in for 1996. 'Like a lot of things in life,' the offer to coach the Cowboys came quite by accident,' Lowe said. 'I was talking to their chief executive Rabieh Krayem one day when we bumped into each other. I had a bit to do with him from my Manly days because he managed Ian Roberts back then. A few hours later he rang me back and said he'd spoken to the club president Ron McLean and they wondered if I'd be interested in coming back to coaching. I said that I wouldn't coach again but that didn't deter them. They said they had a unique proposition—to coach the team for 12 months until Tim Sheens arrives. Not many people would want a job like that, but they thought it might suit me. They asked me to come up to Townsville and have a look around. So I did and straight-away I fell in love with the place. I spoke to them and we were on the same wavelength. I also admire Tim Sheens and feel it an honour to be selected to help set the place up for him. It is a tough task—for me and Tim—I have no illusions about that. But I'm keeping it in perspective and see it as a big challenge.'

Lowe is an old-fashioned character with old-fashioned views on football and coaching. 'The most important trait a coach needs is to be honest,' he said. 'Footballers are seen by many people as not having too much in the way of brains. And in some cases, that stereotype is quite close to the mark. But all footballers, even the dumbest ones, know when you're bull-shitting them. They can pick it straight-away when you try to kid them. So if you do that, you'll lose their respect. If you're honest with yourself and with the players, you'll survive. You have to be fair with them, but firm at the same time. To me coaching is a people business; if you treat everyone the way you want to be treated yourself, you'll get their loyalty. And I also believe what goes around, comes around. You watch players and coaches and you know they'll get their comeuppance sooner or later. I've never been into all these trendy modern sayings like "Football's not life or death; it's much more serious than that". To me the game is not life or death. What happens with your football team isn't as serious as what's happening with Sarajevo. So many people lose their perspective. Some coaches act like they're working for the CIA. I've never felt like that and like to keep it simple. I enjoy the company of the players and like mixing with them. I've always got on with the media and part of that is because I've never been a "no comment" person. I've got an opinion on everything and don't mind expressing it. That has sometimes got me in strife but so be it. I'm an individual and have never wanted to be a robot like a lot of others. I'm a big believer in discipline and making players follow you to the letter. You certainly need good players to be a successful coach and that's where I've been very fortunate. Guys like Mark Graham, Wally Lewis and Ellery Hanley have played a huge role in the Graham Lowe story. Without them, who knows whether I would have been a success.'

Despite his playing down the importance of football in the grand scale of the universe, Lowe admits he has struggled to come to terms with losing. 'Like most coaches, I hate it,' he said. 'I find it hard to take. I've learned to cope with it and that comes with experience. But I've never fully learned how to handle it. The hardest thing with losing is having to front up again next week. But I think that learning how to handle winning is every bit as important as handling losing. I think coaches, myself included, kid themselves a bit when they win and aren't as analytical as they should be in those situations. You don't seem to put as much time into figuring out why you won as you do analysing why you lost.'

Lowe wears his heart on his sleeve—his players will always know exactly what is on his mind. 'I get pretty emotional at times. If I'm pissed off, I'll let them know. But I balance that out; if I'm happy, I'll let them know as well. They can usually work it out themselves, so I don't try to hide my emotions. I went through a ranting and raving period early in my career but have mellowed my approach as I've gained experience. Coaching is a pretty fashionable business . . . you hear of things other blokes do successfully so you try them. But I think your own gut instincts are your most valuable asset and you've got to follow them.'

The Sultan
of Slap

ROY MASTERS

CLUBS
Wests 1978–81,
St George 1982–87

PREMIERSHIP RECORD
Games 250, won 142, lost 98, drew 10.
Winning percentage 56.8%.
Semi-finals
1978–80, 1983–85
Grand finals (1)
1985

OTHER COACHING ACHIEVEMENTS
Coached Australian Schoolboys on undefeated tour of
England 1972.
Coached Wests to under-23 premiership 1977.
Coach of the Year 1978, 1985.
Dally M Coach of the Year 1980, 1985.

Roy Masters will always be remembered for bringing two things to rugby league—the class struggle and face-slapping. An innovative and shrewd observer of the game, Masters was the key figure in Western Suburbs' last great era in the late 1970s. It was Masters' labelling of the Magpies as the battling fibros—and arch rivals Manly as silvertails—that had the fans charging through the turnstiles nearly two decades ago. Packed houses at the Magpies' old home base of Lidcombe Oval were the order of the day as Masters' side, containing Wests legends like Tom Raudonikis, John Donnelly and Les Boyd, took on all comers. It was at Wests that Masters introduced the infamous face-slapping psych-up that was to become a Magpie trademark. Masters then went on to further success at St George, bringing the Dragons agonisingly close to a premiership in 1985. Now a respected member of the media, Masters remains a close confidant to many of the players he coached at both Wests and Saints.

The young Roy Masters played rugby league at school in Lismore before turning his hand to rugby union at university while studying for his diploma in education. 'I was then posted to Tweed River High School and played league there before moving to Armidale and then Tamworth, where I began to teach,' he said. 'It was very important there to coach junior kids, so I made the transition from very ordinary player to interested and involved coach.' Masters coached Tamworth High School to victory in the University Shield, the prestige school competition at the time, with such monotonous regularity that even the league hierarchy in faraway Phillip Street was forced to sit up and take notice. When the first Australian Schoolboys side was selected in 1972, Masters, although an unknown in the eyes of the public, was named as coach. And what a team it was. Masters' eyes still light up when he thinks of the talent he had at his disposal as the Joeys, as they became known, embarked on a ruthless rampage through England and France. 'We had players like Craig Young, Royce Ayliffe, Ian Schubert and Les Boyd who all went on to play for Australia at senior level. Then there were Robert Finch, Brian Hetherington, Tony Graham and Jack Jeffries, all of whom played regular first grade in Sydney, and several other players who did very well in the bush. We had just one try scored against us in the entire tour and scored a phenomenal number of points. We were actually down 3–0 at halftime in the final Test against Great Britain but stormed home to win comfortably. It was the first schoolboys tour of either rugby code and probably the best. It set the standard for many league and union tours in years to follow.'

It was late in the tour that Masters was almost lost to Australian football before his coaching career ever began in Sydney. 'The boys really made a lot of English clubs sit up and take notice with our style and one—Wakefield—was so taken they made me an offer to coach them,' he said. 'It seemed a huge gamble for them to take on an untried Aussie schoolboy coach in first grade, but they were prepared to sack the current coach and do it. We had a lot of moves and creativity in the schoolboys side and that was what convinced them. They felt their game needed opening up and I was the man for the job. It was a pretty good offer but the problem was that I was locked into the Department of Education back home. I had about eight years seniority up by that stage and was slowly climbing the promotional ladder. The old public service mentality that I'd lose my seniority and superannuation worried me, as well as the fact I'd have to relocate my family. It was a bloody big step and one I wasn't ready to make at that stage. I knocked them back, returned to Tamworth and was immediately approached by several Sydney clubs that had also been impressed by the deeds of the schoolboys, who had attracted a lot of publicity back home. Jack Gibson called me—I think he was with Newtown at the time. Easts flew me down for talks as well, but it was Penrith who made the biggest impression. They were on a huge recruitment drive and had already signed a couple of my Tamworth High kids—Barry Le Brocq and Ritchie Thornton. In addition to that, I wanted to continue teaching and in those days the only teaching positions you could ever seem to get in Sydney were on the western outskirts of the city. So I took a senior position at Doonside High School which allowed me to accept a coaching job at Penrith in 1974. To be honest, I would have preferred one of the stronger inner-city clubs, but living out west it seemed practical to join Penrith.' In the early '70s, the Panthers were still struggling to find their way in the big league and Masters admits these were trying times. 'We had this crazy bloody coaching panel headed by Jack Clare. Barry Harris, Tommy Wilson and myself were on it. The way it worked, you weren't in charge of a team as such. Someone would look after the forwards, someone else would look after the backs, or the ballwork, or the tactics—for all three grades. The ballwork and the tactics were my areas and we had a fair year—we made the final of the Amco Cup and had some good wins in the premiership. But the set-up just didn't work. There were too many jealousies and in-fighting became a problem. The following year I took on the under-23s and then in 1976 I moved to Wests where I also coached the under-23s. We won the premiership in that grade the following year. I had a few good players in Alan Neil, George Moroko and Bob Cooper but basically it was just a team of good, honest battlers.'

Masters' success with the under-23s saw moves within the Magpies ranks to have him installed as first grade coach the following year. 'There was a player-led push to get me in as first grade coach led by Tommy Raudonikis and Les Boyd. The committee were pretty much onside and I got the job with the blessing of the man I was replacing, Keith Holman, so it was about as harmonious a transfer of power as you could have. Of the 14 board members, 12 voted for me and the other 2 abstained. And after a while, they both became strong supporters of me too. It was good to have everyone in the place backing me and they stayed loyal for most of my time there.'

Masters quickly forged a friendship with Raudonikis, the team captain, as the pair went about whipping a young Wests team with potential into a premiership contender. 'I'd always been a players' coach and Tommy and I hit it off from the start,' he said. 'We took the players off into training camps in remote parts of the bush—funnily enough, Tommy did something similar when he took over as Wests coach at the start of 1995. But back then, we really did it tough . . . there were no five-star hotels where we stayed. We bought our own cornflakes, we used powdered milk and the players and their wives or girlfriends would sleep in sleeping bags on the verandahs of old homesteads. We were running in grass that was knee-high, training in the most primitive conditions. We even shopped around for bloody sausages . . . that's how little we had. It all created an ethos that stayed with the club a long time. We were battlers and we roughed it; very different from what the players get today. It wasn't contrived in those days; it was largely forced upon us by the economic circumstances the club was in. You could hit the players for around $50 each for a training camp but the club gave bugger-all. At that stage, the licensed club was cutting back its grant to the football club so we felt the pinch. But the players really bonded together through it all and we started the 1978 season well. We finished third in the pre-season and that's when we played the infamous game with Manly in Melbourne that everyone remembers.'

The clash against Manly in an 'exhibition' match to determine third spot in the pre-season competition—in effect a nothing game—developed into a bloodbath. Players from both sides ripped into each other in a brawling, spiteful affair before a small, bemused crowd in Melbourne. The match proved the beginning of the infamous 'fibros v silvertails' clashes, as Masters labelled them. It was a label that would stick to games between Wests and Manly for years to come. The image of the battling Magpies, coming from their fibro houses in Sydney's west, against the affluent Manly superstars was a Masters creation and a cunning ploy that always brought out the best in his players. 'I must admit it was a little bit contrived in that often after those ferocious games at Lidcombe, we'd go and have dinner with some of the Manly players at a Chinese restaurant at Concord,' Masters admitted. 'And we'd all say, "We know this is part of some big spectacular hatred bullshit, but it seems to work for us." We got huge crowds at Lidcombe, they got good crowds at Brookvale and when we went out onto the field, we really DID rip shit out of each other. We knew we were using each other, and being used, but no-one seemed to care. It was the same with the fibro business. Once Les Boyd came up to me and said, "Roy, I don't believe any of this fibro bullshit one bit; I'm a Liberal voter and I want to have the biggest house in the country. But I make myself believe it when I play and when I get out there, I play better." So we weren't really fooling each other. But on the field, it was full on. Tommy used to hate Manly and especially their halfback Johnny Gibbs. I remember in one Manly–Wests game a brawl broke out and you could just see Tommy looking for Gibbs. There were big forwards bashing each other left, right and centre but that didn't interest Tommy. He just wanted to get hold of Gibbs and tear him apart. He reckoned later Gibbs was hiding in the hole where the cornerpost went. And Les Boyd didn't get on with John Harvey. The two of them loathed each other from way back and would often be the first to rip in. That was another genuine feud. "Dallas" Donnelly always went looking for Stephen Knight, who was his team-mate at Wests a couple of years earlier. The citing by video process had just come into the game at that time and was whipped out by the officials just about every time the Wests–Manly clashes came around. After one game Dallas Donnelly and Les Boyd were cited and copped four and three weeks respectively. But to this day the players will absolutely insist that (Manly's) Terry Randall, who got off free as a bird, started it. I still see Terry and we have a laugh about it. The media loved the violence but in a very hypocritical way. For weeks beforehand they would talk about the game and say there would be bloodshed. Inevitably, the bloodshed would come as we got carried along by the tide of it all. And afterwards, the media got very sanctimonious about it, saying how dreadful it was. But at the same time, the journos were licking their lips and waiting 11 weeks until we belted the crap out of each other again. A bloke wrote me a poem once which I thought summed up the situation very well. He said:

"The media declare it's violence we dread,
You can savour the scenes in our full colour spread."'

Playing in front of capacity crowds at Lidcombe with an exciting team including Boyd, Raudonikis, Donnelly, Graeme O'Grady and John Dorahy, Wests proved themselves genuine title contenders in 1978, winning the minor premiership for the first time in many years. Playing an aggressive style mixed with touches of pure class, the Magpies were the most feared team in the game but lost their way in the finals, going down 14–10 to Cronulla and then losing 14–7 to Manly just a game short of the grand final. After the controversial loss to Manly, a fuming Masters blasted referee Greg Hartley, who disallowed what appeared a fair Wests try at a vital stage of proceedings. In a blast that would nowadays have earned him a $10,000 fine, Masters told the media: 'Eight weeks ago Hartley was in reserve grade. Then suddenly he makes first grade and is now number one. How do you justify it?' The Sea Eagles went on to win the grand final—again under Hartley's control—in a result that still sees Masters grit his teeth with rage.

The Magpies again reached the finals under Masters in 1979 but the biggest impact Wests made that season was on the television current affairs show *60 Minutes*. The show featured the now infamous face-slapping scene in the dressing room prior to a game in which Magpie stars worked themselves into a rage by whacking each other on the face. The graphic behind-the-scenes footage, which included a couple of players having to be separated after taking the 'slapping' too far, stunned the league world. It was replayed for weeks afterwards and condemned by many senior officials and critics. Masters never lived down the 'face-slapping' image but now finds the fuss all very amusing. 'Everywhere I go now, it seems that's my legacy,' he said. 'But I must say that we were suckered into that a bit by the *60 Minutes* people. They rang us up and said they wanted to do a story on us. I said no and then they said they reckoned we were on drugs and that's why we didn't want to go on television. That made us bloody furious and it simply wasn't true ... we didn't need any drugs. In fact, they were the last thing we needed. We fired ourselves up enough without them. So we opened our doors to them and told them they could come to every training session, every dressing room and social function just to prove to all and sundry that there were no drugs in the place. And I've got to give it to them, Ray Martin was the reporter and he and his crew followed us around everywhere for six solid weeks. I woke up one bloody morning, went out to get the newspaper in my pyjamas and there they were filming. They were very, very vigilant. Anyway, we had a trainer in those days called Dave Dickman and he was a real fiery bloke—he liked nothing more than to wind the blokes up before a match. As a coach, you have days where the players turn up to play and you can tell they just aren't interested. They're rugged up in their big warm jackets to escape the cold and the last thing they want to do is play football. You can see they're just not in the mood. Dave noticed this one day and said, "Look at these pricks; you can tell they don't want to play. Let's rev them up." And did he rev them up. He got them to slap each other around and the *60 Minutes* cameras were there and didn't they lap it up. I remember in the room at the time, Ray Martin said to the cameraman, "Did you get that?" I thought to myself, "Oh no, here we go . . . this is going to come back and haunt us." And when the show went to air, they showed the face-slapping maybe five times in the 20-minute segment. When you think they shot many hours of film over six weeks, I think they went a little bit over the top. We definitely started the face-slapping but I remember other teams didn't mind following us in. In one of those games against Manly, their players ran onto the field and three or four of them had blood pouring from their noses at the time . . . they must have really got stuck into each other. Terry Lamb even told me that the Canterbury players did it a few years ago. It's

Jack Gibson: coach, thinker, revolutionary.

Chris Anderson—a tough shrewd coach who retained a dash
of 'country'.

Harry Bath and hooker Steve Edge celebrate the victory by 'Bath's Babes' over Canterbury in the 1979 grand final.

Bob Bax—his record leaves no doubt he had the key to winning
football.

Wayne Bennett makes the most of the Brisbane sun at pre-season training.

A youthful Clive Churchill heads the line up at an Australian team medical in 1953. Behind him are Harry Wells, Noel Pidding, Keith Holman, Ken Kearney and Greg Hawick. (Pic credit: *Daily Telegraph*)

Clive Churchill watches his superb South Sydney side in action in the early 1970s.

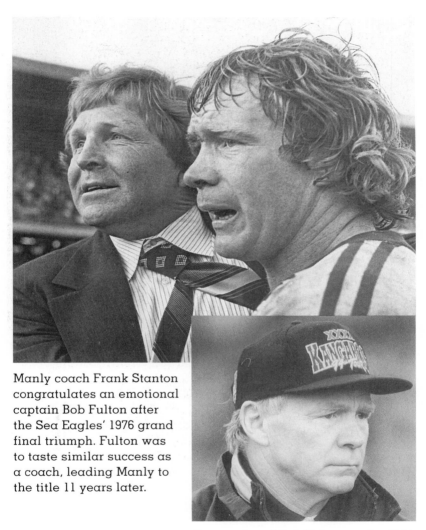

Manly coach Frank Stanton congratulates an emotional captain Bob Fulton after the Sea Eagles' 1976 grand final triumph. Fulton was to taste similar success as a coach, leading Manly to the title 11 years later.

A stony-faced Bob Fulton on the 1994 Ashes tour. Fulton is as tough and demanding as a coach can be but his success cannot be denied.

How sweet it is. Graham Lowe celebrates yet another triumph with Wigan. (Pic credit: Varley Picture Agency)

Roy Masters savours victory in the St George dressing room. Surrounding him, his players. Back row (left to right) Steve Rogers, Brian Johnston, Steve Morris. Alongside: Craig Young (left), Brian Johnson, Graeme Wynn, John Chapman. In front: Michael Beattie.

Masters looks far from impressed with proceedings as he surveys the action from the Western Suburbs bench. The Magpies enjoyed great success under Masters in the late 1970s.

John Monie learned his coaching under Gibson and became his
own man.

A youthful Norm Provan. The rangy second-rower had a
memorable career in league, first as a player and later as a
player-coach and coach.

Malcolm Reilly holds court with the media, with Great Britain manager and close friend Maurice Lindsay (left) at his side.

Reilly strains to get a better view of the action in an Ashes Test. He put much-needed pride back into the Lion jumper. (Pic credit: Andrew Varley)

Warren Ryan–he picked up where Jack Gibson left off.

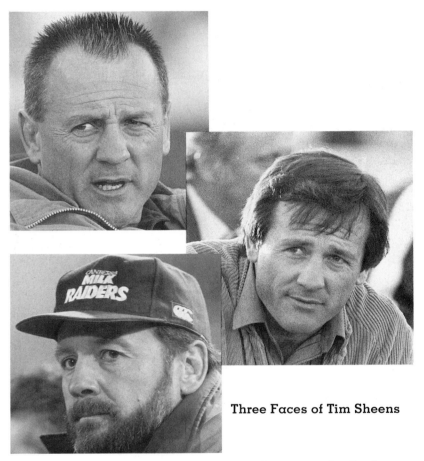

Three Faces of Tim Sheens

Clockwise from top: Sheens casts a critical eye over the Canberra Raiders from the sideline. Sheens made history by taking the premiership out of Sydney for the first time when the Green Machine won an epic grand final in 1989.
Rookie coach Sheens in the mid 1980s. Sheens brought a new professionalism to the Penrith Panthers.
A bearded Sheens, pictured during the Canberra Raiders' premiership winning campaign in 1994.

A pensive Brian Smith during his stint with St George. Smith led the unfancied Dragons to two grand finals.

Smith barks out instructions during the heat of the battle.

Every coach needs a friend now and then. The German shepherds, Max and Elsa were constant companions for Jack Gibson in the coach's 'den'.

something you wouldn't use often but occasionally it was a good way to fire the blokes up.'

Always on the lookout for a psychological edge, the crafty Masters found a way to use the face-slapping characterisation of his team to an advantage. 'I've got to admit that we used the image that was painted of us to suit our own ends,' he said. 'An ethos developed that all you had to do was match Wests on the field with aggression and you could beat us. And I think that all that hype and alleged aggression tended to mask one very important thing—that we had a very talented football team at Wests. Our tactics were often to start the brawl in the first 10 minutes—not always, but when we thought the football abilities of the two teams were about level—we'd start something ferocious. The result was that the opposition was still trying to get square in the 79th minute, where we just absolutely turned off the aggro after that early stink and started to play football. A lot of teams fell into that trap to their own peril. Some of those tries we scored against Manly would be length-of-the-field jobs but were often forgotten because of all the hysteria over the violence. We had blokes in the side who didn't like the biffo at all but knew it was a necessary part of the overall match plan. Bob Cooper, Ray Brown and John Dorahy were magical ball handlers . . . the fights didn't turn them on. I remember a while ago Cooper and John Ribot— before all this Super League stuff started—came over and we watched some videos of us in action back in those days. And we all agreed some of the ball skills were better than what you see today. Opposition coaches would say, "Wests are just boof-heads and face-slappers" and we were happy to be portrayed that way. It often meant they underestimated us. So in a sense, it was all a big con.'

Masters firmly believes the Magpies had the talent to win a

title in those days, but it was not to be. 'Our best team was in '78 and that was the year that Hartley made it tough for us. But having said that, I must admit we didn't play well in the semis. In '79 we were still right up there but Tommy broke his thumb in the finals and that was a disaster for us. Then in 1980 we did well to beat St George in the semis but then were thrashed by Easts in the final. The thing I firmly believe is that a team needs some solid semi-final experience before it can win at that level, just as a team needs grand final experience before it can win a title. The statistics are so hard core that there is no doubt. Look at Cronulla—they just can't win finals games. Before I got there, Wests had barely been in the finals for the past 15 years and that counted against us, without doubt. You need to have a tradition of winning in semi-finals and we didn't have that.'

Over his time at Wests, Masters had to suffer the frustration of regularly losing star players to richer and more ruthless clubs. Wests lost key players like Les Boyd, John Dorahy, John Ribot and Ray Brown to Manly, Tom Raudonikis, Graeme O'Grady and Steve Blyth to Newtown and Ron Giteau to Easts. By 1981, Masters knew his hopes of winning a title at Wests had long gone and after four years at the helm, decided it was time to move on. 'Late in the 1981 season, we were playing St George at Kogarah Oval and their secretary John Fleming and coach Harry Bath came up to me after the game. Harry was stepping down at the end of the year and they asked me what I was doing the following season. I told them I wasn't sure and John replied, "The coaching job at Saints is yours in 1982. We will have no further contact with you until the season is over." It was as simple as that and typical of the efficient, no-nonsense way Saints operated. I read reports in the next few weeks that Saints were going to appoint Ian Walsh and a few other people but I wasn't worried. I took them at their word. Wests played their last game of the year on a Saturday in late August and the following day I went out to watch a Parramatta game. Jack Gibson had asked me to come out to help them with a few tap plays and drills and I was glad to be of assistance. Anyway, I got home on the Sunday night at around 6:30 and Saints had also played their last game that day. Minutes after I got in the phone rang and it was John Fleming, ready to discuss the job for the following year. Saints had followed it through to the exact letter of the law. Their season had finished at five o'clock and a couple of hours later they were on the phone. I went over to the leagues club opposite the ground at Kogarah a couple of days later and they made me an offer which was good and I decided to accept it. It wasn't easy to leave Wests but I knew my time had come. I'd had two years in the lower grades and four years in first grade and I just instinctively knew it was enough. The words that worked so well a couple of years earlier were falling on deaf ears. Losing all those players to Manly over the years was very frustrating. I knew I was going to a club that would hold onto any player it wanted to keep.'

But coaching the famous St George club wasn't the picnic Masters had anticipated when he saddled up for his first season in 1982. 'Saints had their troubles the previous year and I, quite arrogantly, assumed that all they needed was a change of coach to make things right,' Masters said. 'But it didn't work. Saints were going through a period of transition and it took time to get things right. We needed to replenish our playing talent and '82 proved a year of change for both me and the club. After a bad year in '81, the club decided to give a lot of players one last chance to see if they could produce the goods under a new coach. And many didn't. So we decided to open the purse strings in 1983—Graeme O'Grady signed from

Newtown, Michael O'Connor came over from rugby union and we also picked up the experienced Steve Rogers and Steve Gearin to handle the goalkicking. We started slowly, probably because of all the new faces in the team. But we began to click mid-season and charged into the finals at full throttle.' The Dragons thrashed Easts 44–16 in a midweek playoff for fifth spot and then downed Balmain 17–14 in extra time only four days later. But Saints' gallant run came to an end the following week when they were downed 26–24 in a fast-paced, open game by Warren Ryan's Canterbury Bulldogs. Overall, Masters was satisfied with the progress made but nothing could prepare him for the disappointment that was to come just 12 months later.

'I really felt in my bones that 1984 was going to be our year,' Masters said. 'We were a much better side than the previous season and were clearly a threat to the likes of Canterbury and Parramatta. We did well in the preliminary rounds and came into the finals in good shape. But it all came to grief in the final against Parra and I'd say without doubt that was the worst bloody day in my life—I don't think I'll ever get over it. It was the most critical game I've ever had anything to do with and we won it everywhere but on the scoreboard. It was just shattering.' With title favourites Canterbury already in the grand final, Saints met the Eels for the right to play the Bulldogs in the big game. Playing a tight, well-disciplined style, Saints held the whip hand for much of the game and led 7–4 as time appeared to be running out for the three-time premiers. But with three minutes remaining, Eels winger Eric Grothe—the best finisher in the game at that time—broke away down the right flank. Despite the veteran Steve Rogers clinging to his legs, Grothe had enough power to reach the try-line, planting the ball centimetres from the corner. The try gave the Eels an 8–7 win and a spot in the grand final, putting Saints out of business in the most heartbreaking manner.

'They received three penalties from (referee) Kevin Roberts in a row leading up to that and it just killed us,' Masters recalled, still showing the signs of frustration. 'If it hadn't have been for that, we probably could have hung on. That game was the only occasion in my life when I just didn't know what to say to the players in the dressing room afterwards. I always knew what to say: "Well played . . . bad luck . . . you played bloody terrible . . . you were robbed." The words always came easily under normal circumstances. And I'm vain enough to say that most of the time my post match summary was pretty accurate. But after that game, I just had no idea what to say to them. I walked into the dressing room—there was a numbing silence as you'd expect after such a devastating loss and I just told the players, "Look, I'm sorry, I just don't know what to say." It was devastating, we'd played really well and were the better team by far. But Roberts really killed us with those three late penalties and that got Parramatta home. The club needed desperately to win that game to get into the grand final and cap a good season but it just wasn't to be. There are some things in life which are forever printed on your mind, such as the death of a son, which I sadly went through. I'm not equating the two, nothing could be worse than losing a child. But they are things you can't forget. I remember coming home that night—it was a typically cold September night—I went out in the backyard of my Blakehurst home in short pyjamas and sat for I don't know how long under the clothes line, just boiling. The worst part of it all was that the loss denied us the experience that would have been so valuable the following year when we did make the grand final. Even if we'd lost to Canterbury the next week, it would have prepared us for 1985.

As I said earlier, I believe you've got to lose a grand final before you can win one and it was shattering to come so close. But that loss just mucked everything up and I'll never live the game down . . . it still gets to me.'

Masters was convinced he would overcome the devastating disappointment of that loss to Parramatta the following season in 1985. From the premiership kickoff in March until grand final day in September, 1985 appeared to be St George's year. The Dragons won the club championship by an incredible 92-point margin and were minor premiers in all three grades. Saints won the under-23 grand final against Canterbury and the reserve grade grand final against Parramatta and were on the verge of a historic clean sweep of titles. But come three o'clock, it all went horribly wrong for Masters and his Dragons. Saints came unstuck against the well-drilled Canterbury machine, coached by Masters' long-time rival Warren Ryan. Premiers the previous year, the Bulldogs were a noted big-match side that thrived under the pressure of the tight games.

In keeping with grand finals in the mid '80s, there were few tries scored. Each side managed just one four-pointer, with a field goal to Andrew Farrar proving the difference as Canterbury ground out a 7–6 win. In the post mortems, both clubs conceded that the Bulldogs' relentless tactics of bombarding young Saints fullback Glenn Burgess proved the difference. Canterbury spent long periods camped in the Dragons' quarter, with high kicks from Steve Mortimer hemming Burgess in his in-goal area time and again. Ironically, it was that match that eventually saw the league change the rules, allowing the team that took a bomb over its own tryline to retain possession through a quarterline tap, rather than surrendering the ball through a line drop-out. 'Canterbury exploited that rule to perfection,' Masters rued. 'Mortimer's kicking was pinpoint accurate and we just kept giving them back the ball every time. Had we been able to keep the ball on the quarterline, things may have been different. But on the day we just couldn't overcome the weight of possession.' Masters also admits, in retrospect, the remarkable feat of having all three teams in the grand final counted against his team. 'Everything was club-driven at Saints and the prospect of winning all three titles was our aim, which was understandable. But that meant Canterbury had four fresh reserves at their disposal and I had only one. If I had my time over again, I would have kept a couple more fresh players.'

With several key players passing their prime, Masters knew his chance to win a title at Saints had come and gone. 'I must admit I was very keen to get out at the end of 1985,' he said. 'I'd had enough by then and didn't think we could come any closer to a title than we did. But the committee was keen for me to have another year and we bombed out badly in 1986, missing the finals. Suddenly the roles were reversed; I didn't want to end on such a bad note and wanted another year and the committee was probably thinking twice about rehiring me. In the end, the 1987 season wasn't much better and we again missed the finals. But a lot of the fault in those two years was the move to the Sydney Cricket Ground. It was a bloody disaster as far as I was concerned. To give up your home base is just suicide in modern football. And while the SCG is a lovely ground, when it's only got a small crowd it can be like a morgue; the atmosphere isn't there and the players find it hard to rise to the occasion. Anyway, at the end of '87 it was like the final year at Wests . . . I knew my time had come. I was saying the same things every week, I was getting frustrated and I'd just had enough. As I'd said, I was ready to give it away at the end of '85 so by then, I'd reached the end of my tether. It was my tenth straight season in first grade and I knew I really needed a break. In that time, Jack Gibson, Warren Ryan and Frank Stanton had all had one or two years off whereas I'd done it straight—it was just too hard.'

The progression into journalism was perhaps in Masters' genes. His mother Olga was among Australia's best authors, writing five books. Brother Chris is one of the country's leading current affairs reporters, working on the ABC program 'Four Corners'. It was Chris' sensational expose on corruption in the game in 1983 that led to the demise of league boss Kevin Humphreys and changed the game forever. Sister Sue is head of television drama at the ABC, while another sister, Deb, is a producer on the ABC's '7:30 Report'. Brother Ian hosts a radio show in Los Angeles while yet another, Quentin, is a film producer in London. 'As the eldest of seven, I was forced to take a more traditional line of employment years back,' Masters recalled. 'My father was a schoolteacher and I had it drummed into me from an early age that I had to get a degree and a public service job—it was crap, but the way people thought at the time. My brothers and sisters had a bit more freedom and were able to take jobs that were more creative. They've all done well but it makes family reunions pretty difficult. In fact, I think the last time we were all together was at my wedding in 1963.' Although originally planned as a break from coaching for a year or two, Masters has taken to the media and is now among the foremost sports critics in the country, writing for the *Sydney Morning Herald* and appearing on the Seven Network. 'I'd done a fair apprenticeship as I'd been writing one or two columns a week for the old Sydney *Sun* while I was coaching since 1980,' he said. 'It was never hard or a chore and something I really grew to enjoy. Over the years I've had a couple of offers to return to coaching. I've thought about it, but I get my kicks nowadays, so to speak, from dealing with players I've coached who are now coaches themselves, such as Tom Raudonikis. Players still remember you as a coach and seek out your opinion. David Gillespie asked my advice about a few things while I was in England for the 1995 World Cup. They don't forget the involvement you've had and will ask your opinion on things. The biggest reward in coaching is helping players and talking to them and I still get that a bit, even though I'm not directly involved any more. One of the high points of the job is the links you maintain after you finish. I'm still very close to a lot of blokes.'

Having spent many years in the coaching battlefield and several more observing others in action, Masters has firm views on what makes a good coach. 'First and foremost, you've got to be very, very honest. That's the most important thing, to be extremely truthful. Players are quick to detect duplicity or dishonesty. You can't bullshit with them. They live a life whereby they have to detect weakness quickly in others and they will see it in a coach who isn't straight with them. Admittedly, some coaches survive by being amazing liars, but I think eventually they get caught out and they don't have long-term relationships with their players. Secondly, you have to be a good technocrat. You really have to know the game on two levels—the actual skills of the game and the tactics. With the skills, you have to be able to show the players subtle little things like how to shift the ball quickly or use their footwork to best advantage. As far as tactics, the game has evolved to such a stage that a coach needs to be able to find weaknesses in the opposition and alert his players to them. Thirdly, you have to be a good communicator. Players don't like humbug. They know when you're bullshitting them. You've got to get straight to the point and be concise in conveying your message. Fourthly, you have to be a diplomat. You have to be able to get on with your board, the players, the fans and the media. We all fall away in that area from time to time because of the absolute pressures that come with the job. The pressures get you down, but they never make it unbearable in my opinion. To me, there is nothing in this world as good as coming into a crowded dressing room after a big win. Everyone has worked well, you've stuck to a plan and it's all come off. You've planned it all week, and if you went into the match as the underdog, it feels even sweeter. The joy in that is something that I still miss. On the other hand, there's nothing worse than a loss. It's a horrible feeling to lead in a game and get done in the last 20 seconds by a lucky intercept or by a referee's decision. Your whole week's work and all that effort is just gone in a tenth of a second. I must admit that for me, the contrasting win–loss feelings became a problem. I found that a win at St George might last 24 to 48 hours; you'd still be fairly relaxed on the Tuesday night but starting to think ahead to the next game. At Wests, you could maybe add another day. The winning feeling would still be there on Wednesday at which stage you got back down to business. But I found a loss—at both clubs—hung around like a bad smell for the entire week. And if you've lost three or four games in a row, you're looking at a lot of nights without much sleep. Some coaches can cop a loss and shrug it off as just a bad day at the office. I think Wayne Bennett is like that and Warren Ryan, surprisingly, could also handle defeat very well. But people like Jack Gibson and myself couldn't. Losing would stick with us for a week and there was nothing we could do to get rid of it. Basically, you didn't get rid of it until you won another game. As far as I was concerned, I was willing to trade four wins for every loss.

I thought that was a fair ratio and I'd be getting enough good nights' sleep to get by. But in the last couple of years at Saints, we were winning a lot less than four games out of five—it was more like a 50–50 ratio which made for a lot of sleepless nights. And the other things that caused me a lot of aggravation in the latter years was the blasted trend towards citing by video. You'd win a game and often within 15 minutes of fulltime, somebody would come into the dressing room and say, "They want to cite Craig Young on video evidence." It would totally take away that feeling of satisfaction you got from winning. I'd have to go back to the club on Sunday night and go through the video time and again. It wasn't that Saints were a violent club; I spoke to other coaches and they went through the same feeling. I remember one coach said to me, "When can we start enjoying the game again?" The video citing system meant you had to get straight down to business after the game—win, lose or draw—as most hearings were held on the Monday night. And it wasn't just a matter of coaching the players to play to the letter of the law. There are so many things that happen on the field on the spur of the moment or by a reflex action. A coach has no control over them. A player can lash out with his boot while trying to get free in the play the ball and accidentally get a bloke in the head; the ball carrier can raise his elbow a split second before impact to protect himself and break his opponent's jaw. These things happen and the increasing use of citing made it very stressful. And at Saints, I was the players' advocate; I had to go in with players from all three grades. Even if first grade won well and there were no dramas, I'd often find myself in the leagues club office late on Sunday night trying to find out what happened to some young under-23 player who had been sent off earlier in the day.'

Masters has mixed views on the modern game and the way

it is heading. 'There is no doubt that players are fitter and faster than even just a few years ago,' he said. 'Work-rates are higher and players seem more adept at keeping the ball alive. But there are some things that seem to have declined. Players don't seem to draw and pass as well as they used to. And they don't seem to think as well, as a whole. Some do, of course— the top players are always very clever in any era. All the off-field stuff is much less enjoyable than in our day—I'm sure the mateship and camaraderie were greater in my time. But still, if a bloke's getting $300,000 a year, he's getting enough enjoyment through his bank balance. A lot of the joy we received at Wests were from the off-field things. That was the compensation for the lack of money at the time. The friendships last a lifetime and the coach often continues to represent a father figure role. When Michael Beattie, who I coached at Saints, was in trouble with the law in 1994, I was only too glad to help. I still talk to Tom Raudonikis a few times a week about league and other things. I'll often drive from Sydney to Melbourne and stay over with Les Boyd in the bush along the way. You can't buy the mateships we forged back in those days and the modern players, for all the money they earn, will probably miss out on this one important aspect of football and be poorer for it.'

The Iceman

JOHN MONIE

CLUBS
Parramatta 1984–89,
Wigan 1989–93,
Auckland 1995–

PREMIERSHIP RECORD
Games 171, won 99, lost 71, drew 1.
Winning percentage 57.9%.
Semi-finals
1984–86
Grand finals (2)
1984, 1986
Premierships (1)
1986

ENGLISH CHAMPIONSHIP RECORD
Games 104, won 82, lost 19, drew 3.
Winning percentage 78.8%.

OTHER COACHING ACHIEVEMENTS
Coached Wigan to four Challenge Cup victories 1990–93,
four first division championship victories 1990–93,
Lancashire Cup 1993, Regal Trophy 1993,
British premiership 1992, World Cup championship 1991.

J ohn Monie is the iceman of modern rugby league coaches. A quiet, calm character, Monie seems to always be in control of any pressure situation. The man who started his coaching life as Jack Gibson's unknown offsider at Parramatta has become a respected coach in his own right. Monie was the first coach to win major titles in both hemispheres, guiding Parramatta to the Winfield Cup in 1986 before moulding Wigan into a trophy collecting machine four years later. Monie is known as a gentleman's gentleman within the game, a deep thinker who rarely lets his emotions get the better of him. His quiet, almost shy nature is at odds with many of the other successful coaches in the game. In fact, the initial impression of John Monie is that he is too nice to be in such a cut-throat business. But he has used his own style to become one of the game's elite coaches—a man destined to be at the top of his profession for years to come.

Monie was born and bred on the New South Wales Central Coast, 90 minutes north of Sydney, and remains a favourite son of the area. 'I was a Woy Woy junior and broke into first grade there when I was just 17,' he said. 'We had a good strong side and I made the Southern Division side in 1967, which led to me joining Cronulla the following year. I took over the five-eighth spot from Jack Danzey, who went on to become a referee, and I played more than 60 first grade games and a handful of matches in reserves. Cronulla was still new to the premiership but we had a fair side; Warren Ryan was outside me in the centres and our halfback, Terry Hughes, won the inaugural Rothmans Medal the year I came to the club. Ken "Killer" Kearney was the coach and he was a very shrewd tactician compared to most blokes around at that time. I liked the football in Sydney but by the third year there, I began to get homesick for the Central Coast. I wanted to surf more and just didn't have time when I was training most days and playing on the weekend. I used to enter surfing contests on the Saturday and make the finals, but couldn't participate in them because Cronulla were playing the next day. Once I was off injured for a while and thought I'd sneak up the north coast for some surfing. I looked back a while ago at some photos of myself then and noticed that even though it was the middle of winter, I was as brown as could be with the best suntan. At the time, I didn't think anyone would know that I skipped up north. When you're young you don't think of those things. But in retrospect, I'm sure they knew.'

Monie concedes that if surfing was as well organised in the 1960s as it is in the '90s, he may never even have contemplated a career in rugby league. 'Surfing was always my passion,' he said. 'But back in those days, it was pretty hard to make a living out of it. The sport was still in its infancy and didn't have the structure or status it enjoys now. If it did, I would have been a pro surfer, no question about it. I also loved league, but just spent every spare minute in the water. My first contract money at Cronulla, I spent going to Hawaii. I spent the next year's money going to Bali before it was famous.' The lure of the Central Coast lifestyle and a less rigorous training schedule which allowed more time for board-riding saw Monie return home. 'I went back to Woy Woy as captain-coach and stayed there a few seasons before going on to Wests in Newcastle as a paid player under Dennis Ward in the mid '70s,' he said. 'I went back to the Central Coast for a year at Umina and then got my old job back at Woy Woy as player-coach. Eventually, I broke my arm at about 32 and decided to retire and concentrate on coaching. It was fairly soon after that in 1981 that I got a call from Jack Gibson, who'd just taken over the job at Parramatta. The call was something of a surprise as

I'd had very little to do with Jack over the years. He was a selector for a year when I was at Cronulla but we didn't have much contact then. Jack had a little too much foresight for them at Cronulla and didn't last long. Apparently, he followed my career as a player-coach and non-playing coach. Word got to him that I'd won a couple of titles at Woy Woy with sides that probably weren't the best in the competition. He asked me if I'd like to come down as skills and reserve grade coach. It was a great opportunity; I always knew I could communicate with players well and wanted to make a go of it; this seemed my big chance. Jack put a big broom through Parramatta when he joined the club in 1981 and it was like starting afresh. He sacked a few more after that first year but fortunately I was one bloke who got on well with him. I found I wasn't that intimidated by him and I just treated Jack the way I treat everybody. It seems he liked that in me.'

Monie was Gibson's deputy throughout his three-year term at Parramatta, which saw the Eels rule the league roost. The club won three straight premierships, with Monie's reserve grade side also reaching the grand final in 1981. When Gibson decided to stand down at the end of 1983, Monie was the man he endorsed as his successor. That was all the encouragement the Parramatta board needed. Despite being virtually unknown outside the club, Monie was handed the reins for the following season. But there were plenty of tough times for Monie to overcome when he inherited the job from Gibson, who was then—and many say still is—regarded as the best coach in the game. Gibson's departure prompted many critics to speculate that the magic had left Parramatta—and for a while it looked like they were right. After an impressive start to 1984, the Eels lost six second round matches to enter the finals looking decidedly vulnerable. But the Eels' big match players—Peter Sterling, Steve Ella, Brett Kenny, Ray Price, Eric Grothe and Michael Cronin—rose to the pressure of finals football. The Eels edged out St George 22–16, before going down to Canterbury 16–8 in the major semi-final. The Eels then had to beat St George in the final to earn another crack at Canterbury in the grand final. And beat them they did, but only through a late try to wing powerhouse Grothe in the right corner minutes from fulltime. That set the scene for an epic grand final between the two teams of the 1980s—Canterbury and Parramatta. And in a grinding, trench-warfare match, two key injuries proved the Eels' downfall. After just seven minutes, star centre Steve Ella, one of the Eels' main strike weapons out wide, limped from the field with a leg injury. Then midway through the second half, with the Eels ahead 4–0 after a Cronin try, Ray Price went down injured with Canterbury on the attack. Bulldog hooker Mark Bugden, sensing that the Eels' defence was stretched to cover for Price, darted out of dummy-half to race 25 metres for the Bulldogs' lone try. And with Chris Mortimer's conversion, that was all it took. The Bulldogs held on for a hard-fought 6–4 win to break Parramatta's three-year domination of the game. The critics immediately declared it was the departure of Gibson that proved the Eels' undoing but Monie insists the talk never got to him. 'I knew what people were saying but I can honestly say it never worried me,' he said. 'I've always been a relaxed person. I've got on with everyone and never made a big deal out of anything. The pressure of the job has never been a factor with me. I read the papers, like everyone does. Those who say they don't are just lying. But I've never taken a great notice of things other people say about me and have been happy to get on with the job. I'm not immune to criticism, but I don't let it bug me to the extent that I put pressure back on myself. I've always believed that if I work as hard as I can and prepare the team to the best of my ability, then what happens on Sunday at three o'clock just happens. That's not to say that I accept losing, like any coach I want to win. But as I've gained more experience, I've learned to accept a loss and not get into a state of depression. In the early days, I did it really tough for quite a few days after a loss. But I take it in my stride more now.'

Cool, calm and collected is the best way to describe John Monie's attitude to both life and football. 'I rarely get excited,' he admits. 'And that's the way I want my team to be. I figure that if before a match, I'm uptight and on edge, then the team will be the same way. And I don't want them to be like that. I want them to be relaxed, confident in their own ability. That's the way I want them to play. I can't see any advantage in having them edgy or afraid to try something because they might make a mistake. I want them to be adventurous and I want them to try to be as good as they can be. The English experience probably helped me develop that attitude. Over there, they are more prepared to take risks and be adventurous and it is a good way to play the game.'

Monie's ability to stay detached during a game also has its down side, however. The coach recalls an incident when he watched his son playing in a junior game several years ago. 'He was 14 and dislocated his shoulder midway through the match. Afterwards he was upset because I didn't go down to see how he was when it happened. It didn't hit me until then— I was just trained to watch the game and see it through. As a coach, when a player gets injured, your first thought is, "Can he do the job?" But after the game, I'll be as concerned as the next guy. I care for my players like anyone else.'

Any doubts about John Monie's coaching capabilities were forever cast aside following the deeds of his Eels in the 1986 season. Parramatta began impressively, winning their first five games and set the scene for the finals by taking the mid-week Panasonic Cup. They won the minor premiership and club championship, breezing through the finals, only to set the stage for another meeting with arch rivals Canterbury in the grand final. The clash proved another 80-minute war of attrition and earned the two clubs a dubious place in history for producing league's only tryless grand final. But this time it was the Eels who triumphed by the barest of margins—4–2—thanks to two penalty goals by Cronin to one by Canterbury's Terry Lamb. After the game, all the attention focussed on Eels greats Cronin and Ray Price, who decided to end their Sydney careers on that triumphant note. Monie's coming of age as a coach was almost forgotten in the hysteria over the two long-serving stars, but not by Price. Before the match the Eels captain told his players: 'Win this game firstly for yourselves and secondly for John Monie.' In the victorious dressing room a couple of hours later, Price sought out former coach Gibson and told him: 'John's finally jumped out of your shadow. I'm happier for him than anyone else in this room.'

Monie took the victory, typically, in his stride. 'We won the grand final 4–2 and that score reflected the closeness of the two teams in that era,' he said. 'We could have just as easily won the '84 grand final and lost in '86—there was so little between us in the two games. It just came down to luck on the day on both occasions. Parramatta and Canterbury took defence and mistake-free football just about as far as it could go at that time. Towards the end of the 1980s, sides started to open the game up. But I will always have fond memories of '86 because of our consistency over the year. We won every title that was up for grabs and very few teams have done that in the history of the game. It was very rewarding and a great way to send

Pricey and The Crow out of the game. They deserved that finale after their great service to rugby league and to Parramatta.'

But the Eels' fairytale premiership in 1986 was to prove the end of an era. Parramatta never recovered from the dual departures of Price and Cronin, and subsequent retirements of fellow match-winners Sterling, Ella, Kenny and Grothe. A decade later, the Eels still haven't reached the finals since the heady days of 1986 when they made a clean sweep of all the trophies on offer. 'Sadly, it was all downhill and I saw the writing on the wall in 1989 when we finished in eighth spot on the ladder,' Monie said. 'I remember telling the officials I'd over-achieved to get the club there—really we should have finished a lot worse. Denis Fitzgerald (the Eels' chief executive) had a great theory of bringing as many local juniors into the team as possible but it's been proved since that it just doesn't work. You've got to have a blend of good imported players and locals. It put Parramatta into a spin and one they've taken a long time to get out of. I knew it was time to get out but when the call came late that season from Maurice Lindsay, the Wigan chairman, I barely considered it. I'd never met the bloke and had barely heard of him. When he rang, he said, "I'm Maurice Lindsay and I'm talking to the next coach of Wigan." Coaching in England didn't hold the remotest interest for me at that time. I'd never thought of England as a possibility and just wanted to get back onto the Central Coast in the sun and the surf. I told Maurice, "Bullshit I'm your next coach . . . I'm off to the beach." He called again the next day and asked, "Am I talking to Wigan's next coach?" But I turned him down again. That went on for quite a few phone calls . . . he would have been chasing me for over a month. But I've got to give it to him— Maurice finally convinced me and I DID become the next coach of Wigan. His enthusiasm for the game, particularly the English game, and his vision of the future won me over. Maurice believed the sky was the limit. Nothing seemed to stop him getting what he wanted. He spoke about rugby league in terms and with a passion I'd never heard before. He was the exact opposite of Jack Gibson, for example. Jack was always low key and very dry. Then this English gentleman gets on the phone to me talking dreams and visions. He told me to picture Wembley Stadium with 100,000 fans in it on Cup final day. I instantly liked the bloke. I'd also spoken to Peter Sterling and Brett Kenny who had very fond memories of Britain and they said it would be an excellent move, so I went.'

Monie knew he would be filling big shoes at Wigan when he arrived in the winter of 1989–90. Former coach Graham Lowe had firmly established Wigan as the top team in the land, winning a host of silverware to prove the point. Monie was, in effect, on a hiding to nothing. If he failed to continue Wigan's mighty run of the Lowe years, he would have been branded a failure. And if he did bring home the titles, he would merely be doing what the fans and directors expected. 'People warned me it was a dangerous situation taking over such a successful club,' Monie said. 'But again it comes back to my personality. I didn't ever let those things worry me. And people over there didn't realise how absurd it was to tell me, "You're in a no-win situation taking over from Graham Lowe at Wigan." After all, I was the bloke who took over from Jack Gibson at Parramatta. If only they knew the situation I'd been in a few years earlier in Sydney, they wouldn't have bothered trying to warn me of the perils of the job. Graham Lowe had done a great job and he was the real start of the Wigan monster that has dominated the code in Britain. The thing is, though, I didn't feel any pressure about taking over from Graham, or the enormity of the job. To me, it was a coaching job like any other and I wasn't going to let it worry me. And looking back, I was probably rather naive because I didn't realise how much rugby league meant to Wigan. I was just a boy from Woy Woy and had never seen anything like their love or feeling for the game.

'The passion that English fans have just isn't in our game in Australia or New Zealand. When I was over there I met people who had been standing at the same spot on the terraces for 40 years. It's almost a religious fervour and their singing during games reflects that. I'd been there for a couple of years when, during one game, all the usual chanting and singing was going on. I was sitting in the coach's box on top of the grandstand on the far side of the ground to the fans concentrating on the game when one of my stats men said, "Well, why don't you?" To which I replied, "Why don't I what?" He said, "Why don't you give them a wave?" I started to listen closely for probably the first time and suddenly realised what it was they were singing. They were chanting, "Monie, Monie, give us a wave." They'd probably been doing it for the past two years and it never registered because I'd always been putting all my thoughts into the game. So I gave them a little shake of the hand and the whole place erupted. It almost stopped the game because all of the players looked around wondering what the hell this almighty roar was about when nothing was really happening on the field. You just can't imagine that sort of thing happening over here . . . it's hard to explain why.'

Monie admits he was rather tentative taking over a team full of superstars as an outsider from Down Under. The new coach knew he would have to win over the respect of seasoned internationals like Martin Offiah, Ellery Hanley and Shaun Edwards. 'When I arrived, I didn't try to do too much coaching in the first month or so,' he said. 'We didn't play all that well—I think we lost two of the first four games. But I didn't jump in to try to change things. It's not in my personality to be overpowering and I didn't feel it necessary to come in and wield a big stick. When Graham Lowe left, he was at logger-heads with several of the star players. The likes of Ellery Hanley and Andy Gregory had gone missing for a while; Shaun Edwards also had a blow-up with him and left for a week or two. I reckon these guys would have thought when another coach from Down Under came in, "Oh no, here we go again." So I was very conscious of how I took over and didn't try to tread on any toes, even when it may have been necessary. I like to think I can handle people well. I probably shocked them at the first team meeting when we went through the video and then I told each of them I wanted them to get a diary and take notes. I didn't want them just staring blankly at a video for three hours while I told them what they were doing right and wrong. I wanted them to write down the positive and negative aspects of their own performance, how many tackles they were making, how many dropped balls and the like. They were a bit taken aback by that and Ellery started to question a few things I was doing, which I found great. I don't mind players having the balls to stand up and say what they think or asking for an explanation of what you've said. We had some good discussions and a few times he asked me to leave so he could talk to the side alone. Again, I didn't really mind and it was good for the overall functioning of the team. Far from being trouble, Ellery was a brilliant player to coach and an inspirational captain. He was great—a man I counted as a close ally in my time at the club. My only problem with Ellery came when he announced he'd accepted a fair bit of money to say he'd signed with the London Monarchs gridiron team. It was a good publicity stunt for them but in the end it wasn't much more than that. The whole experience over there worked out well for me and well for Wigan. I think time proved my method of handling the players to be the right one. In my four years at Wigan, we didn't have a single player dispute, even though the coaches before and after me (Lowe and John Dorahy) had plenty. I had a lot of good times with players like Andy Goodway and Andy Gregory and for me, taking a great player like Gene Miles over there was a highlight. Watching Martin Offiah play outside Miles was sensational. There was one game there when Offiah scored 10 tries which is a record—one that may never be beaten. You can't forget something like that. Offiah, I thought, improved under my coaching, even though he's come back to the field a bit since then.'

Monie found the Wembley experience every bit as special as Lindsay had promised. And he had plenty of chances to sample the atmosphere at the most famous of football grounds. In his four years at Wigan, the club won every trophy on offer—including four Challenge Cup finals at Wembley. 'The atmosphere at Wembley is just unique,' he said. 'And the roar as you go out onto the field is awesome. Maurice told me it was something to savour and he was right there. But winning the four first division championships was actually more important to me than winning at Wembley. And I'm not belittling Wembley or the Challenge Cup by saying that. But for me, being a professional rugby league coach, to be the most consistent team over the whole season was the target I was always aiming at. To win that was my goal and we did it every year as the Wigan monster, as they call it over there, just got bigger and bigger.'

Monie's initial fear that he would quickly become homesick for the sun and surf of Woy Woy never eventuated. 'I really thought I would miss the life back home being so far

JOHN MONIE

away and spending so much time in a cold climate,' he said. 'But it never happened. I quickly learned that when you're winning at Wigan, you are doing everything first class. My wife and I would fly to Spain for a weekend when we had a break to get some sunshine. And we made so many great friends there. Even though the current chairman, Jack Robinson, has been waging a vendetta against me in the newspapers over there since I left, my memories of Wigan and Central Park are nothing but happy ones. It was a great time in my life and I'm just glad I took the plunge and gave it a go. I could have easily knocked it back and never experienced all the things I grew to love over there.'

During his fourth season, Monie did finally get a case of itchy feet to return home. 'I'd originally planned to go for just two seasons and here was I, now in my fourth,' he said. 'I was beginning to think enough was enough and I knew if I kept staying there, eventually we would lose our mantle as the best team in Britain. A few offers came from back home and that's when I made plans to return to Australia.' But, much like his move to Wigan, Monie took some convincing when he received his initial call from the Auckland Warriors. 'My thoughts were to return to Sydney and coach one of the top sides,' he said. 'And then I got the call from Auckland, which didn't even have a team yet. The idea seemed too daunting . . . the club hadn't played a game and didn't have any players. But the more I thought about it, the more I warmed to the idea. It was the ultimate challenge for a coach. To be able to set up the Warriors from scratch, and recruit exactly the type of players that I wanted, was a rare opportunity. It was a great opening and a chance to be involved in decision making at the club right from the start. I really enjoyed being involved in the recruitment, which is an area of the game I hadn't had a lot to do with prior to that. I still copped out a little bit because as soon as it came time to talk money, I left the room. I left that part of the job up to (Warriors chief executive) Ian Robson and he did a great job. He was like the Mounties—he always got his man—and for a new administrator, I thought he did outstandingly well. The way he could talk to players and discuss money with them was great. Just about every player we targeted, we got and he gave us a real leg-up in recruitment. I remember we thought we'd signed Ian Roberts but he changed his mind at the last minute. Ian Robson and I were in a lift in a big hotel in London and Andy Platt stepped in as we got out. Ian immediately said to me, "Well, what's wrong with him?" I told him I didn't think Platt would leave England. A week later we found out Roberts wasn't coming and Ian jumped straight back on a plane from Auckland to Manchester to talk to Platt. He could have done it on the phone but decided to do it face to face instead and I think that proved the difference—Platt signed and has been a huge asset to us. He also signed up Denis Betts by using the same type of persistence.'

But it was Robson's determined recruiting, netting former Wigan players Dean Bell, Frano Botica, Platt and Betts, that resulted in a rare situation for Monie—at the centre of a controversy. New Wigan manager Jack Robinson, clearly feeling the pressure at having lost several star players, began a bitter campaign against Monie in the British media. The Wigan boss accused the club's former coach of treachery and of ripping the club to pieces. Monie, always keen to avoid drama, at first chose to ignore the accusations. But when the tirade continued, he fired back in kind as the British tabloid press ate up the war of words. 'The truth of the matter was very different from what Robinson was spouting,' Monie said. 'Of the guys we signed, Wigan didn't offer Bell, Botica or Platt new contracts. So the only bloke we recruited that they wanted was Denis Betts. Wigan wasn't going all that well under John Dorahy while all this was going on and I think Robinson was feeling the pressure. He got a lot of back pages with his bleating that I was ripping his team apart. He was painting me out as a devil. But we both knew the real story. When I returned to Britain for the World Cup in 1995, I was greeted well by all the Wigan people so they didn't let the stories he was putting out worry them.'

Always the gentleman, Monie harbours no grudge against Robinson despite having at one stage threatened legal action against him. 'I've always thought you've got to be bigger than that sort of thing,' he said. 'I saw him when I was over there and shook hands with him. But whatever he thinks or says isn't going to worry me. It was unfair because he was having a field day at my expense in the press while I was thousands of miles away concentrating on my new job with my new club. It was annoying at the time, but I try not to let those sort of things get to me.'

The Warriors played some fine football in their opening season in the Winfield Cup, but were hampered by a lack of consistency. A key moment came in a round three clash against Western Suburbs, which the Warriors won convincingly to record their maiden premiership victory. After the match, it was discovered the Warriors had used five replacements—one more than the rules permit. The club was stripped of the two points and at the time, there was a definite feeling that the mistake would come back to haunt the club. Ultimately, the loss of the two points cost the Warriors a finals berth. It is believed a member of Monie's coaching staff made the blunder, but the coach was quick to take the blame. Further, to make light of the situation and prevent it affecting morale, Monie wore a dunce's cap around the training paddock the following week.

'The buck stops with me as head coach,' he later declared. 'It was my mistake and I have to accept responsibility.'

One occasion when Monie did lose his cool was at halftime of the Warriors' last game in their maiden season against Brisbane at ANZ Stadium in August 1995. After being in finals contention all season, the Warriors faded badly in the run home to narrowly miss a top eight spot. But Monie was still hoping to finish a mixed year on a high note against the Broncos in front of their home crowd. 'I really went berserk that day,' Monie said. 'I consider we'd had a good season and been competitive and learned during the year. But that game we just lost our way completely and played like novices in the first 40 minutes. Being a new club with a lot of players new to the Winfield Cup, I think they decided the season was already over before we played round 22. Mentally they just lost it. We made five or six unforced errors, failed to find touch from free kicks, gave away silly penalties and so on. These were things we had eliminated from our game early in the piece but for some reason we were falling into the same bad old habits again. And the Broncos, great side that they are, punished us for our mistakes. I wanted our guys to finish strongly as it would have been a good morale booster for the off season and the club's second year. It was also Dean Bell's last game and he deserved to end what was a very fine career on a good performance. That was important to me and I knew it was important to Dean. But we hit the self destruct button and when they came into the room at halftime, I just went crazy. That's not something I do often; I like to think I'm helping the players at halftime. The players are generally looking for guidance at the break ... they don't need a ranting, raving lunatic yelling at them. Anyway, the players were dumbfounded; they were literally in a state of shock. Unfortunately, when I do go off like that, every second word starts with "f" and I get so worked up that it doesn't make any sense. It didn't help the team but our second half wasn't that bad. The game was already gone, but at least we played a more disciplined and controlled game. I don't know why they turned it around, maybe I scared them into it.'

Monie shrugs his shoulders when asked to describe what makes a good coach. 'That's the hardest question in rugby league, even harder than what makes a good player,' he said. 'Look around . . . there aren't a lot of successful coaches. A lot of blokes who were great players just can't make the transition to coaching. Tactically, you've got to be very aware and up with the latest trends. But it's a lot more than that. You've got to be part mother, part father, part psychologist. You have to understand the game from its most fundamental aspects to the most complex. You've got to be able to pick strengths and weaknesses in the opposition and there are times when you have to be smart. Other times you have to act naive. Communication is important; you've got to be able to get your message through to the players. Man management, being able to relate to both players and officials. It's a complex question and who knows what combination makes a good coach . . . I haven't really got a clue. The other thing that many people don't realise about coaching is it's a job you don't leave at the office. I think the man in the street thinks it's a great lifestyle but he isn't aware of the pressures. At times it's the world's best job, at other times it's the worst. You could say the peaks are high, but the valleys can get pretty deep. You've got to be prepared to look at other sports, the latest training methods from overseas, sports psychology and the like. The mental state of players is an area that is still being explored but can obviously play a huge part in getting a winning unit. It's a field where we've barely scratched the surface. Within the next five years, I think most clubs will have sports psychologists playing a major role in their organisations. I can see them playing an important part with the players in goal-setting and preparation. The whole coaching scene is changing fast. We've now got dietitians to tell the players what they should and shouldn't eat, strength coaches, sprint coaches, training co-ordinators. It's an ever changing game and you've got to keep moving with it. You've got to be prepared to keep changing, keep learning. If you stick your head in the sand for even one season, you can be left behind. If you're not a better coach now than you were 12 months ago, then you're in big trouble. As a coach, I hope I get better all the time. If you stop improving, you get sacked. I've been around since 1981 and so far I've managed to avoid the sack, which is pretty rare in this business. If I'd stayed at Parramatta one more year, I might have come close, though. The threat of the axe is forever over your head and hopefully I can avoid it for a few years yet.'

Sticks Provan
Walked Tall

NORM PROVAN

CLUBS
St George 1962–65 (captain-coach), 1968,
Parramatta 1975,
Cronulla 1978–79

PREMIERSHIP RECORD
Games 181, won 124, lost 49, drew 8.
Winning percentage 68.5%.
Semi-finals
1962–65, 1968, 1975, 1978–79
Grand finals (5)
1962–65, 1978
Premierships (4)
1962–65

OTHER COACHING ACHIEVEMENTS
Coached Parramatta to pre-season title 1975,
coached Cronulla to Amco Cup victory 1979.

I f you believe statistics maketh the coach then Norm Provan is the best coach in rugby league history. While the likes of Jack Gibson, Warren Ryan and Tim Sheens are often brought up when discussing league's great coaches, Provan's record beats them all. His winning percentage at the three clubs he coached stands at 68.5 per cent—clearly superior to Gibson (62), Ryan (56) and Sheens (60). As a player, Provan was a born leader—a man who, in a different era, would have been a knight of the round table or a polar explorer. A gentleman's gentleman from the old school, he was a modest performer on the field renowned for his loyalty and fair play. Provan coached for eight years in the big time at St George, Parramatta and Cronulla, taking his teams to the finals on each occasion. He led Saints to the premiership in each of his four years as captain-coach, before steering young Parramatta and Cronulla sides to impressive finals performances. Add that to his amazing effort in playing in 10 consecutive winning grand finals and Provan can lay claim to being the most successful individual league has known.

Norm Provan was born near Wagga in 1932 but grew up in Sydney's northern suburbs when his family moved to town during the Great Depression. He played his early football for Willoughby D Grade, before the family again moved to the Sutherland Shire. Young Norm, now a strapping teenager, and his four brothers played for the Sutherland Gravediggers, who at that time were part of St George's junior league. The brothers were very close throughout their careers and at one stage there were four Provans playing grade for the Dragons. Coach Norm Hollingdale was the major influence on Norm Provan's development and, as a former Easts player, took the 17-year-old forward to the Roosters in 1949 for a trial. Easts couldn't find a spot for Provan in their third grade side and he returned to the Gravediggers, only to get a call from Saints the following year. Provan began his time with the Dragons in reserve grade but was given his chance in top company a year later, remaining in first grade for the next 15 years as he chiselled out one of league's most impressive careers.

Standing well over six feet and tipping the scales at over 100 kilos, Provan soon made his name as a hard-running attacking forward and punishing defender. He played in his first grand final in 1953 and experienced what was to prove a rare feeling in his career—losing. Souths, with fullback Clive Churchill in grand form and winger Ian Moir scoring three tries, crushed the Dragons 31–12. It was to be Provan's only loss in 11 grand finals, however. He narrowly missed selection with the 1952 Kangaroos but made his Test debut against arch enemy Great Britain at the SCG in 1954. His international career had a dream start, with the lanky forward crossing for a try after just eight minutes as Australia cruised to a 37–12 win. It was in that series, won 2–1 by the Aussies, that Provan first played alongside Queenslander Kel O'Shea. Because of his tall, lanky frame, Provan was nicknamed 'Sticks'. The pair, dubbed 'Sticks and Twigs', played together for many years on the international scene, steamrolling all comers.

In 1956, Saints won the grand final, beating Balmain 18–12. The crowd of more than 61,000 at the SCG marvelled at the skills of the young Saints side, which included Provan, Bobby Bugden, Billy Wilson and Ken Kearney. But no-one at the ground that day could have realised they were witnessing the beginning of the greatest winning streak rugby league—or any other football code for that matter—has ever seen. 'We were just happy to win that first title and have it under our belts,' Provan recalled. 'Not at any time did we realise the enormity of what we were about to achieve. And over the next 11 years, we just kept trying to play our best and nothing more. Often people talk of the pressure we were under, but I never felt it and most of the other blokes will say the same thing. We just went out to play, to have a good time and hopefully to win. Any pressure was created by the media and the public and didn't worry us.'

Provan was rewarded for Saints' 1956 triumph by winning Kangaroo tour selection, although injury hampered him throughout the English leg of the tour. He recovered in France as the Aussies scored a 3–0 series win over a strong local side. Always something of a loner, Provan spent much of his spare time on tour studying electrical engineering. While his teammates were out drinking and enjoying themselves, Provan was up in his room reading textbooks. The life on tour, while a delight for many, did not agree with Provan. He never toured with the Kangaroos again, declining selection with the 1959 squad to spend more time with his family and tending to his thriving electrical retail outlet.

But at home, Provan remained a force on the international scene. He played 14 Tests in all, as well as contesting two World Cup campaigns. He starred in the World Cup victory in 1957, as Australia scored a clean sweep of wins over New Zealand, Great Britain, France and a Rest of the World combination. Meanwhile, on the club scene, there was no holding Saints. The club went from strength to strength as outstanding talents such as Reg Gasnier and Johnny Raper joined established stars Provan, Wilson and 'Poppa' Clay. Saints had one of the keenest minds of the era in Ken Kearney as coach and Provan learned many lessons from the man known as 'Killer'. Kearney revolutionised training in Australia, bringing a new expertise to the Dragons. He introduced torture circuit sessions that the players endured on a weekly basis, despite much grumbling. But the benefits were there for all to see—Saints were fitter and stronger than any of their rivals. For most clubs, training in the '50s and '60s consisted of a few laps of the oval, a game of touch . . . and a visit to the pub. Saints worked relentlessly on their attacking moves and their fitness, as well as defence. Saints had the skills to beat most opponents, but when they did find themselves in a tight spot late in matches, their fitness would come to the rescue. 'We always knew we would be stronger in the last 20 minutes than opposition sides,' Provan said. 'And that gave us a tremendous edge.'

Provan watched and learned from Kearney, a shrewd campaigner with years of experience in the trenches of both Australian and British rugby league behind him. Kearney captain-coached the Dragons with a ruthless professionalism from 1957 until the beginning of the 1961 season when a knee injury forced him to hang up his boots. But he continued as coach for the remainder of 1961, leading the Dragons to their sixth straight title before Saints' policy of having a captain-coach saw him move on to Parramatta. And when he left, Saints had no hesitation in asking Provan to take over the captain-coach's role. 'It was a fairly smooth transition as Killer had a successful formula and I saw no reason to change it,' Provan explained. 'The players were comfortable with it and so was I. There were slight variations, like some new moves in attack I introduced, but other than that, we kept largely on the same course. One change I brought in was getting the players to train in the sandhills around the area. I was a great believer in running in sand for building strength and endurance and although the players didn't like it at times, they did it nonetheless. We also played touch footy on the sand. I felt variety was important and was keen to get the players away from the oval. The hard ground took its wear and tear on the body, whereas the sandhills created less jarring.'

Many players who step up from being one of the boys to coach have had difficulties handling the transition, but for Provan it was not a problem. 'It could have been, without doubt, and I was aware of that,' he said. 'But I was lucky in that I never went out and drank with them—either before or after I got the job. Drinking at the pub was never my style. I was described at times as intimidating because I wasn't one of the boys as such, but I think it did give me an advantage when I took over. There was always that bit of distance between us and I think it helped. The players were very professional and accepted me as coach. Even the ones with the larrikin reputations like Billy Smith and Johnny Raper would always give 100 per cent at training and in games. Good players are the easiest to coach. They know what's required and have the professionalism to do the work. I never found internationals a problem.'

But former centre great Reg Gasnier remembers one time when he and Raper decided to test just how stern Provan really was. 'In Norm's first season as captain-coach, Johnny Raper and I didn't turn up to training one mid-week session,' Gasnier said. 'But we had what I thought was a very valid excuse—we'd been out all night drinking. It was getting near the end of the season and we both felt like lashing out. It had been a long season. But that didn't interest Norm; he rang our wives to warn us we'd better be at training. But it was no good—they couldn't raise us. When we came to training the following night, he really hauled us over the coals. We were pulled aside and told we acted like a couple of idiots and should be in reserve grade. He got the point home all right; I remember feeling like a naughty schoolboy. And I don't think we ever missed training again. Next weekend, "Chook" won the man of the match and I came second. We were both determined to make it up to Norm. We respected him, as did everyone at Saints. He was the sort of figure who commanded respect. As coach, he was a good reader of the game but his strength was that he led by example. No way would he ask us to do something he wouldn't do himself. He was principally a forwards coach and let us backs run ourselves. That suited us fine and we enjoyed the free rein. But if we stuffed up, he pounced on us, so we were never reckless or carefree. He was not a tyrant, but believe me, you didn't want an angry Norm Provan if you could help it.'

Provan adopted a strict attitude to training to ensure his squad achieved maximum fitness levels. 'My policy was to treat every player the same, from a Test player to a kid just out of third grade. And I think they all respected me for that, even though the odd nose may have been out of joint at times. If someone was out of condition, he was in trouble no matter who he was. I knew from my playing days that you could cheat on conditioning. You could go through a whole session without really pushing yourself to the maximum. Anyone who wasn't up to scratch had to do the extra work and they copped that sweet. They understood why I was ordering them to do it and they responded. When we started playing in that first season as captain-coach, there was an early hiccup when we lost the pre-season competition in 1962. That was my first challenge and I wanted to win it, but we couldn't manage it. But we won the pre-season in my remaining three seasons there, as well as all four premierships. So apart from that first pre-season, I had a perfect record in my time at Saints.'

Champion wing man John King remembers Provan's strict training regime as the strongest characteristic of the new coach. 'He was a very hard man and really drove us at training,' King said. 'Sessions started at 5:30pm sharp and finished exactly two hours later. Discipline was high on Norm's priority list but that wasn't a problem as the players already had it drummed into them by Killer Kearney. Norm revelled as a captain-coach. I think his own play improved because he tried that little bit harder.'

Provan's first grand final as captain-coach in 1962 provided an incident that has become part of league folklore. Rival clubs in that era developed a theory—'Stop Provan and you stop St George'. Wests' Jim Cody decided to test the principle on grand final day, flattening Provan with an almighty stiff arm in the first half. Johnny Raper takes up the story. 'The mood was fairly ugly in the dressing room at halftime, as "Sticks" lay there dazed in the corner. Plenty of blokes were talking about getting square. But Billy Wilson, who had taken over as captain, suddenly jumped to his feet and made it clear there would be none of that.

'"I know you blokes are all fired up after what happened to Sticks but I don't want you to go out there and look to get even with them," Wilson said. We all took his advice and no sooner had we kicked off than I saw Jim Cody flat on his back. Apparently, Billy had hit him with the best left hook you'd ever want to see. Cody was carried off and Billy was waved straight off by referee Jack Bradley.' Despite Provan being a virtual passenger and the team being reduced to 12 men following Wilson's dismissal, Saints kept their golden run alive with a 9–6 win.

Wests again gave Saints an epic struggle in 1963, when the two teams met on another heavy field to contest the grand final. But with rookies Graeme Langlands and Billy Smith providing Saints with new spark, the Dragons were again victorious, this time by 8–3. It was after this match that *Sun-Herald* photographer John O'Gready snapped one of the most famous photos in sport. O'Gready captured the moment when Provan consoled Wests' tiny skipper Arthur Summons seconds after the siren. On a glue-pot field, both players were covered in mud, giving the appearance of a couple of bronze statues. The photo—entitled 'The Gladiators'—won the prestigious British Press Award and nearly 20 years later was used as the model for the Winfield Cup trophy. Provan, always a stickler for etiquette, admits that both he and Summons had their doubts when asked to lend their image to the trophy. 'It did concern me at first, the fact that we were going to help promote cigarettes,' Provan said. 'And I actually knocked back Winfield's initial approach. But I had a long talk to one of the Rothmans people who came up to see me and he assured me we wouldn't have to do any endorsements or anything else. And they were true to their word. They never placed any demands on us and in the end, it was a very flattering experience to be on the Cup that symbolised supremacy in the game for more than a decade.'

Provan faced a formidable challenge extending Saints' winning run in the grand final of 1964. Sticks found himself up against a talented young Balmain side coached by former Saints team-mate Harry Bath, a shrewd operator who knew the Dragons' game plan intimately. If ever there was a coach who could devise the tactics to end the Dragons' streak, Bath was the man. Saints were well below strength on grand final day, with key forwards Dick Huddart and Ian Walsh sidelined through injury. For Provan, the grand final had a special touch of added spice. The Saints veteran was up against younger brother Peter, who began his career with the Saints before moving to the Tigers in 1961. The clash was the first meeting of brothers in a grand final. And while this was big brother's day, Peter's turn would eventually come. The younger Provan led Balmain to one of the great league grand final wins some five years later—in the 1969 boilover against South Sydney. The pair remain the only brothers to captain premiership-winning teams. But for Norm, the family reunion was anything but a day to savour. 'People have to understand that in those days, it was so deadly serious, particularly in a grand final,' he said. 'This was no friendly family get-together where we could look after each other or share a joke in the middle. It was a jungle out there in the forwards and I distinctly remember it wasn't a good feeling knowing I was coming up against my brother. In fact, I would have much preferred it if he was sitting in the grandstand. I didn't go out to hurt him, but I remember accidentally sticking my finger in his eye, which naturally caused him a fair bit of discomfort. And it was an incident I later regretted, because I was roused on something awful by my sister over it.'

The grand final of '64 was close and hard, with Bath's tactics of forward aggression designed to contain Saints up front. Only a freakish try from grand final specialist Johnny King, his sixth in five grand finals, got Saints home. King crossed for the lone try of the game after a Langlands break to give the Dragons an 11–6 win.

Provan had retired more than once leading up to 1965, but decided to have one last season. And the grand old SCG has seen few more emotional scenes than after the Dragons' grand final win over Souths, played before a record 78,056 crowd. So many fans streamed onto the ground after the game to congratulate Provan that he was unable to complete a lap of honour. But he was content—after more than 250 first grade games, enough was enough. 'We'd won 10 straight titles and I thought it was a good round figure for me to quit on,' Provan said. 'Grand finals were extremely hard, especially on a captain-coach, and I didn't fancy the prospect of going through another. You have to do extra in a grand final. I tried to do in that game what I did 10 years ago by covering the whole field. In a normal game, you don't charge after every opposition movement; you have faith in your team-mates and their ability to defend. But I always decided that in a grand final, you should follow the play . . . just in case. I was 34 by this stage and my body was starting to feel all the wear and tear. I had spent almost half my life in grade football and felt I needed something new. My wife and the kids had come second to football for too long. And I knew we had to lose sooner or later. Saints were still a great side, but the law of averages suggested to me we couldn't keep the run going indefinitely. As it was, they won the next year with Ian Walsh as captain-coach, but the run ended the year after that in 1967. Like all the blokes, I was sad, but not devastated. We'd had a great trot and it was time for someone else.'

Provan faced his first assignment as non-playing coach the year after his retirement in 1966 with an under-10 team in his local neighbourhood at Caringbah. After several years of building up his business, he made a return to senior coaching in 1974 when he took a young Illawarra team to victory in the Country championships. The following year, he was given charge of a Parramatta team that had finished last on the ladder the previous season. 'Dave Bolton, the English five-eighth, coached the Eels in 1973–74 without much success and when he left, they gave me the call,' Provan said. 'I never applied for a coaching job in my life actually; the work was too hard to go looking for it. But I decided to take them on and it was a tremendously hard year. We had a lot of work to do whipping them into a force. They had no tradition of winning and confidence wasn't at all high. They had some fair players, but they were used to losing and they also had too much weight on that had to be got off. The preparation was hard for them, which meant it was hard for me. In those days, I used to do it all with them. I told them at the start of the year, "I'm going to do horrible things to you guys; you'll probably hate me now but hopefully by the end you won't bear a grudge."

'Fortunately, they responded and got on a roll to finish equal fifth with Wests and Balmain. That led to a dreadfully hard passage of football; we had to play Wests on the Tuesday, Balmain on the Thursday and then Canterbury on the Sunday. Somehow we managed to beat them all and it was a really top effort by the players. I think we'd played something like eight games in 20 days at the pressure end of the season. Manly finally knocked us out of business in the minor semi-final, but everyone still finished the season with their heads held high.'

Current Eels chief executive Denis Fitzgerald, then a lanky young forward, believed Provan's attitude, more than anything, was the key to his success. 'He was a boyhood hero to most of us and the players felt extremely flattered to have such a legend of the game suddenly take charge,' Fitzgerald said. 'We doted on his every word and would have run through brick walls for him. As soon as he took over, Norm made fitness a priority and really worked on getting us in top condition. Those were the days of hard long-distance training but Norm didn't shirk any of it. He led the way on the runs and really impressed us with his fitness. He was hard but fair and always went out of his way to show appreciation for the effort the players put in. We started the year poorly but then had a great run home. We reached the final of the Amco Cup and also had that memorable run in the semi-finals. Looking back, Norm Provan has to take a lot of credit for turning the place around at Parramatta. He didn't accept defeat. He had a winning attitude and that soon rubbed off on the players. He brought the culture of winning to the club, which we needed for the success that was to follow.'

The Eels' memorable run under Provan in 1975 established Parramatta as the sleeping giants of the Sydney premiership. The Eels had never reached a grand final, but the club's new army of fans was convinced better times were ahead under Provan in 1976. But then a shock—the coach stood down after just one year at the helm. 'The travel was probably the thing that got to me,' he said. 'I was living at Cronulla and driving across Sydney to Parramatta three times a week was something I didn't want to do for another season. And I had an excellent back-up in Terry Fearnley. He was my reserve grade coach and I knew he'd do a good job if given the chance. He was keen to take over and I saw no problem with that. I told them when I came into the club that I'd stay for a year. Everyone assumed when we went well I'd stay, but I didn't see the need. I got a lot of satisfaction out of seeing the club reach its first grand final the following year in '76. They kept referring back to my influence when they finally got there and that was very flattering. One of the greatest things about coaching is seeing what you've accomplished. And by that, I don't mean just when you're there in charge. How it flows on after you've gone. To see if the blokes can pick it up and run with it when you're not around any more.'

After two years on the sidelines, Provan accepted his next—and last—coaching post, at Cronulla. 'They were a team of young kids with some promise and so I thought I'd take them on when the opportunity came up in 1978,' Provan said. 'They had finished down the ladder the previous year but I saw something there. Steve Rogers was still playing good football and was a fine captain. In the forwards they had some talented players like Paul Khan and Steve Kneen and hooker

John McMartin had been around for a while and knew plenty of tricks. We made the finals and came in full of confidence, knocking Manly off 17–12 in our first game. We then beat Wests to qualify for the grand final, but I had both Greg Pierce and Kurt Sorensen suspended and we missed them on the day. We held Manly to 11–all in the grand final but that was as close as we were to get to them. In the replay on the Tuesday, we lost McMartin, Gary Stares and Barry Andrews on top of the two blokes who were suspended. In the grandstand before kickoff, I had a bad feeling; I knew we weren't going to win. Manly led 15–0 at halftime and it was all over. We did better in the second half. They only added a field goal, but the crown was theirs.'

Always the gentleman, Provan steered well clear of the drama and controversy regarding Manly's run to the title under referee Greg Hartley. Hartley awarded Manly a dubious try from a forward pass and a seventh tackle try, something he had also done for the Sea Eagles against Parramatta a fortnight earlier. But when pressed on the subject now nearly 20 years later, Provan admits that disenchantment with refereeing was a major factor in his decision to turn his back on rugby league at the end of the following year. 'They were troublesome years in the refereeing department, without doubt,' he said. 'Plenty of people who followed rugby league and were genuine lovers of the game weren't happy with the situation regarding referees. I have to admit I was one of them. And that was one of the reasons I did eventually give the game away. Ironically, after all those years they finally made some changes and the system for appointing referees improved the year after I got out in 1980. It was disappointing for me as a coach, and of course for the players as well, because some of the results we got were influenced by factors beyond our control. At the same time, we had a good year and I looked back on it with a lot of satisfaction.

Most of the guys there were young, on the way up, and had improved out of sight in the space of 12 months. They were talented young players but one of the biggest problems I had with them at Cronulla was that virtually none of them was married. Back in the St George era when I was playing, we were just about all married and, strange as it may seem, I think players are far more consistent when they have a wife. The young guys were less disciplined, didn't have settled home lives, tended to go out partying and didn't always eat the right food. It is far easier to coach a player who is married and settled down, I always found. At Cronulla, they were a brilliant side and people loved to watch them play. I just let them do their stuff with the ball. I have always approached coaching as putting round pegs in round holes. If people are good at doing something, then let them do it. And these Cronulla kids could run the ball, so I encouraged them to do so every chance they got. They liked to throw the ball around, and were good at it, so I wasn't about to stop them. We made the finals again in '79, but lost both our games and were eliminated. For me, that was enough. I'd been in the game a long time, had a couple of businesses to run, and was happy to hand over the reins to someone else.'

Steve Rogers recalls Provan's amazement when he joined the Sharks at the players' free and easy lifestyles. 'He was used to the St George blokes all going home to their wives and regular meals after training,' Rogers said. 'But we were young and intent on enjoying ourselves. Almost all the team were local boys who'd grown up together and were big on the male bonding thing. Norm was from the old school and horrified by it all. I recall him saying once, "How do you guys find time to play football?" But John McMartin, one of the few senior players we had, advised Norm to just let us go because we still worked hard when it came to training and were producing the goods on the field. To his credit, Norm did that, even though it must have been difficult for him. He did tighten things up a bit, though, and brought more discipline to Cronulla than the place had ever seen. He flogged us at training but it was very hard to argue with him because he was right there doing it with you. Norm must have been well into his forties but he was still as fit and strong as a bull. It was a smart move . . . guys 20 years younger could hardly slacken off when this old guy was matching them stride for stride. I enjoyed playing under Norm and he taught us all a lot. He had difficulty expressing his feelings at times but read a game beautifully. He was one of the first people to talk to us about corridors on the field and looking over rucks . . . he knew the game inside out and nobody could ever question that.'

Now in his early sixties, Provan keeps a paternal eye on the game from afar, living in north Queensland. He manages the Norm Provan Oasis Resort at Caloundra on the Sunshine Coast but also spends time at his cattle farm near Cairns. 'I'm still a big fan and do get itchy feet occasionally,' he said. 'You always think you can do better than somebody else. You're not much of a coach if you don't think that. It's probably in the blood. But there's a big difference between thinking you can do it and actually getting out there and doing it. There's so much involved in coaching—it controls your whole life. That's one reason I had to get out in the end. You think you are in control, but the job actually controls you. And it doesn't just control half or part of you—it has a grip on all of you. Only those who have been there can truly understand what I mean by that.'

Provan is modest in assessing his immaculate record as a coach. 'To begin with, I had St George as my first job, which was a great start. They were a magnificent team and would have won a lot of games no matter who coached them. The statistics say I was a great coach, but statistics can be pulled apart. They are just fed into a computer on a "win–loss" basis, but there is a lot more to coaching and success or failure than that. Some coaches take over a side that has done well the previous year and can't carry it on. Others get an ordinary team and make it go well. So with Saints, I had a good head start. But to balance that out, I had young teams at Parramatta and Cronulla that improved a lot under my coaching. Don't forget the Eels were wooden spooners the year before I took them on and we made the semis in my only year there. I suppose the two key ingredients in my coaching were discipline and fitness. I always thought the two went hand in hand. You've got to have both in large quantities. You've got to be as fit or fitter than the next team. And you won't go far, particularly in the modern game, without discipline. When I was playing, fitness and discipline were the two areas I swore by. And I thought when I moved into coaching, what worked for me, would work for them. Another key factor in being a successful coach is having the right management. They must keep the players happy and not give the coach a hard time. There are plenty of instances of committees full of their own importance bringing down a club. At Saints, Parramatta and Cronulla I was lucky. No-one annoyed me. I insisted that I didn't deal with large committees. I always thought that would be too complicated and fraught with danger. At all three clubs, I asked that I just deal with one member of the committee. If I wanted something, I went straight to him and he would try to help me out. And that's how it was. I never had to stop training for a committee member; they knew better than to come near us during a session. They let me get on with my job but in the main were there to support me. Every coach has troubled times when the team is in a slump and has lost three or four games in a row. That's when you feel the weight of the world on your shoulders. But an understanding and supportive committee can make a huge difference."

Provan also gave his players much of the credit for his success. 'I had this style that I like to call communal coaching,' he said. 'It means talking to your players and finding out what works for them. I learned that all players are different; what works for some beautifully won't necessarily work for others. At no time did I ever say, "This is what we're going to do . . . like it or lump it." We would work things through at training and discuss them and finetune them until everyone was happy. It either worked or it didn't. Even if it was my idea, if it didn't work, I scrapped it. If a player came up with an idea, I was more than happy to give it a try. You've got to have the support of all your players and have them confident in what they are doing. And keep it not too complicated, too. When it all boils down to it, rugby league is a pretty simple game and some modern coaches tend to forget that to their own peril at times.'

The Kid from Castleford

MALCOLM REILLY

CLUBS
Castleford (UK) 1975–84 (player-coach), 1985–87,
Leeds (UK) 1988–91,
Halifax (UK) 1993–94,
Newcastle 1995–

ENGLISH CHAMPIONSHIP RECORD
Games 487, won 265, lost 200, drew 22.
Winning percentage 54.4%.

ARL PREMIERSHIP RECORD
Games 25, won 17, lost 8.
Winning percentage 68.0%.
Semi-finals
1995

OTHER COACHING ACHIEVEMENTS
Won Challenge Cup 1985–86, Yorkshire Cup 1988–89.
Great Britain coach 1987–94. Tests 42, won 30, lost 12.
Took Great Britain to World Cup final 1992 (lost to Australia).

Malcolm Reilly can take much of the credit for restoring the roar in the British Lion over the past decade. With the international game on its knees in the mid '80s because of the decline of the British game, Reilly rode in like a knight in shining armour. Straight-talking and uncompromising, Reilly quickly brought out the best in the British team, to the extent where the three Ashes series in which he was in command—from 1988 to 1992—were real contests for the first time in many years. But Australian fans always knew as soon as Reilly took on the job, things would change very quickly. For Reilly is remembered Down Under as a fiercely competitive player who starred for Manly in the early '70s. The world's most expensive player when he joined the Sea Eagles, Reilly gave Manly great service, helping the club to its first two premierships before returning to England to finish his career. Reilly followed a natural progression into coaching with Castleford and was soon handed the national job by a country on the brink of international oblivion. He came tantalisingly close to doing the impossible—wrestling the Ashes away from the Aussies—before taking on a new challenge with the Newcastle Knights.

Like many English youngsters, Malcolm Reilly's first football love was soccer. 'I played a lot more soccer than league in my early years and then combined the two sports as a teenager,' he said. 'I liked the league a lot but was only fairly small at that stage. They played me halfback and I got concussed quite a few times. So my parents weren't happy with me continuing with league. They pushed me towards soccer and I had no complaints . . . I loved the game. But at around 18 or 19, I started playing league again and just found it came so natural. So I went back to league full-time and never looked back.' Reilly believes his time playing the round ball game was far from wasted in later years, however. 'It taught me a lot and most of all, it helped with my kicking skills,' he said. 'Kicking was always one of the strengths of my game in league and I believe I've got soccer to thank for that. It enabled me to get a lot of control in my kicking in league and the two sports had a fair bit in common.'

A talented ball-playing lock or second-rower, Reilly was a spectacular success in his early days with the Castleford club in the late 1960s. 'In my first full year there in '68 we got knocked out of the semi-finals of the Challenge Cup by Wakefield,' he said. 'But the next year we went all the way to Wembley and won the title in the final against Salford. I was awarded the Lance Todd Trophy as man of the match and it was a great experience for a young kid who'd only been playing league for a couple of years. We won it again the following year against Wigan and I finished that season by touring Australia with the British Lions.'

Respected English commentator, former first grade player Ray French vividly recalls his first meeting with Reilly in 1968. 'I travelled over to Hull Kingston Rovers as the confident captain of the Lancashire team to play Yorkshire in the Roses match,' French wrote in his book, *100 Great Rugby League Players*. 'My team and I were hit by a whirlwind in the shape of a young man I had never come across on a league pitch before: Mal Reilly. Although we only lost 10–5, this young player ripped holes in our mid-field defence and knocked us unceremoniously to the floor with the bone-jarring tackles that were to become his trademark for years to come. Mal Reilly, who had been signed by Castleford in 1967 from the amateurs at Kippax Welfore, arrived on the rugby league scene that day. Wherever he played over the next 15 years he wrought havoc among the opposition.'

The 1970 Lions tour gave Australian fans their first glimpse of the young back-rower from Castleford who was to develop into one of the key figures in the game over the next decade. 'That tour was a real eye-opener for me; I learned so much over those few months,' Reilly said. 'I made the Test team and we were given a real lesson by Australia in the First Test up in Brisbane. They had an excellent pack containing the likes of Arthur Beetson, Ron Coote and Jim Morgan and smashed us 37–15. But we learned our lesson from that and recovered very well. We turned it around when we won the Second Test at the SCG 28–7, with Roger "The Dodger" Millward scoring a couple of tries. There was no holding us back in the decider, again in Sydney, and we won a closer struggle 21–17 to regain the Ashes. To finish a very successful tour, we whitewashed New Zealand over there.'

It was midway through the tour that Reilly made a decision that was to have a drastic effect on his life. 'I fell in love with Australia and decided I wanted to play out here,' he said. 'In fact, I saw it as the type of adventure I wanted to embark on ever since I was a kid. I realised very early in my career that playing in Britain wasn't going to be sufficient a challenge for me. While I was in Sydney, I got onto Jim Comans, the leading players' agent at the time, and he spoke to several clubs for me. After some talks with St George, we settled on Manly and I agreed to come back the following year. I returned in January of 1971 and began looking forward to my new life Down Under.'

Manly, with secretary Ken Arthurson wielding the cheque-book, paid a then record $30,000 to gain Reilly's services, but it was money that was to prove well spent. The Sea Eagles finished minor premiers in 1971 but didn't go on with it in the final series. And a major reason for that was Reilly's infamous knee injury that was to plague him throughout his career. Although leading the major semi-final at halftime, the Sea Eagles fell 19–13 to Souths. The following week, in the preliminary final, Reilly failed to go the distance with his knee injury as the Sea Eagles crashed out of contention, losing 15–12 to St George.

But there was no holding back Manly—or Reilly—as the club celebrated its 25th anniversary in vintage style the following season in 1972. The Sea Eagles were the team to beat all year and outclassed Eastern Suburbs 19–14 in the grand final to take their maiden premiership title. Reilly, a key man at lock, was a tower of strength throughout the big games, bringing a new dimension to the team with his ball skills and kicking game. By the end of the season, Sydney scribes had labelled Reilly as 'the world's best forward'—and few could argue his claims to the title. 'We had a very good side in '72 and it was a memorable time,' Reilly recalled. 'We were the best team throughout the season but still had to produce the goods on grand final day. We did that and the celebrations continued for days after the game. In 1973 we again took the title in a very tough game against Cronulla.'

The '73 grand final is widely acknowledged as the most brutal grand final of all time, with Reilly an early victim of the constant skirmishes. The classy forward was a marked man from the opening whistle and copped a late tackle after kicking the ball downfield. He limped from the field, took three painkilling needles in a badly bruised side, and gamely attempted to return to the battle. But it was no use. Reilly, a virtual passenger, was replaced after 25 minutes and took no further part in the game. He was reluctantly forced to watch from the SCG dressing room as Bob Fulton's brilliance earned Manly a 10–7 win. Reilly, nonetheless, picked up a winner's medal, becoming the first Englishman to win two Sydney grand finals.

Reilly admits that, as one of the few Englishmen playing in Australia in the early '70s, he copped more than his fair share of extra attention. 'It was actually very difficult,' he said. 'Opposition forwards would invariably save a little bit extra for me. They certainly didn't relish English players. But I think it brought the best out in me. I had to be tough to survive. I knew I had to be at my best every week if I was going to make it. The experience was undoubtedly good for me in the long run. And I enjoyed the confrontations. Blokes wanted to take me on and I was happy to accommodate them.'

But Reilly was anything but an angel himself, giving as good as he got. He visited the judiciary seven times in his five years at Manly, most notably after a ferocious clash against Souths at the SCG in 1973. Long-time league fans still regard the battle between Reilly and Souths hooker George Piggins, another uncompromising character, among the most vicious one-on-one stoushes seen at the famous old ground.

Reilly paid a heavy price for his five-year stint at Manly. Under international rules at the time, he was barred from playing Test football for his beloved Great Britain in his time at Brookvale. 'That was always something I regretted, but I suppose it was the price I had to pay,' he said. 'I really only had the six Tests I played from Britain before coming out to Oz. And that was when I was aged from 20 to 22. I went back home to Castleford in 1976 but by then my knee was in bad shape. I was really on one leg and only played one more international after my return. It's disappointing to think how many Tests I actually missed. In 1978, (Great Britain coach) Eric Ashton asked me to captain the Great Britain team for the tour to Australia. I was tempted to take up the offer but after a lot of thought, I decided against it. My knee was getting no better and I reasoned that whatever service I had left in me, I should devote to Castleford. They were paying the bills.'

Reilly took his first steps towards coaching when he quit Manly to return to Castleford in 1975–76. 'They appointed me captain-coach and it was a responsibility I enjoyed,' he said. 'I picked up a lot of experience in Australia that I was able to use to good effect in Britain. I was only 26 at the time but felt I was ready for it. To me, coaching was just an extension of the way I played the game. I always liked to be an organiser on the field. I felt I had a fair knowledge of tactics and liked to run the show.'

Despite ongoing problems with his knee, Reilly managed to soldier on for several seasons back in England, playing until his mid-thirties. That feat was remarkable in itself, given the problems he had with his knee from an early age. During his stay in Sydney, Reilly's knee was THE most talked about piece of anatomy in the sports world. It received such regular write-ups in the papers that Mike Gibson, then a young sports writer with the *Daily Telegraph*, devoted an entire column to an 'interview' with the knee. 'It gave me trouble for a lot of years, but it was actually easier back home in Britain,' Reilly said. 'The softer grounds resulted in less wear and tear and enabled me to extend my career. I slowed down a bit and eventually finished up wearing the number 10, but I could still kick and direct traffic on the field. I lost most of my mobility but could still be of some value.' The knee problems are destined to come back to haunt Reilly in later life. 'I can't run and they still give me a lot of trouble,' he said. In fact, recently the doctors told me I'm going to need to have both knees replaced. They said I could delay it for a while, but I'll need to have them done within 10 years. I'm not complaining, though. That's the nature of the game. League is a very physical contest and injuries are a fact of life. I can still keep fit by doing gym work and I try to work out whenever I can.'

After Great Britain lost the Test series against Australia in 1986, the British hierarchy began the search for a new coach. Britain's league stocks had never been lower than when Reilly got the nod ahead of several other applicants the following year. Two Kangaroo tours had come and gone—in 1982 and 1986—in which Australia had not lost a game. The Australians were light-years ahead of the British and Reilly realised the daunting task ahead. 'It was going to be a tough job because physically, tactically and psychologically the Australians had the edge on us,' he said. 'My first meeting with them was mid-way through 1988 in the Ashes series Down Under and I would have liked more time to prepare. I took over the reins late in 1987 and only had a couple of quick tours to France to prepare the players. Of course, that was nothing like the preparation required and we struggled when we arrived in Australia. The First Test was the 100th match between the two old enemies and the occasion seemed to bring out the best in us. We ended up giving the Aussies one hell of a fright. We scored an early try through Ellery Hanley and led 6–0 at half-time. The Aussies gradually wore us down, with Peter Sterling and Wally Lewis taking control of things. But I thought the 17–6 scoreline in their favour didn't reflect how close we came to winning. In the Second Test in Brisbane, we went overboard with the aggressive tactics and for that, I have to accept a large part of the blame. We were very passionate about what we wanted but were misguided; we played with too much emotion and not enough common sense. Our tactics played right into the Aussies' hands ... we didn't stick to the game plan and they beat us easily, 34–14.'

But Reilly's influence came through loud and clear in the Third Test back in Sydney. Although the series had already been decided, a fired-up British team scored an emotional 26–12 win over a shell-shocked Aussie team. Reilly was chaired from the field a conquering hero, with the small but vocal band of British fans celebrating late into the night. 'It was our first win over the Aussies in 10 years and a tremendously satisfying feeling,' Reilly said. 'It was probably as good a day as I've had as coach; to turn the tables on our age-old rivals was really something after living in their shadow for so long. We knew now we could play them on a level field.'

It was a very similar story for Britain in the three following Ashes campaigns. The Lions had clearly arrived as an international force capable of challenging Australia, but lacked the overall class to win a three-Test series. In 1988, 1990, 1992 and 1994 (the last series with Ellery Hanley as coach), the British were beaten 2–1 in their bid for Ashes success. 'It was a recurring pattern,' Reilly recalls. 'That win in the final Test in 1988 was a tremendous morale boost for us for the series that followed two years down the track on home soil. The First Test was a great day for British rugby league. We took on the Aussies at Wembley in front of more than 52,000 fans and won 19–12; it was their first loss in three tours and really showed how much we had improved. We had them on the rack in the Second Test at Manchester but that famous Mal Meninga try in injury time got them home. It was a great try, but frankly, it shouldn't have been allowed. Meninga acted like a defensive blocker; he prevented one of our players from making the tackle by knocking him out of the way. The scores were tied at the time and I've no doubt we would have won the series had that try not been awarded. It changed the momentum of the series; Australia arrived at Leeds on a high for the Third Test and, in poor conditions, they beat us. I've got to admit they were clearly the better side that day; we just didn't produce what we could.

'Even though we lost that series again, I saw it as a real breakthrough for us. As coach, one of your main jobs is to make your players believe in themselves, believe that they can win. And at that time against Australia, it wasn't easy. The Aussies were regarded as something like supermen after their exploits on the 1982 and '86 tours, when they thrashed all comers. And I think some of our blokes still regarded them in that esteem. I found that there were players in the side who just didn't believe they could ever beat them. If they conceded a couple, of tries in the first 15 or 20 minutes, their confidence would go to water. In 1990 we came Down Under again and started very strongly in the First Test. Martin Offiah made a couple of great breaks that could have resulted in tries but good last-ditch defence by Andrew Ettingshausen kept us out. They came home strongly and won from there. But then we produced another marvellous performance in Melbourne to score our biggest ever win over Australia in Australia—33–10. All the lads just clicked that night and played some marvellous football. We then went up to Brisbane full of confidence but the Aussies were again too strong, winning 16–10 in another close one.'

Although both are among the game's fiercest competitors, Reilly and Aussie coach Bob Fulton are remarkably friendly. The pair hit it off in their playing days at Manly in the early '70s and have maintained ties ever since. Surprised onlookers in recent years have seen the pair dining in a quiet corner of a restaurant in Leeds or Sydney, only days before a Test match. 'We've always stayed mates,' Fulton confirmed. 'And there wasn't a problem about going out for dinner even if it was a few days before we'd do battle in a Test. Often, we wouldn't even talk about the upcoming game, just about the good old days and football in general.' Fulton admits Reilly made his job as Australian coach a lot harder than it may have been in the late '80s and early '90s. 'Malcolm was a really whole-hearted player who gave his all and he has brought those qualities into his coaching,' Fulton said. 'He has brought the British team right up to standard after years in limbo and deserves a lot of the credit for the way the Lions have improved in recent years. I don't think they would have made up the ground so quickly had it not been for Malcolm Reilly.'

After three frustratingly narrow Ashes series losses, Reilly has no doubt as to why the Australians have proved so hard to topple. 'The thing we were lacking was the intensity of the Winfield Cup every week,' Reilly said. 'The Aussies were battle hardened by tough games week in, week out. They knew how to play at their peak from one game to the next. Our guys were used to one hard game a month and a few easier ones along the way. As a coach, it was very hard, because I went into each series knowing the opposition was better prepared. But it was something I could do nothing about; it's a simple fact of life that the Aussie competition is a lot more intense than ours, even though the gap is closing. We had to work very hard to match them and managed to do so for one game out of the three, but not through the series.'

The bad news for British fans is that Reilly sees no change in the world order in the foreseeable future. 'The Aussie competition is always so strong and they have so many players to choose from,' he said. 'They showed that in the 1995 World Cup when they left a host of great players at home and still won the trophy. Also, the Super League war has seen a lot of British stars like Lee Jackson, Ellery Hanley and Phil Clarke move to Australia. And while they are still available to play for Great Britain, their absence further weakens the domestic competition.'

Reilly was busily preparing for the 1994 Ashes series when a quiet dinner with a player's agent changed his destiny. 'Mike Tyler, the agent for John Schuster, had dinner with me one night and sounded me out about coaching in Australia. I admitted to him that the idea of coaching Down Under had always been a goal of mine and it all started from there. The opportunity then came up at Newcastle shortly afterwards and I saw it as a great challenge. It was a hard decision to leave Britain, especially as it meant giving up the national job. But as I said, it had been an ambition for some time to coach in Oz and now that the chance was there, I knew I had to take it. If I didn't accept it, in years to come I could see me asking myself, "Well, why didn't you take it?" I would have also been representing Super League over there, which would have been difficult given my views on the subject.'

When Reilly received the offer from the Knights, one of the first people he consulted was Great Britain league supremo Maurice Lindsay. 'Malcolm came to me not as a coach to his boss, but as a mate,' Lindsay explained. 'He asked me my opinion and I told him it would be hard to turn down the type of money Newcastle were talking. His kids were getting to college age and the financial terms would certainly have made the payment of educational fees and the like a lot easier. I had no idea then that Super League was going to start . . . neither of us did. But financially, Malcolm had to take up the offer and he realised that.'

Reilly found himself in the Super League firing line early in the war when he received a massive loyalty payment from the ARL. A key man in the battle plans of both camps because of his links with players in England and Newcastle, Reilly was a prize signing. The ARL had no hesitation paying out a six-figure sum to secure his services in a move that was slammed by several critics. Leading the chorus was another ARL loyalist, radio commentator and South Sydney football manager Alan Jones. The outspoken Jones branded the ARL as treacherous for giving Reilly, an 'outsider', such a massive sum, while not initially giving long-serving ARL coaches like Wayne Pearce or Tom Raudonikis a cent. 'Alan Jones made a song and dance about it, but so what?' Reilly said. 'He had no idea of the circumstances and just shot off his mouth. I'm not interested in his views . . . nor are plenty of other people I've spoken to.'

Reilly was one of the few to caution against Great Britain's decision to jump on the Super League bandwagon midway through 1995. 'I am not a fan of the Murdoch plan for the game and what it has done so far,' he said. 'The way he has bought the game lock, stock and barrel in Britain and New Zealand is not healthy in my opinion. The game started back in 1896 and has always belonged to the people—not just one man. I would have thought rather than selling out, they could have sat down at a round table with everyone involved and worked out their problems together. I was close to Maurice Lindsay in my time as national coach; we went back several years and got on fine. Since all the drama I haven't had a lot to do with him. Whether he is solely responsible for what's happened, I don't know. But if he is, I don't think he guided the English game in the right direction. They have escalated the marketplace, just as has happened here. I'm not sure the game can afford those prices, particularly in three or four years' time if Murdoch pulls out. Then they will have to survive by themselves. And are the gates going to be sufficient to pay the bills? I don't think they will be. We will get back to reality finally, but in the meantime, some clubs in Britain will really suffer.' Can Reilly return home sometime in the future with such strong anti-Super League views? 'I don't think I've burned my bridges over there; I could still go back to coach at some stage if the situation arises. I'm on a new four-year contract with the Knights, which is in line with the contract I signed with the ARL in 1995. I have no plans to go back in the near future, however. I've settled in Newcastle very well. I like the area and I like the people.'

Reilly's switch to the ARL camp could have brought about a parting of the ways with close ally Lindsay. As the driving force behind Super League in Britain, Lindsay suddenly found himself at odds with the man he helped appoint Great Britain coach years earlier. 'But fortunately it hasn't worked out that way,' Lindsay said. 'We had little contact in the initial Super League negotiations, which is a bit of a pity because the bond I have with Malcolm is probably as close as he's had with anyone in his life. But I think we can still call each other friends; we've been through a lot together. We went on what we jokingly call the "tear gas" tour of Papua New Guinea in 1990. We went to New Zealand in the same year and were labelled as no-hopers. But we beat the Kiwis; the first time we'd won a Test series there since 1979. We toured Australia together in 1992, as well as the World Cup later that year. We were good friends and we trusted each other. It has been difficult for us both because we have kept at arm's length. But I would like to think that deep down, we still respect each other.'

Lindsay agrees that Reilly's influence has been a major factor in Great Britain's recent rise on the international scene. 'As a coach, Malcolm is just so dedicated,' he said. 'He places a lot of emphasis on a total commitment from the players, mentally and physically. He wants the players with courage and that has been one of the reasons for his success. The players he has used haven't been afraid of the Australians; they have been prepared to stand up to them come what may. Like any good modern coach, he stresses discipline and doing the right thing. Malcolm is very honest; he'll never lie to you. If there was a war and it was you and him against 300, he wouldn't change sides. That's how loyal the man is. Malcolm does have a reputation within the British game as a mercenary, but then what's wrong with that? Aren't all players mercenaries, when it comes down to it, particularly in this era? I could never criticise him for that. In fact, even though I wasn't paid as Great Britain manager—it was an honorary position—I always fought for Malcolm to get the best possible bonuses. Whatever the players got, Malcolm got as well. If they got five grand a match, so would he. I also insisted on the best treatment—the best hotels, the best buses and restaurants. Nothing was spared. I was criticised back home for that, but I think both the players and Malcolm appreciated it.'

Lindsay concedes that Reilly was somewhat behind the best Australian coaches when he inherited the Lions' job in 1987. 'Malcolm probably didn't have the sophisticated touch or know-how of the top Aussie coaches like Tim Sheens, John Monie and Wayne Bennett when he took on the role nearly a decade ago,' he said. 'But that wasn't his fault; it was more the environment he worked in. Great Britain was so far behind Australia in just about every department at that stage. But he was only a short head behind them and had he been working in similar conditions, he may well have been better than them, because he's got all their qualities and more. There's no doubt that he helped us get closer to the Aussies, but funnily enough he got a bit of help from Aussie coaches, particularly John Monie. Key Great Britain players like Shaun Edwards, Martin Offiah and Gary Connolly all came out of a Great Britain coaching system that was improving. And the man responsible largely for that was John Monie. It's no coincidence that Denis Betts and Phil Clarke, two of our leading players who are both playing in the Australian competition at the moment, came through as teenagers at Wigan under John Monie. Malcolm put a lot into the coaching scheme himself and the results have been forthcoming. He had a good team, particularly his assistant in Phil Larder. But Malcolm was the one who led the team and put it all together.'

Lindsay claims that the image of Reilly as a fire and brimstone coach is nothing more than myth. 'I think it came about because everyone remembers what a fearsome character Malcolm was as a player,' Lindsay said. 'But as a coach, he rarely even raises his voice. He exudes lots of passion, but it is disciplined and controlled. There were times he expressed his displeasure with a poor performance at halftime, but after the game he said nothing. He restrained himself and saved it for the team meeting the next day. He dominated the players by his presence. I think the players were largely in awe of him . . . with the possible exception of Ellery Hanley. The two of them didn't get on, particularly in the latter stages of their relationship. It's a pity, because they began with tremendous respect for each other, but it all broke down. There were times Malcolm didn't see eye to eye with a particular player, but that's hardly unusual in this business. Overall, I'll never say anything bad about the man. We worked very well together.'

After many years as both a player and coach, Reilly has firm views on what is necessary to produce a winning team. 'As coach, I see preparation as probably the most important factor in getting the best out of the players every weekend,' he said. 'And I don't just mean physically. The psychological side of the game is so important, particularly nowadays when there are so many class athletes at every club. Often it's the team in the right frame of mind that will win the tough games. Confidence is all-important; you've got to build the players up and make them believe in themselves. If you prepare well and do the hard work during the week, then the individual should feel confident enough to perform at his peak on Sunday. It's difficult to explain, but the players will know what I mean; you've just got that winning feeling if you know the preparation has been spot-on. I believe a major key to coaching is similar to that of playing—to let your strengths grow out of your weaknesses. You can't run away from a weakness, particularly on a football field when it is there for all to see. It's something you've got to work on; you've got to adjust your make-up. And there's no time like the present to do that, otherwise you'll fall behind.'

Reilly also sees moving with the times as a vital ingredient in a successful coach. 'Even if you're on the right track, you'll end up getting run over if you just sit there,' he said. 'I have particularly learned that coming from English football to the Aussie game. I've had to update and change aspects of my game and adjust my thinking. It is often only minor things, but they can end up being important in the long run.'

Reilly is fortunate to have gifted players like the Johns brothers and Jamie Ainscough as game-breakers with Newcastle. All three are among the most exciting attacking players in the game and are given maximum chance to shine. 'In coaching, you have to assess the individual and his capabilities,' he said. 'And you have to make sure the players use those capabilities, but don't over-stretch them. It's like trying to get a golfer to drive a ball 250 metres if he's not capable of doing it. You have to make sure the player doesn't over-stretch his limits. You get him to do what he's good at. With Matthew and Andrew Johns, they are both very elusive players with good kicking and passing games. And if they've got weaknesses, I approach it like I would with any other player. Let's identify the problem and work hard on it to make them better players. The Knights played a more structured style of game before I got there but that's not for me to judge why. Maybe the team hadn't matured sufficiently to play a more open, attacking style. You've got to enjoy what you're doing. People who enjoy what they're doing invariably do it well. It's up to the coach to help ensure the players enjoy themselves.'

Pressure has always been a factor in the game that hasn't worried Reilly. 'There is a lot of pressure in coaching and that can be a negative factor for some people,' he said. 'But I see pressure as opportunity. You've got to learn to act on it and make the most of any given situation.'

Reilly has had his problems with the media, and more than once has 'asked' a reporter to leave his dressing room. The Malcolm Reilly, 1990s style, seems a more diplomatic version of the original model. Most people who know him see Reilly as having mellowed from his early days in coaching, but not the man himself. 'I don't think I've mellowed much at all over the years,' he said. 'The fire is still very much there within me, there's no question about that. I just expect fairness; I'll be fair with people if they're fair with me. I've had my run-ins with the media. If people misreport me or make interpretations of my team that I don't think are just, I'll be offended. I don't forget very easily. I don't see any point in ranting and raving with the players before or after a game or at halftime. You've got to be clear and concise and make sure you get your message across. You've got to tell them where they are and what they've got to do. And to do that, you've got to be fairly rational in your approach. One thing I've learned is that rugby league players are very complex and very different individuals. You treat one with a kid glove to get the best out of him, while another may need a good old-fashioned kick up the arse.'

Playing Wazzaball

WARREN RYAN

CLUBS
Newtown 1979–82,
Canterbury 1984–87,
Balmain 1988–90,
Wests 1991–94

PREMIERSHIP RECORD
Games 362, won 203, lost 146, drew 13.
Winning percentage 56.1%.
Semi-finals
1981, 1984–86, 1988–92
Grand finals (6)
1981, 1984–86, 1988–89
Premierships (2)
1984–85

OTHER COACHING ACHIEVEMENTS
Coach of the Year 1981, 1984.
Dally M Coach of the Year 1991.
Country Origin coach 1987–91.

here are two schools of thought when discussing Warren Ryan and his contribution to rugby league. The more popular is that the man was the most controversial coach the game has seen, an egotistical despot who made his teams play a ruthless, relentless defensive brand of football. But the second, and perhaps more accurate, is that Ryan was an astute thinker on rugby league, a revolutionary who mastered the game to such an extent that administrators were forced to make rule changes to prevent his total domination of the code. Ex-St George coach Brian Smith once said: 'There have only been two coaching greats—Jack Gibson and Warren Ryan. Gibson gave us all jobs. And Ryan is a genius and hasn't received the real credit his achievements deserve.' Former coach and television commentator Bill Anderson expressed a similar sentiment when he said: 'Gibson made coaches important but Ryan made coaching a science.'

Two things invariably followed Ryan throughout his 14-year Winfield Cup career—success and controversy. Ryan coached nine teams to the finals, reaching six grand finals for two wins. While he pioneered an awesome defensive brand of football, he also showed an ability to get the best out his players in attack. Ryan is convinced his controversial reputation—and the clashes with officials and senior players at all four clubs he coached—Newtown, Canterbury, Balmain and Wests—were beaten up out of all proportion by the media. The much-travelled Ryan had a stormy relationship with the media throughout his career and ironically, now maintains contact with the game by writing a regular newspaper column and appearing as a commentator on ABC Radio.

Ryan grew up in Newcastle and learned his football with Marist Brothers at Hamilton. 'I played junior league for Central (now Central Charlestown) before giving it away for a couple of years for athletics,' he said. Ryan achieved great success as a shot putter and represented his country at the 1962 Commonwealth Games in Perth. 'That was a great experience, but I probably wasn't ready for it,' he admitted. 'I was only 21 and finished seventh. I was still raw and well short of my peak as a shot putter. A year after the Games, I was throwing much better in practice than what I'd actually thrown at the Games.'

After the Commonwealth Games, he returned to league and was offered a trial to play at the then mighty St George in 1964. 'I jumped at the chance, as any young kid would, even though it meant the end of my athletic career,' he said. 'In those days, as Michael Cleary found out, they barred you from the sport as soon as you took money to play football. Saints decided they wanted to sign me and my Newcastle club whacked a 400 pound transfer fee on me, which was a lot of money in those days. They thought they'd get their pound of flesh for me out of the rich Saints club. Frank Facer (Saints secretary) swore about it, but paid it up and we got on with life. Playing in the centres, there weren't many chances to get into first grade with the likes of Reg Gasnier and Billy Smith ahead of you. I played just one first grade game, against Souths at the Cricket Ground, when all the good 'uns were away in New Zealand. But it didn't bother me, it was no great shame playing reserve grade at St George in those days. On the day of the record crowd for the 1965 grand final when they were hanging from the rafters, I played lock in the reserve grade grand final which we lost to Balmain 9–7. The Tigers had a great pack— John Spencer, Dennis Tutty, Gary Leo, Geoff Connell and Norm Henderson were there and all went on to play a lot of first grade.'

Ryan admits he was somewhat surprised by the lack of scientific approach to the game at Saints. 'I came from the bush expecting them to really have it all down to a fine art,' he said. 'But I was asking the coaches questions they just didn't have answers for. The game still hadn't evolved technically to any great point. Often they'd say to me, "Go ask Poppa Clay—he might know." Don't get me wrong, they were great players and they knew how to win. But they didn't apply any great principles to coaching. I mean, my God, imagine if we went back to the unlimited tackle rule they played under—nowadays the opposing teams just wouldn't get the ball. Coaches would ensure their team just never surrendered it. The rule would last a week before they threw it out and returned to six tackles.' After his stint at St George, Ryan moved to neighbouring Cronulla, where he was a regular first grader in 1967 and '68 before finishing his career at Wests in Wollongong. 'We won four comps in a row at Wests and in 1971 and 1972 I was fortunate enough to be selected for NSW Country, captaining them the second year,' he said. 'I retired at the end of the 1972 season. The key man in getting me to make the transition into coaching was a local official down there, Peter "Buck" Buchanan. He was a great judge of football and spotted John Dorahy for us when "Joe Cool" was only 16. Buck said to me, "When Don Parish retires, we want you to take over as captain-coach." They were thinking about getting a coach from outside but I remember him telling me, "We're the Red Devils and the devil we know is better than the devil we don't." That really got my career on the road, although I'd done a bit of coaching of school teams in my capacity as a teacher. I coached Collegians in Wollongong in 1974 and they went okay but were really struggling financially. So I suggested to them they could save some money by making the captain I brought down there, Darrell Bampton from Souths, the captain-coach. That got the club out of paying a bit of money and I thought that would be the end of my coaching career there and then. I had no great aspirations to be a coach and never did any courses or anything like that. But in 1978, two of the players I'd captain-coached at Wests in Wollongong, John Dorahy and Shane Day, were playing first grade for Wests in Sydney. They appealed to the committee there to get me up in some capacity. The only opening was the under-23 job, which Roy Masters had held before moving up to first grade that year. I was left wondering how I'd help my two guys coaching the lower grades, but it soon became apparent. I was dragged up to first grade teaching this, teaching that. At one stage they asked me to teach Les Boyd to play in the centres . . . imagine that. I worked on their defence and the first grade finished minor premiers with the best defence in the league. My under-23s became the first team to make the grand final from fifth spot that same year. We were beaten by Penrith who were nicely stacked with some players who should have been in the higher grades. Ken Wilson was at Penrith at the time and joined me at Newtown the next year. I remember him saying to me, "Gees, they did a job on your kids last year. They had eight first graders in the grand final side." It was Penrith's first title and I guess it meant a lot to them so they planned it well in advance. They had class players in that side like halfback Henry Foster, hooker Steve Martin and a good ball-playing forward, Tim Armistead. Anyway, getting the team to the grand final coupled with the work I did with first grade obviously made an impression. I got a call towards the end of that year from Frank Farrington, the Newtown secretary. He'd seen the under-23s play and liked what he saw and asked me if I'd coach Newtown the following year.'

Taking on the battling Jets proved a formidable challenge for Ryan. 'They'd won three wooden spoons in a row when I went there and I remember people questioned the wisdom of taking the job on. But it was my break into first grade and it was largely a case of beggars can't be choosers.' Ryan was confident, however, after talking with Jets officials that the club had the ability to pick up its act. 'The provision was there for improving, I could see that after sitting down with the officials,' he said. 'It's when the administration is failing that you've got no hope. But they had some idea at Newtown and the drive to climb up the ladder. The first couple of years were hard but at least we got off the bottom of the table. That set the scene for the club's big year in 1981.' Ryan's feat of taking the Jets to within a whisker of a premiership in 1981 ranks as one of the great coaching miracles of modern times. As former Norths coach and current metropolitan selector John Hayes observed, 'The only great achievement in recent coaching times was Ryan's getting that Newtown to the grand final in 1981.' But Ryan admits the Jets of 1981 were a better team than most critics gave them credit for. 'I'm not silly enough to believe there was no ability there,' he said. 'There were some very good footballers there and guys who were mentally very tough and hungry. They hadn't achieved anything and were eager to show the world they could play. We embarked on a program of playing the game differently from the way it was played elsewhere and I like to think that Newtown side were the pioneers of a new style of football. They were great to watch; a top fullback in Phil Sigsworth, exciting wingers in Ray Blacklock and John Ferguson, good centres in Brian Hetherington and Mick Ryan, a crafty halfback in Ken Wilson and a very tough pack with the likes of Steve Blyth, Steve Bowden, Mick Pitman and Graeme O'Grady. No-one really noticed us until it was almost too late. Every week in the finals, whoever we were playing was supposed to knock us out. I remember saying to the boys in the lead-up to the grand final that the critics had a week to get it right. They were wrong every week and it was really their last chance when we played Parramatta. We were in that game with a chance, but the Eels just proved a bit too strong at the crunch.' It was during the run-in to the finals in 1981 that Ryan earned the wrath of critics by replacing the popular but ageing Tom Raudonikis at key stages of matches with another veteran, but a player of vastly different style in Ken Wilson. 'I was cursed to be coaching ageing halfbacks—both Raudonikis at Newtown and later Steve Mortimer at Canterbury,' Ryan said. 'They both seemed to blame me for growing old. Tommy brought a lot of spirit to the club, I can't deny him that. But he really was over the hill as a player.' Ryan claims that he inherited Raudonikis from arch coaching rival Roy Masters, who was glad to wash his hands of the veteran halfback. 'When Tom left Wests for some John Singleton dollars at Newtown, he seemed oblivious to the fact that Masters was leading him towards the door with an arm around the shoulder and the paternal advice, "Take the money, Tom. Wests can't match it." The real agenda though was the selection of the rising red-headed halfback star Alan Neil to replace Tom. The opportunity for Tom to switch to lock was blocked by the extremely gifted Graeme O'Grady. Tom's departure solved a major selection headache for Masters. Tom and Roy went out on the town to celebrate the signing of Tom's big contract but Masters would have been silently celebrating for his own reasons. Tom was from a past era. He thought belting blokes was the way to play the game. That may have worked back when he started, but the game had well and truly changed by 1981. There was citing by video and referees just weren't letting players get away with blatant illegalities any more. As soon as Kenny Wilson got onto the paddock, the whole team functioned so much more smoothly. He understood what I wanted, had a great kicking game and could move the team around the field. Tommy, great player that he was in his prime, found it hard to tolerate that I was giving Wilson a slice of the pie. Ken was the real brains of the side, our quarterback, you might say. But because Tommy was a high-profile player and a media favourite, I was crucified. I don't think it's all that uncommon. A host of coaches will tell you they have problems with senior players. These guys have been around for a long time, earning rave reviews in the media, and can't take any criticism.'

The Jets were the big surprise packets of the 1981 season, battling through to the grand final and beating strong Manly and Easts sides along the way. The Jets gave hot favourites Parramatta a real run for their money, too, leading early in the second half before going down 20–11 to a late Brett Kenny-inspired burst. Ryan left the Jets 12 months later and despite the club's fine showing in 1981, wasn't surprised when the Jets folded just two seasons down the track. 'In the end they had dreadful financial problems that they just couldn't dig their way out of,' Ryan said. 'And the area only seemed to grow ethnics and factories. At that time, league hadn't managed what Canterbury has achieved by winning the support of the ethnic community. If you haven't got money, you can't get corporate support or people through the gate. It's a spiral—there's just no hope and that's why the Jets were doomed.'

While he had done well with the Jets and their limited resources, Ryan came to realise that if he was to achieve his destiny of coaching a premiership-winning team, he needed more talent to work with. 'I'll always remember an American basketball coach who once said, "There are a hundred coaches who may well be able to do what I do but they lack the one ingredient I've got—talent. Not everyone can win with talent, but nobody can win without it." Anyone who deludes himself that he is going to make a contribution to coaching should think twice and take a look at the talent he's got, because that is more than likely to determine if he will succeed or fail.'

With Ryan on the lookout for a club with strength both on and off the field, Canterbury's interest in his services midway through 1983 for the following season couldn't have been better timed. Ted Glossop, after winning the Bulldogs the 1980 title, had fallen out of favour and the Bulldogs looked to Ryan as his successor. The partnership was to prove a stormy, but highly successful marriage. 'The Bulldogs had some great players and signing Terry Lamb that year from Wests really brought it all together for the club,' he said. 'Coaching there appealed as a marvellous opportunity, although I was warned before I arrived about factions within the club. The club was split into the family and the rest—you were either part of (chief executive) Peter Moore's family or you weren't. A lot of the players' contracts reflected that. Luckily for me, the family influence wasn't as strong as it had been just a couple of years earlier. Only Garry Hughes remained of the Hughes clan and he was on one leg. Chris Anderson was past his best and eventually got dropped. There was only Steve Folkes left and the Mortimers, who weren't members of the Moore family but were like adopted sons. There were suddenly more of "us" than "them" and that made it a lot easier.' The 1984 season was a red-letter one for the Bulldogs. The club celebrated its 50th year in the best possible style, ending Parramatta's three-year premiership reign to take the title. In an epic grand final that produced just two tries—one apiece—the Bulldogs triumphed 6–4. The match was straight out of the Ryan copybook—rugged defence characterised by gang tackling and a no-mistake game in attack.

The following year St George went into the grand final as firm favourites, having won the minor premiership and club championship getting all three grades into the grand final. But in another dour, defensive match, the Bulldogs triumphed 7–6 to make it back-to-back titles. Despite the on-field successes, there were clearly troubles in the Bulldogs camp. Ryan's disputes with senior players Steve Mortimer and Anderson and chief executive Peter Moore made for a traumatic time and often exploded into newsprint on the back pages of the tabloids. 'Dropping Anderson to reserve grade was something Moore, his father-in-law, never forgave me for,' he said. 'Yet I gave him every chance to keep his spot and the other selectors will back me in what I say. He was playing dreadfully but I stuck by him for six weeks—he was an international and deserved a chance to get back to form. Eventually we had to drop him and bring young Steve O'Brien into the team for the big games in 1984. And it was Steve who came up with the play of the grand final that year against Parramatta. The Eels were on the attack when he came in and intercepted a long pass to Eric Grothe. If Grothe took that ball, he would have scored and there's every chance they would have beaten us for the title.' Ryan is angry at the media's coverage of his differences with Mortimer. 'There was this great nonsense, perpetrated by Steve and repeated in the media, that he was shackled. My only problem with Steve is that he wouldn't run with the football. Even the kids at the school where I was teaching could see it. Yet he kept saying I shackled him. I used to beg him, "Steve, be brilliant . . . for God's sake, be brilliant." No coach denies a player the right to be brilliant. The "shackle" angle was never defused because it was a great excuse for Steve. He was past his best and didn't have the pace any more to regather his chip-and-chases. But he wasn't about to admit that and blaming the coach was a far easier solution. It wasn't always a struggle and there were plenty of times we got on fine, though. I'm convinced that Peter Moore had stooges in the media who would invent stories about me and Mortimer constantly having arguments. I'd get to training and say to Steve, "I see we're fighting again; what are we blueing about now?" But in retrospect, the damage was done because the Canterbury faithful must have thought the situation was no good and it was time to get the son-in-law (Anderson) in as coach. There was a strategy associated with it all. Phil Gould, who was given a caretaker coaching role when I left in 1988 because son-in-law Anderson was tied up in England, eventually dropped Mortimer for the same reasons of diminishing pace and involvement. However, it was never reported that way in the press. Mortimer, according to the scribes, had a virus, but that wasn't the first time the truth never reached the public and I'm sure it won't be the last.'

Ryan tried to put the factional fighting at Canterbury into the background as his team fought its way towards the premiership in 1984 and '85. 'I can honestly say the situation didn't bother us that much at the time,' he said. 'We used to laugh about it. I remember one day we were all sitting around after training thinking about the future. A couple of the players must have been visionaries. They said one day one son-in-law, Chris Anderson, would be coach, the other son-in-law, Steve Folkes, would be conditioner and all the girls would be working in the office at the club. That was 10 years ago and it's all come true. In the end, I must admit it did get to me, all the petty politics. After my fourth year I said I'd had enough and walked out of the place.'

There remains little love lost between the Moore-Bulldog dynasty and Ryan. 'I have had nothing to do with the place since I left,' Ryan said. 'I enjoyed my time there and the results were marvellous. We made the grand final three years in a row, won the first two and I felt we should have won the third as well. That was the grand final we lost 4–2 to Parramatta and I think (referee) Mick Stone got swept up in the emotion of the farewell to Mick Cronin and Ray Price. By halftime, the penalties were three to one against us. On the last play of the game, Mark Bugden went himself from dummyhalf to the right. If he'd passed to his left, Geoff Robinson had just come onto the field and I'm certain he would have scored. I know it's a big "if", but that's what coaches always come back to—"If . . . If . . . If". You can't imagine how many times I've gone back and tried to change the video. Leaving Canterbury eventually was a sour parting and I couldn't handle the way family was put ahead of club.'

Ryan's relentless pressure game—defined as 'Wazzaball' by his critics—saw the league finally decide to change two key rules. The Bulldogs bombarded the living daylights out of St George fullback Glenn Burgess in the 1985 grand final, constantly pinning him in his own in-goal area and then regaining possession through the line drop-out. Not long after that, the league ruled that if a player caught the ball on the full over his own line, his team retained possession through a tap-kick on the 20 metre line. 'Our own chief executive Peter Moore took the film of that game over to England to show it to the international board,' Ryan said. 'He played it to them, showing how we just hemmed Saints in their own territory and starved them of the ball and asked them, "Is this what you want?" That's all it took to make them change the rule. We'd actually advocated at Canterbury that the team who takes the bomb should retain possession. We knew that with the old rule, defensive teams could be placed under unbearable pressure.

So we said, "It's a bad rule, let's just show them how bad and why it needs to change."'

And Ryan's ruthless defensive pattern made officials finally realise that defensive teams had to be kept back further than five metres, with the League gradually bringing in a 10-metre rule. 'In the mid '80s you invariably had the two best defensive sides in the grand final. By 1987, the League started to change things and kept the defence further back and speeded up the play-the-ball. The result? You got the two best attacking teams—Manly and Canberra—in the grand final. Now the field is even marked in 10 metre grids and hallelujah, we're getting a bit of football. But even then the press had a field day and blamed me for being defensive. God, if I could have attacked and scored tries with the equipment I had, I most certainly would have. Even Parramatta, the great international Parramatta backline, couldn't score a try in the 1986 grand final. There wasn't a try scored; the pendulum had been weighted in favour of defence through the rules. It took teams like Parramatta and Canterbury to play a tryless grand final for officials to look up and say, "Hey, wait a minute, what's wrong with our game?" We took the game to the point that something had to be done. In retrospect, we probably did league a favour by playing that tryless grand final. Two great sides both being unable to get across the line finally showed the administrators that changes were needed. You work to the nth degree within the framework of the rules and it seems a natural evolutionary process that the rule makers sit up, realise the flaw is there, and make changes to improve the game.'

Ryan denies popular theory that his players deliberately gave the opposition the ball in early stages of big matches to belt the living daylights out of them. 'That is a silly idea; the opposition gets enough ball as it is without you giving it to them. We never went out to give the opposition the ball. Logically, you just wouldn't do it. There were times when we strategically kicked on an early play. But that usually came after a good run to take the action down from our end of the field to their end. After a ground gaining run, there would be less pressure on the kicker and it was an ideal time to really turn the opposition around. But that was the decision of the kicker. And what was "Wazzaball" anyway? The ability to defend well? Our ability to hang onto a lead for three days? I never understood what guys like Roy Masters were implying with that sort of term.'

Ryan's move to Balmain in 1988 resulted in immediate success for the Tigers. After several years on the fringe of making the big time, the Tigers clicked under Ryan's iron-fisted game plans. The club reached the grand finals in both 1988 and '89, although both games finished in bitter disappointment for Tigers fans. 'The people at Balmain were marvellous and I really enjoyed my time there,' Ryan recalled. 'The club had a great pack of forwards but there was a definite weakness in the outside backs. And the extent of that weakness was fully illustrated when we got (Great Britain skipper) Ellery Hanley late in 1988. You know what you've been missing when you suddenly get it. He just set our backline alight and showed what could be done with some pace and power out wide. I kept telling (chief executive) Keith Barnes, "Keith, your forwards will die of old age before you buy them a backline that can strike." One game against Canberra at Leichhardt in '88 before Ellery arrived sticks in my mind. I remember thinking our forwards would hold them until halftime and then their speedy backs would cut loose. And that's exactly what happened—it finished in a cricket score against us. Our backs were just substandard. I knew the club had a bit of money at the time, but apart from getting Hanley, they refused to spend any more on backs.' The Tigers won the hearts of the league community with a marvellous late run in 1988, fighting their way through from a playoff for fifth spot to the grand final. But Ryan is bitter about the circumstances of his side's 24–12 loss to his former club, Canterbury. 'Two things really got to us,' he said. 'Steve Roach got rubbed out and Ellery Hanley got knocked out. Roach copped a nice, neat four-week suspension that put him out to grand final day even though Chris Mortimer, the player involved in the tackle that got him in strife, was happy to go into bat for him. Suddenly Mortimer clams up and won't help us . . . I don't think it was any coincidence that we were to meet Mortimer's old club Canterbury in the grand final. Then the plan was hatched to send "Blocker" to Britain to serve out one week of his suspension, clearing him to play in the grand final. But the League quickly clamped down on that. In the game itself, Ellery, our main strike weapon, was knocked out cold in the first half and we were leading at the time. I'm not suggesting we would have won the game as in the end we were beaten quite comprehensively, but we would have been a lot better side with Ellery and Roachie out there. I'm always amazed that there were no post mortems or enquiries into the Hanley incident. And they wonder why some people tried to break away from the Australian Rugby League . . .'

After the experiences of 1988, the Tigers were confident that 1989 would be their year. Ryan's men breezed through the preliminary rounds and this time were the first team into the grand final, installed as comfortable favourites to take the trophy. Up against the Tigers was a brash young Canberra side that had all but emulated Balmain's feat of 12 months earlier by fighting through to the big game from fourth spot. The match was a classic—arguably the greatest grand final ever played—but another day of sadness for the Tigers. 'There's no doubt it was a great grand final and I'm proud that we were there and able to take part,' Ryan said. 'Sadly only one team can win a grand final. Looking back, Canberra were a great side about to take off, just as the Parramatta team we met with Newtown in 1981 were a great team on the verge of a golden era. Canberra were truly one of the gun sides yet we almost halted their run before it started. It was such a close game and a few vital things went against us. We led 12–2 at halftime but still weren't playing all that well. I remember saying to the players at the break, "You've got a big enough lead to win two grand finals. But you're lucky to be this far in front and you're going to have to play a lot better." As it turned out, Canberra finished on top of us in the second half and extra time and we just weren't on our game on the day.' The critics again had a field day at Ryan's expense after the Tigers' 19–14 loss, blaming him for replacing Test forwards Paul Sironen and Steve Roach late in the match. Ryan was merely following a tried and tested policy of replacing tiring attacking forwards with fresh defensive men to protect a lead, but when the Tigers were beaten, the critics—and the two players concerned—cried for his blood. 'By the time I replaced him, Roach was our worst defender. He was slow coming back into the line and the Canberra little men were running from dummyhalf and just carving us up. I had a fresh bloke in Kevin Hardwick on the bench and he was a workaholic tackler.' After four grand final losses, Ryan has firm views on how the vanquished should be treated after the big match. 'The losers just want to get out of there—the last thing they want is to see the opposition yahooing and cracking open the champagne,' he said. 'The first thing that should happen when the presentation begins is that the losers receive their medals and are allowed to leave the ground quickly and with dignity. Having lost four of the damn things, I've had plenty of time to think about it,' he adds with a wry grin.

Ryan shifted to Western Suburbs in 1991 and his arrival saw an immediate resurgence in the perennial battlers from Campbelltown. Critics will argue that Ryan did bring some big names to the Magpies—David Gillespie, Paul Langmack, Andrew Farrar and Joe Thomas—but his Midas touch was again evident nonetheless. After a decade in the doldrums, the Magpies made the finals in both 1991 and 1992 and won over the hearts and minds of fans at their Campbelltown base. 'It was a happy marriage initially and we had some success,' he said. 'But the officials failed me ultimately, not the other way around. They conned me by telling me all these grand plans and how they were going to spend big; then a few weeks after I'd signed my second contract with them they suddenly announced they had a cash crisis. They allowed the older players to retire and failed to replace them. There was no planning for the future and that brought about our undoing. I pleaded with them to keep Jim Dymock one day in the boardroom but it fell on deaf ears. They made a token offer to him and he left for Canterbury—look what a great player he's become. I got the impression when I talked to the board they had just no idea about football; I was banging my head against a brick wall. There wasn't a person there with the faintest idea of how to mount a premiership campaign or accumulate the money for someone else to do it for them.'

Ryan's sacking by the Magpies late in the 1994 season after a fallout with officials and senior players has left the much travelled coach with a bitter feeling towards officials in general—especially those at Wests. 'Survival is the main aim of most administrators,' he said. 'They are there to serve themselves and anything left for the coach or players is a bonus. Wests told me they were prepared to run on recycled footballers. That was ridiculous. It's like buying second hand cars; you're just inheriting someone else's problems. You'll endure the same defects as the prior owner—if the player was any good, his previous club wouldn't have got rid of him. Wests even admitted to me privately one day they weren't in there to compete; they were in survival mode and just there to make up the numbers. Once they told me that, I knew we were on a collision course. I was there to win, not just to play a token role in the overall scheme of things. I said to them, "Well what the hell are you doing here if you're not going to compete?" I was stunned. The Wests players were doing better on the field than the administrators off it. The officials were the wooden spooners of the League—when they were begging their creditors to accept 20 cents in the dollar, they definitely ran stone, motherless last. Wests have won more wooden spoons than any other club and the officials are the reason. Wests always seemed to be struggling. St Jude should be their patron saint—he's the hope of the hopeless. And their club should be called the orphanage—the home for players no-one else wants. When Wests sacked me it was largely because the officials couldn't cope with some home truths I told them. Yet all the media concentrated on next day was everything they perceived I'd done wrong—from not filling the players' drink bottles to failing to wash the windows of the sponsors' box. Sacking the coach is the easy solution for clubs that have no idea and Wests have been doing it for years, even before I got there. You start to fail at the top. To say that everything is rosy other than the coach and once he's gone, all your problems will be over, is laughable. Someone should have a look at Wests' record of sacked coaches and sacked chief executives over the last decade—it

WARREN RYAN

says everything. When Tom Raudonikis took over as coach, the then new president Jim Marsden praised him for being a coach who lived in the area. I mean, how in God's name is living in Campbelltown going to make Tom a better coach? Did Jack Gibson ever move from Cronulla to Easts or Parramatta when his teams won premierships there? What relevance has this got? It just shows what little idea they've got . . . how can they think something like that is important or relevant?'

Ryan believes the Magpies' new-found policy of relying of local players under his successor Tom Raudonikis is doomed to failure. 'That's merely trying to make a virtue out of necessity. Anyone who relies on their juniors like Wests are now is kidding themselves. Every junior worth his salt now has a manager who will sell him to the highest bidder. There is no loyalty in league, especially nowadays. The word doesn't even have any meaning any more. The players' motto has become "I've got to look after myself", and I can understand that. The only reason players stay where they are and appear loyal—and I emphasise *appear* loyal—is that no-one else wants them or that their current club gives them an offer that is as good as, or close to, the one from the opposition so they decide to stay with their mates. It's taken until now to prove that loyalty comes at a price. I just wish that players would stop throwing dummies and simply say, "I'm in it for the money—I went to the highest bidder." I've lost count of the number of times a manager has come to me and said, "So and so wants out of his club because he can't get on with the coach." When they start that routine, I just tell them to cut the bullshit and tell me how much they want.'

Ryan has little time for the modern player, who he believes has developed a prima donna character. 'Players are very spoilt—most league players are selfish brats. They receive endless praise from their friends and in the media and go around big-noting themselves in discos and nightclubs. When a coach dares to come up to them and say they can't pass or tackle, they spit out the dummy. But it's the coach who has the tough job of bringing the player back to reality. So many players become big-headed because of the constant praise and back slapping they receive. They haven't got the mental strength to cope with it all and actually change personalities. Terry Lamb is a rare exception. He was always level headed and a great bloke and is the same unassuming person now as he was 15 years ago, to his great credit.'

Ryan is a deep thinker on the modern game and his weekly columns in the *Sydney Morning Herald* are compulsory reading for close followers of the code. 'Harry Bath said in the '70s there wasn't enough room to play football under a five-metre rule and things gradually got worse,' he observes. 'Canterbury showed in the mid '80s just how a defence can bottle up the opposition. The 10 metre rule has given us more room to play and I think everyone acknowledges that it is a better product. We're seeing more tries but the game is now weighted heavily in favour of the super athlete. The problem there is there aren't enough of those players to go around 20 clubs. Take 1995—we had the ridiculous situation where three clubs went to the halfway mark in the competition without a loss. That highlighted the disparity in standard between the top teams and the cellar dwellers and also the fact that there aren't enough super talents to go around 20 teams. A few years back, if you had no stars but a very good defensive side, you were in with a chance of beating the Manlys or Brisbanes or Canberras. But a very good attacking side will usually triumph these days.'

Ryan has little time for critics of the selection policy of him and other coaches. 'There's no doubt that team selection is one of the toughest jobs for a coach,' he said. 'But I've always been amused when people come up and say, "So and so should be in the team SOMEWHERE." I'll just say to them, "But where? At whose expense? Drop someone for me." Once you pin them down, they have no answer. They don't want to abide by the rules of mathematics that only 13 players can run onto the field.' Ryan insists that despite differences of opinion with players at times in his career, he has never allowed his team selections to get personal. 'Your survival as a coach depends on picking the best team available,' he said. 'You can't afford to get petty, for your own sake and the team's. You've got to go for the players who will do the job, regardless of how you feel about them.'

Like Jack Gibson, Ryan has spawned his own coaching empire. Former Ryan players Phil Sigsworth, Ken Wilson, Bob Lindner, Andrew Farrar, Phil Gould, Allan McMahon, David Waite, Peter Tunks, Chris Anderson, Wayne Pearce, Tom Raudonikis and John Dorahy have all moved into coaching. And two of Ryan's former reserve grade coaches, Peter Mulholland and Graham Murray, are now respected first grade coaches. Watching teams coached by these men in action, it is not hard to see how many have copied Ryan's distinctive style.

With his imposing record of nine semi-final appearances in 14 years, including six grand finals, Ryan's statistics speak for themselves. And talking to the man shortly before the start of the 1996 season, I got the distinct impression that despite his disenchantment with many aspects of the modern game, he is ready for one last tilt at coaching. 'There could be something there in the near future, but I don't know for sure,' he said. 'Frankly, I see modern coaching as a fairly dishonest business. It's plagiarism without giving acknowledgment. But it's also dishonest in another way. For reasons of self preservation, coaches these days have to develop the art of telling players and officials exactly what they want to hear, even if it's 10 miles from the truth.' Ryan did, however, acknowledge former St George coach Brian Smith had been honest enough to admit copying the Ryan blueprint. 'Brian studied my teams for hours early in his coaching career to see just how we dominated matches and it was refreshing to see him come out and say it. I'm in two minds about coaching again but if I do, it will only be at a strong club. There's no future in coaching recycled second raters that have been accumulated by chook raffle administrators who are a combination of geriatrics and hillbillies. I've been there, done that and am not interested in going through that aggravation any more.'

Sweet Shine of Success for Mr Sheen

TIM SHEENS

CLUBS
Penrith 1984–87,
Canberra 1988–

PREMIERSHIP RECORD
Games 295. Won 178, lost 111, drew 6.
Winning percentage 60.3%.
Semi-finals
1985, 1988–91, 1993–95.
Grand finals (4)
1989–91, 1994
Premierships (3)
1989–90, 1994

OTHER COACHING ACHIEVEMENTS
Coached NSW 1991.
Games 3, won 1, lost 2.
Coached City Origin 1991.
Dally M Coach of the Year 1984, 1990.

Tim Sheens has the most imposing big match record in modern football. A history-making coach who rewrote the record books with the two clubs he has coached, Sheens is a players' coach who has developed a tremendous rapport with the athletes in his charge. An honest front-rower who at one stage held the record for most games for Penrith, he took on the Panthers when the football club was close to folding in 1984. Just twelve months later, the Panthers were the pride of the league when Sheens steered a young side into the finals for the first time. But it was at Canberra that he really made the league world sit up and take notice. He transformed a talented but erratic Raiders team into one of the most exciting attacking units the game has seen. Over the past decade in vital semi-finals with Canberra, Sheens' talent for winning big matches really came to the fore. The Raiders came from fourth spot to take their maiden title in 1989, fought from fourth again to make the grand final in 1991 and won the premiership from third spot in 1994. A conservative coach who is happy to let his players take the accolades, Sheens has always put his team first. But it is that determination to do the right thing by his players that has seen him run foul of officialdom more than once in his career.

After copping many thrashings in the Penrith engine room during the Panthers' bad old days in the 1970s, Sheens spent plenty of time reflecting on the game. 'As a player, as you get towards the end of your career, you start to think about your future,' he said. 'In league, there are only two main avenues— administration or coaching. My aim was to captain-coach in the bush in my early thirties and when I finished at Penrith, I went for a year to Campbelltown. I was the captain and even though I wasn't the coach, I assisted him a lot. There were times he wasn't around and I'd be in charge. My plan the following year was to captain-coach in Townsville; I wanted to stay on in football . . . it was the thing I knew best. I didn't know if I'd be good at coaching but I was keen to have a go at it. I did have a back-up plan if things didn't work out, however. I was a partner in a real estate business in the Penrith area and when the offer to coach the Panthers came up I told my partners, "I'll see you in 12 months." The list of coaches that Penrith had gone through over the years was as long as your arm and I wasn't sure I'd be there for long. I couldn't be confident I'd still be welcome 12 months later, particularly under the circumstances that prevailed at Penrith at that time.'

Sheens inherited a club that was in dire straits in 1984, after spending much of its 17-year existence in the doldrums. 'It was late November '83, most teams were already in full training and Penrith only had half a dozen players on contract and no coach,' he recalled. 'Several of the few class players we had, including Des Hasler and Henry Foster, had left and even guys like Roycie Simmons were knocking on secretary Roger Cowan's door asking for a release. For a while the club didn't even look like fielding a team in 1984, things were so grim. Roger held a seminar and people from all around the area came to give their views. There had been nearly two decades of turmoil with little success . . . coaches getting sacked, big name signings proving to be duds, chief executives going, boards resigning. To that stage, every coach Penrith had ever had was booted out; nobody left on good terms. A lot was discussed by people on all facets of the game and it was left to Roger to piece it all together. I actually had to leave after saying my piece to attend one of my kids' birthday parties and didn't think much more of it. But I got a call from Roger the next day out of the blue and he asked me if I'd coach the team.' Unbeknown to Sheens, the Panthers' few remaining players, headed by captain Simmons, had fronted Cowan the previous afternoon and pushed for Sheens to get the coaching job. Ironically, Sheens managed to return the favour exactly a decade later. When Phil Gould quit the Panthers midway through 1994, leaving the club in tatters, Cowan was again in a quandary. The Panthers' boss put in a call to Sheens in Canberra, who promptly recommended Simmons for the job.

'Most people said I was crazy to even think of taking on the position because of the lack of personnel and the club's history of failure,' Sheens recalled. 'The club had no money; apart from the six players on contract, no-one else received sign-on money. For the rest, it was pay for play. But after my wife Rhonda and I went to see Roger to talk it over, we decided to give it a go. Given the circumstances, Roger's expectations were very low. In fact he said, "If you win one game, I'll be happy." But he was confident that with the new leagues club opening that year, they would be among the richest clubs in the game in five years. "By then, we'll be able to sit Wally Lewis on the bench if we want," he bragged to me at the same meeting. And Roger was pretty close to the mark because five years later—the year I left—they paid record fees to sign Chris Mortimer and Peter Kelly from Canterbury and they were two key signings for the Penrith club.'

Sheens began the task of moulding the few players on his books together with new recruits into a competitive unit. 'We started in December and my office was more like a closet; I couldn't have sat two people in there. I was lucky to be able to put together a good staff; my two lower grade coaches in Harry Hackett and Cliff Cartwright were known and respected in the area and my trainer Ron Oxley was great for morale. Len Stacker and Dave Bolton were put on as assistant coaches and both had vast experience. They made me full-time coach and from memory, I was the only coach in that position apart from Jack Gibson. And Jack had other business interests as well so technically, I was probably the first full-time coach. I also had a manager-coach role, which was a first. It meant I put in a lot more hours but also gave me more control over my own destiny. My assistant coaches knew the local players and Cliff was especially valuable because he got kids from St Mary's on board. Penrith and St Mary's had always been rivals and most of the St Mary's players wanted nothing to do with Penrith. But when they saw Cliff was giving their players a go, they all jumped on board. I was fortunate in that while we had few senior players, those we did have were good people.

'They were strong of character and a reliable bunch to put the younger blokes around. The ones I'm referring to were Royce, Mark Levy, Lew Zivanovic, Warren Fenton, Brad Waugh and Ken Woolfe. Brad Izzard was still a kid but a good player coming through. They were regular first graders but it really was a struggle after that. We trialled a heap of players in the local area—hundreds and hundreds of kids. Anyone who wanted a chance we looked at and what we pushed is that they were playing for real opportunity. They weren't going to be coming into a club with established first and reserve grade sides so anyone who could play was going to get a start. Amongst it all we found some fair players.'

Sheens realised the importance of making maximum use of the Panthers' vast junior ranks. 'We standardised everything right through the club,' he said. 'The under-17s used the same moves and training drills as the first graders. And they could compare their times over 100 metres to the best players in the club. I went to every game . . . I was probably the only coach within 100 miles of an SG Ball game at that time. That's where we found the likes of Mark Geyer, Steve Carter and later Brad

Fittler. I didn't grade Fittler, but I put him on contract to the club when he was just 14. Even at that age, you could tell he was going to be some player.'

Sheens knew the player who was to be the key to his plans at Penrith was a youngster from the Panthers' SG Ball side who had never played a game of grade football. 'Greg Alexander was in that team, as were some great kids like Steve Robinson, John Cartwright, Ben Gonzales and Colin Van Der Voort. They won the final of their competition by 40 odd points and were obviously something special. I hadn't seen much of young Alexander but he was already a big name in the district because of his exploits in junior football. Parramatta and Canterbury were both chasing him but they had a couple of established halfbacks in Peter Sterling and Steve Mortimer, who were fighting it out for the Test spot at the time. Greg realised he had the best chance to play first grade in his favourite position of halfback at Penrith and when he came on board, it was a big coup for us.' Sheens, mindful of the dangers of bringing the teenager to grade too soon, planned to keep Alexander in the lower grades for at least half a season, if not more, to develop. 'But it didn't work out that way,' Sheens mused. 'He was just too good . . . I think he played one game in reserve grade and then I brought him into the team. I realised I couldn't hold the kid back. He was very young, but his class and his skill made a huge difference to the team. We had to do a lot of work on Greg, but the raw skill that you just can't find in most cases was there in abundance. He could make a break and chip and chase and do a lot of things he won't attempt now. I don't know why it's out of his game now; maybe it was coached out of him over the years or he feels the game is too stereotyped to take the risks. The chip and chase men like Mortimer and Alexander seem to be gone. But back in those days, Greg was a real one man band; he'd set up or score four to five tries a game and save as many in defence. He was just an unbelievable athlete.

'In the end we graded 52 players with an average age— would you believe—of 19. Only three were married and around 46 were local juniors—quite amazing figures. By the season kickoff everyone was super fit but we lost our first four or five games and looked like we were in dreadful trouble. But then we won our first, and five more in a row after that as the team started to click. What we couldn't do with skill, we did with sheer enthusiasm. We recycled a couple of blokes like Ross Gigg and David Burnes and later Geoff Gerard, who a lot of people thought were over the hill; we got great mileage out of them. I remember our three back-rowers Craig Connor, Peter Burgmann and Warren Fenton weighed 87 kilos, 85 and 83. I used to pick the lightest of the three at lock and the other two in the second row. Nowadays most halfbacks weigh as much as that. But all three would make 30 tackles a game and would chase the ball all day. We'd get Greg Alexander to kick the ball deep and these guys would pin the opposition down in their own half.'

Sheens is certain the Panthers were underestimated by many teams in that first year, in which they narrowly missed a finals spot. 'Clubs were used to an easy game when they played Penrith,' he said. 'We had no big name players and were supposed to be going nowhere; there's no doubt that we caught a few teams napping.' Despite missing the finals, the young Panthers were the rags-to-riches story of the 1984 season. Sheens was named coach of the year but received a word of warning from the experienced Cowan mid-year. 'I remember Roger came up to me one day and said I was making a rod for my own back by winning so many games—and he was right. By the kickoff in 1985, everyone expected us to make the finals. We showed our form in '84 was no fluke and finished equal fifth with Manly after the 22 rounds. It all came down to a Tuesday night playoff against them at the SCG and we won 10–7 in extra time. It was a great way to make it into the finals for the first time, beating a top side like Manly. The emotion was high and it was a night I don't think anyone at Penrith will ever forget.'

Sheens occasionally browses the video of that game more than a decade ago and is still stunned by the quality of play. 'Even by today's standards, it was a great game,' he said. 'The intensity of play was really something.' Sadly, the Panthers' joy proved short lived as they were thrashed 38–6 by Parramatta just four days later. 'Both Royce and I knew that the win over Manly was just the first stage,' Sheens recalled. 'But trying to keep the lid on it when you had been nobodies for nearly 20 years and suddenly reached the finals was next to impossible. It went to the heads of some of the young blokes and they could barely concentrate on the game. The district also went wild and that was something we just couldn't keep them away from. The champagne was cracked after the Tuesday night win and I couldn't blame them for celebrating . . . a few of our guys thought they had played their grand final and Parramatta brought us crashing down to earth. But it was still a very emotional time and a great year for Penrith as a whole. Those two years—'84 and '85—gave Penrith the credibility the place had always lacked. Prior to that, players always went to Penrith to finish their careers. Now, all of a sudden, they started looking at Penrith and thinking, "It may not be such a bad place to play after all." We put up a fair fight in '86 and '87 but by then, for me the time had come to move on. It was still a hard decision, though, as I'd played all my football at Penrith and had a lot of friends in the area. But I felt as a young coach, I wasn't learning anything new. I wasn't going anywhere and needed a change. The players probably needed a fresh face in charge too. I was actually going to leave Penrith at the end of '86 as I'd only had a three-year contract, but Roger asked me to stay on for the one extra year and I relented.'

Sheens would have been happy to take a year's break from coaching at the end of 1987 before fate stepped in. 'Midway through the year Wayne Bennett decided to leave Canberra to go to Brisbane and I got a call from (Raiders chief executive) John McIntyre. Canberra really belted us in a pre-season game early in 1987 and it was then I knew they would be a good side. We had our strongest team in but they gave it to us; they'd signed players like Kevvie Walters and Peter Jackson to go alongside the likes of Gary Belcher and Mal Meninga and were developing into a real force. But when I agreed to coach them midway through 1987, they were struggling to reach the finals. As it turned out, they finished superbly and got all the way to the grand final, which suddenly placed enormous pressure on my shoulders as incoming coach the following year. I came into the club and everyone expected us to win the whole thing in my first season. Unfortunately, we had a lot of injuries late in the season; Mal Meninga had a broken arm and several other key players were also missing. We ended up losing 19–18 to Canterbury in the semis and they went on to win it. We came third and some people down here weren't happy about it at all.'

Sheens declined to elaborate, but it is known that early the following season in 1989, when the Raiders lost a couple of games, there were calls from some prominent officials within the club to sack Sheens, particularly after the team had lost its opening two games. Less than six months later, those same officials were dousing their coach with champagne after the Raiders' epic grand final triumph over Balmain.

After a poor start to 1989, the Raiders were in strife at several stages during the year and even looked like missing the finals altogether at several stages. But a late spurt saw them grab fourth spot. Playoff wins over Cronulla, Penrith and Souths earned them their grand final spot for the historic showdown with Balmain. Sheens believes much of the Raiders' success in 1989 was due to a golden run with injury when they made their challenge late in the season. 'There is very little between the top teams in most years and injury can often mean the difference between winning and losing those big end-of-season games,' he said. 'We kept our top team on the park for the last eight or nine games as we stormed home from fourth spot and I've no doubt that was a major factor in winning it. It's luck, but well-managed luck, that enables you to keep key people on the field.' The Raiders rewrote the record books with their extra-time victory over the Tigers, becoming the first team to take the title from fourth or fifth spot and, more significantly, the first premiership winner to come out of Sydney. In what is widely accepted as the greatest grand final ever played, the Raiders outlasted Warren Ryan's Balmain Tigers 19–14. 'Like Penrith's win to reach the finals for the first time a few years earlier, the win couldn't have come in better or more dramatic circumstances,' Sheens recalled. 'We had to come back from a 10 point halftime deficit and those tries by "Chicka" Ferguson and Steve Jackson that got us home will always be very special moments in the hearts of Canberra people. As a player, I'd never even played in a semi-final let alone a grand final so it was a great feeling for me. There's no way you'll ever forget your first win and to come in such a great game made it even better. It was a top game of football and I watch it occasionally on video. But by today's standards, it's starting to fall away—that's how quickly the game is changing.'

Nostalgia was very much the order of the day for Sheens in the 1990 and 1991 grand finals, when he came up against the Penrith side he had helped groom into a premiership force only a few years earlier. Sheens was firm friends with the likes of Royce Simmons, Greg Alexander and Mark Geyer and knew the capabilities of the Panthers intimately. 'People always said I must have had mixed feelings at the time but they were honestly just another team I thought we had to beat,' Sheens said. 'In 1990 we again had a great run with injury; the only player we lost was Brad Clyde, and Nigel Gaffey and David Barnhill filled the spot for us well. We were too good for Penrith in the grand final but in 1991 it all caught up with us. We had a string of injuries and most of our key players had exhaustive representative campaigns with Tests and State of Origin matches. And don't forget they were backing up after a Kangaroo tour and many hadn't had a proper break over the summer. In the grand final, we were in there for a while, but Penrith just outlasted us and Royce of course led the way with two tries. People said to me afterwards that if I had to lose, at least it would have felt better losing to my old club. Like hell it did. I don't like losing—to anyone. There were eight or nine guys in the Penrith side I brought to grade and while that gave me some satisfaction on reflection, it didn't make losing any easier. But they still had a lot of coaching between me and that game—I'm not about to try taking any of the credit for Penrith winning its first title. At least I could shake their hands and congratulate them when they beat us, but I was still dirty, don't worry about that.' Sheens was adamant that Simmons, his old mate who recommended him for the Penrith coaching job years earlier, would have a fitting farewell in his final game of football—win, lose or draw. Although Simmons didn't know it at the time, Sheens decided days before the grand final that if his Canberra side won the game, he would present his winner's medal to the Panthers skipper. As it turned out, however, it was Simmons' memorable two try performance that proved the difference between the sides. The former Test hooker bowed out of the game in a blaze of glory.

Sheens still bears a grudge against the high ranking Australian Rugby League officials who dumped him as NSW State of Origin coach in 1991 after the Blues' narrow 2–1 loss. In one of the closest and best series on record, each of the three games was decided by two points, yet Sheens found himself booted out at the end of the year. Officials gave the excuse that Sheens was axed for failing to keep his players on the field for the official presentation after the deciding game, but Sheens insists he was the victim of football politics. 'I don't want to comment on the reasons they sacked me—that is gone and forgotten,' he said. 'But the so-called reason, that we didn't stay on the field, is a load of crap. They wanted to knife me for things I said to them behind closed doors and eventually they got me.' Sheens believes he went into his first—and only—representative series with a deal of naivety and was taken for a ride by officials. 'If I had my time over again, I probably wouldn't have been fooled by them and the pseudo politics they went on with,' he said.

Two key incidents still leave a sour taste in his mouth when recalling that origin series. Firstly, the suspension of Mark Geyer after the infamous rain-soaked match in Sydney in which he clashed with Wally Lewis after the halftime siren. And secondly, an edict from officials to the Blues to keep it clean before the final game—a warning that NSW heeded but

Sheens believes went largely ignored by the Queenslanders. 'The giving up of Geyer by the NSW people when Lewis should have gone to the judiciary as well really upset me,' he said. 'They were all patting him on the back after the game but he was later made a sacrificial lamb when Queensland put on the pressure. In the third game we were lectured by the powers that be that we had to keep our hands down or there would be repercussions. The second game was quite a fiery affair and so I heeded the warning and coached accordingly. Queensland played it differently and given that experience, I now realise in that grand final-type atmosphere, you don't play it soft. No-one is going to get sent off in those games and I should have realised that. I also didn't handle it too well afterwards by letting a few officials know what I thought and that is why they got rid of me. To me, as well as a bitter experience, it was also an opportunity lost because anyone could see the balance of power was changing at Origin level. Queensland's best players like Lewis and Miles were on the way out while NSW had some great young players coming up. And sure enough, the Blues won the next three series just to ram home that point.'

Sheens suffered another major setback while in camp with the Blues' State of Origin side in 1991. 'We picked up a newspaper and read that the Canberra club was over a million dollars in debt and there were problems with the salary cap—the Canberra players and I couldn't believe it,' he said. 'That made it difficult for the rest of '91 and at the end of that year a heap of players left us. But we had a meeting and most of the senior players vowed to stay together. I signed first, Meninga signed next and the others gradually followed. But a few had been targeted and trying to keep them under what was suddenly a very tightly scrutinised salary cap became very difficult.' The Raiders lost a staggering 30 of their 55 players over the summer and suffered accordingly in 1992. The team missed the finals for the first time in seven years and many believed the era of the Raiders was over. 'Even though they were tough times, I was always confident we could turn things around,' Sheens said. 'We had the nucleus of a top side—Daley, Clyde, Meninga, Stuart and Steve Walters—and just needed to find the right young kids to play beside them. And coming through the ranks were Jason Croker, David Furner, Brett Mullins and Brett Hetherington. I knew these kids would make it, but it might just take them a year or so to acclimatise.'

It was at the end of 1992 that Sheens produced a scouting master-stroke, breaking new ground by bringing Fijian rugby international Noa Nadruku to the club. Sheens was impressed by the flair and speed of the flying centre/winger and was confident he would thrive outside Meninga and Daley. But not even Sheens could have predicted the impact Nadruku would have in his maiden season in 1993. The powerful winger topped the tryscoring list with a club record 22 tries and established himself as one of the game's real personality players. Sheens' success with Nadruku saw many other Winfield Cup clubs sign Fijian players. Just two years later in 1995 some 30 Fijians were playing in the Winfield Cup, although none had managed to emulate the deeds of the remarkable Nadruku. 'I have always thought that the island players with their flair and athleticism would make natural league players,' he said. 'And to me, signing Noa wasn't as big a gamble as some people suggested; the guy had played more than 30 rugby union Tests all over the world. The problem was getting him to acclimatise to the cold and foreign conditions in Canberra and to make sure he felt welcome and happy. We did a lot of work in that area and it paid off very nicely. In the same year we also brought Ruben Wiki, John Lomax and Quentin Pongia to the club from

New Zealand and the fact that all four managed to fire was a significant turning point as we attempted to climb back into premiership reckoning.'

Sheens is loath to compare the teams he has coached at Canberra over the years but is realistic enough to admit the most recent teams may well be the best. 'The game improves a percentage every year, there's no doubt about that,' he said. 'You mightn't see it over 12 months but you can certainly see it over a period of three to four years. And bearing that in mind, you'd have to say the '94 team that won the premiership was better than the '89 team that did the same thing. I also thought that our 1995 team, even though we didn't make the grand final, was as good as any team I've had down here. We only lost two games over the 22 rounds and had an excellent year all round.'

Without doubt the toughest day in Sheens' coaching career came at Belmore in a club match against Canterbury in 1990. For the first time, the Raiders' coach revealed how he had to quell a near on-field mutiny by several senior forwards against the captaincy of Mal Meninga, who had only recently inherited the leadership reins from the respected Dean Lance. 'Belmore is a very hard ground to win at and I remember Canterbury were really giving it to us in the first half on this particular day,' Sheens recalled. 'Their forwards were hammering us in defence and they scored a couple of tries up the middle. As captain, Mal didn't take kindly to it and really blasted our forwards behind the tryline after one of their tries. Glenn Lazarus always was—and still is—a fairly cantankerous type and he took exception to Mal's outburst. As a relatively new captain, Mal was really getting into the forwards and telling them to have a go. But Lazo and Brent Todd obviously sneered at Meninga—probably the biggest athlete on the football field—

who was playing out in the centres and had his shorts still clean. "You can go and get #@*&%$," was their reply to Mal's pleas for more effort. At halftime, Mal made a beeline to me and told me what had happened and demanded some action. In the corner of my eye, I could see the two big fellas, sitting on the bench on the opposite side of the dressing room, waiting to hear my answer. It was a tricky situation and I was stumped for a few seconds. But then the old front-rower in me came out and I just said to Mal, "If I'd been out there, I would have told you the same thing. You're the biggest bloke out there and you've got to lead by example." Mal didn't take too kindly to that; he'd obviously expected me to rip into the two props and tell them to toe the line.'

The dramatic dressing room confrontation could have had dire consequences for the relationship between Sheens and his new captain but fortunately for the Raiders, the encounter produced a happy ending. 'To Mal's credit, he bit his tongue and went back onto the field determined to lead the way to victory,' Sheens said. 'He took the ball from the kickoff to the second half and smashed through the defence and led the way for us. We fought back strongly in the second half and ended up winning a tough game 28–20. And I think in many respects that game proved the turning point in Mal Meninga's captaincy. He became an excellent leader from that day and had the respect of the players he commanded. I would often ask the players to set a goal before a game and Mal would give me a variety of answers prior to that. But from that day on until the end of his career, his goal was always the same and just four words—"To lead by example". And I think it's fair to say he achieved that. He realised what was expected of him and produced the goods and became a very inspirational leader.'

Sheens has been an innovator during his time at both

TIM SHEENS

Penrith and Canberra, always looking for the edge to give him even the slightest advantage over the rest of the field. One day at Penrith, he ran his entire 13-man squad onto the field wearing headgear; at Canberra he introduced the 'heat-tank' to acclimatise his players to the warmer conditions in Sydney at finals time. He trialled a system where a trainer on the sideline would flash up a card showing a number to the players on the field after penalty kicks to signal a particular move (although this was subsequently banned by league officials). Sheens has constantly contacted the league hierarchy in Sydney with ideas and rule changes to improve the game, although often his approaches have been ignored. Like most good coaches, he has never been afraid to take a gamble and no better example can be found than in the 1994 grand final. With prop John Lomax suspended just days before the big game, the Raiders were in all sorts of trouble against a Canterbury team that had beaten them a fortnight earlier. Sheens was expected to bring one of his 'young guns', David Westley or Brett Hetherington, into the front row but shunned them both, going for a wild card—Paul Osborne. Written off by many critics as a spent force, Osborne really had no right to even be in the Raiders' squad for the big game. The chunky front-rower hadn't played in over a month and was heckled by team-mates with good-natured jibes as he trained by himself through the final series before the first graders took over the field. But Sheens saw in Osborne a special quality that he could use to his advantage on grand final day. Four days before the premiership decider, in a cafe in icy Queanbeyan, Sheens said to me: 'The thing about Ossie is that he wants to win a premiership more than anyone I know. If I send him out there for the first 20 minutes, he will give me everything he's got and may catch them napping.'

They were prophetic words as Osborne tore the normally

disciplined Canterbury defence to shreds. His selection proved one of the great grand final gambles of all time, with Osborne laying on the opening two tries as the Raiders scored an emphatic 36–12 win.

While the motives of some converts to the Super League cause can be questioned, no-one can point an accusing finger at Sheens. The highly respected Raiders coach beat his head against the door at Phillip Street for much of the past decade, suggesting rule changes that have been ignored and urging reform. Officialdom responded by branding Sheens a 'whinger' and have invariably snubbed his ideas. The lingering discontent over his State of Origin sacking proved another reason for his disenchantment with the establishment. Sheens also believes the standard of play in 1995 was a major reason that Super League was able to gain a foothold. 'The 20-team format saw the game suffer,' he said. 'It became like playing in the juniors again—there were games where you just knew you would win, and win easily. In other years there were a couple of games you could say that about, but nowhere near as many. I've never seen that situation before in grade football, not even when I was playing. There was always a team or two—often it was us at Penrith—who clubs knew they were likely to beat. But it was never a foregone conclusion like it was in '95 and the game definitely suffered as a result.'

Sheens refused to nominate a best player among the stars he has coached, unable to separate the likes of Greg Alexander, Ricky Stuart, Mal Meninga and Laurie Daley. 'It's like someone asking you to name your favourite child . . . you just can't do it,' he said. 'They all have their own personalities and strengths. I've been blessed to have been associated with so many gifted athletes; I've had something to do with their careers and they have had something to do with mine. I don't consider them my athletes or anything like that. I have worked with them and we've had our ups and downs and had input into each other's careers. You don't do well without good athletes but I firmly believe that athletic performance is coach driven. Otherwise, why do people pay so much for coaches? And why do sportsmen, even individual sportsmen like tennis players and runners, hire coaches? They know that the coach can get that extra bit out of them, the bit that often makes the difference. The Canberra team here would still win plenty of games if nobody coached them, but you can bet they would do better if they had a coach, be it me or someone else. Coaches are more important than most people realise. Some people have stated that coaches have too much say and maybe they do; the egos of some coaches are bigger than the game and the players. But the coaches are under a heap of pressure because whenever there is any drama in a club, they are the first to go. There are very few coaches who can leave a club on good terms. I've managed to do it a couple of times (at Penrith and Canberra) but it's not too easy. Most of us go out the back door . . . like players . . . fighting, kicking and screaming,' he added with a laugh. 'Although these days they don't scream as much, otherwise they don't get their payouts.'

It's a tribute to Sheens' strength of character and popularity that he has been able to stay with the Raiders for nearly a decade. In an era when three years is considered a healthy stay at a club for a coach, he began his ninth season in 1996. The quietly spoken Sheens rode out the tough times of 1988 and early 1989 and is now among the most popular and respected men in the ACT. 'When I came down I probably didn't envisage staying this long,' he conceded. 'But I think it boils down in part to the fact that while there are a lot of top players around, there aren't so many top coaches. I'm not presumptuous enough to put myself in that category; I'm confident in my ability to do the job and my record has been fairly good. If you are continually trying to learn as a coach, which I am, then there is always a new challenge. You don't get bored. In addition to that, we had a massive turnover of players in 1992, which was about halfway through my career here, and it was almost like coaching a new club. And the players who I've had here since day one, the Daleys, Clydes, Stuarts and the like, I've always got on with. I've never run foul of them and have never gone stale with them. Again, we are always looking to change what we do and stay a step ahead of the opposition. That's the secret of coaching as I see it—to always be looking to improve and learn. The day a player isn't learning anything under you is the day he doesn't know where he is going. The game is changing and you have to change with it. And it often changes because of the style the coaches adopt.'

A coach who is used to success, Sheens knows he faces his greatest challenge with the North Queensland Cowboys in 1997 and beyond. But he sees the move north as his fate—he had signed to captain-coach in Townsville in 1984 before Penrith stepped in and the move 13 years later will ensure peace on the home front. Sheens' wife Rhonda, a strong and silent supporting hand, has yearned to return home to her family in her home town of Townsville for several years. 'It won't be easy and I'm not going to make any outlandish claims about winning the comp,' Sheens said. 'But my philosophy when I take on a coaching job is that I want to leave the place better than I found it. If I do that with the Cowboys then I'll be happy. I'm going to have to work hard to identify talent in the local area and set up a support team. But I do see a future there. The district is a great nursery of players and another plus is that the area is unified because it is so isolated. That was the case when

I was at Penrith and also at Canberra and I can see real advantages in that. No-one wanted to come to Penrith in the old days, or Canberra that long ago. That's the situation with North Queensland now but it can quickly change. As far as the juniors go, they've got heaps and in winter, all they do is play football. It's an area that will produce good players if they are identified and well coached from an early age. There will be plenty of enthusiasm there and that will be good for me too. The club is certainly better than Penrith when I started coaching them. When I started there all we had was a handful of players, some footballs and a few witch's hats so I'm not worried by the challenge.'

Sheens is certain the pressure of coaching the lowly Cowboys will be no less or greater than being in charge of the mighty Canberra Green Machine. 'The pressures are just as great at both ends of the ladder—and I know because I've been at both,' he said. 'If you're coaching a good team, you're expected to win and if you don't, you're in trouble. When you don't have a good team, the expectations are there to improve. But it's a lot harder to improve at the top than at the bottom. Understandably, most coaches would prefer to be at the top of the tree, but it's tough for a coach no matter where you are.'

Mr Precision

BRIAN SMITH

CLUBS
Illawarra 1984–87,
Hull (UK) 1988–90,
St George 1991–95,
Bradford 1995–

PREMIERSHIP RECORD
Games 214, won 101, lost 110, drew 3.
Winning percentage 47.2%.
Semi-finals
1992–93
Grand finals (2)
1992–93

ENGLISH CHAMPIONSHIP RECORD (1988–90)
Games 69, won 44, lost 24, drew 1.
Winning percentage 63.8%.

OTHER COACHING ACHIEVEMENTS
Won under-23 premiership with Souths 1983,
University Shield 1982–83,
took Hull to premiership final 1989.

Brian Smith is the pick of the new breed of coach to hit rugby league in the 1980s and '90s. Well spoken, refined and cool under pressure, he reflects the changing face of the game over the past decade. After impressive results at schoolboy level and in the lower grades, Smith broke into the big time with Illawarra in the mid 1980s. But after a frustrating time with the Steelers, a club with little financial or playing resources at that time, he moved to England to make his name. That he did with the Hull club, where he became revered as the man who put perennial battlers Hull back on the map after years in the doldrums. That feat earned Smith another crack at the Winfield Cup—with the famous St George Dragons, the club he played for as a promising halfback in the early '70s. It was at Saints that Smith really made his mark, taking a run-of-the-mill side to back-to-back grand finals in 1992–93. The Super League war, and its devastating effect on the Dragons, saw Smith return to England to another challenge, the struggling Bradford Bulls. But he is keeping a close eye on the Australian scene and has vowed to return home in search of new challenges when his Bradford contract lapses at the end of 1997.

Brian Smith didn't start playing football until he reached high school—he had little choice growing up on the NSW north coast. 'My primary school wasn't big enough to field a team, so I had to wait until high school at Maclean and then Casino. But I was always a fan. Dad used to take me a lot to games when I was little and I loved it for as long as I can remember. In 1971 and '72 I played for NSW Combined High Schools and that opened some doors for me. Some people up there who knew St George secretary Frank Facer got in touch with him and he invited me down for a trial. That was in 1973 and after a couple of games, they signed me up.'

But Smith didn't have a speedy rise to first grade—ironically because of another halfback also named B. Smith. 'Billy Smith was still in the place and he was a legend—one of the greats,' Smith said. 'I learned a lot from him; he was such a competitor and a real professional. He was among the best players of his time and if he was playing now, he'd be even better. He had such an appetite for the game. He just lived for it. But he was also smart and tough and that's what enabled him to stay at the top for so long.'

Smith played 13 top grade games in his second season with Saints in 1974 before moving on to Souths. 'The Rabbitohs' golden era of the early '70s was coming to an end, but there were still some great players there,' he said. 'Bob McCarthy, Paul Sait, John O'Neill, Gary Stevens . . . we still had a formidable pack. I had two years there but it was when I started work as a teacher that I realised coaching was the area I wanted to be in. I was working with schoolboy sides and that gave me the taste of it. Coaching was something I began to enjoy more and more. I had a good side at James Cook High School and we won a couple of University Shields, which was great for the school. It also helped kick me along and I got the opportunity to coach under Paul Broughton in the under-23s at Newtown in 1976. But it was a disaster; Paul got the sack after around six weeks and I straightaway rang him up and told him I was going to quit in protest. But he talked me out of it. "You are going to have a career in coaching, I know it," he told me. "I want you to stick at it. It will be good experience for you." He was half right; it was experience, but it wasn't good. It was disgusting . . . despicable . . . the worst time of my life. The whole place was just a joke. The officials didn't know how to run the club and gave the coaching and playing staff just no support. I learned more in that one year about how NOT to run a football club than I have in the 20 years since. The lessons remain with me even now. I was only 23 years old at the time and I owe Paul a great debt for making me stick at it that year. It was long and hard and I've never been able to forget it. I had a couple of years off the grade scene just to recover and then made a comeback as a player in 1979 with Souths. They made me reserve grade captain and I played every game so it was a satisfying season for me. The following year, Bill Anderson took over first grade and appointed me as coach of the under-23s. I hung up my boots and started to concentrate solely on coaching. They were exciting times at Souths; in 1980 we reached the finals in all three grades, with the first graders storming home without a loss in the final nine rounds. In 1981 the first graders took out the mid-week Cup and I had a very memorable year, winning the under-23s premiership. We had an exciting young side, captained by Craig Coleman and with Mario Fenech at hooker. From day one, they were both destined to be top players.'

Fenech looks back on his early days in grade under Smith with great affection. 'Brian had a profound effect on my career from the day he came to watch us play the President's Cup final in 1980,' Fenech recalled. 'He came into the room after the game and asked me to come into grade football. It was a moment I'd dreamed of all my life and one I'll never forget. And when I arrived at Souths, he opened up a whole new game to me. The communication, the skills training, the tactics . . . it was like another world. Brian ran the team with so much discipline. His knowledge of the game was so vast and he could analyse the strengths and weaknesses of any team or player. I played under a lot of coaches in my time but there's no doubt even at that early stage of his career, Brian was among the best. It was a very special time for me under him.'

BRIAN SMITH

Bill Anderson saw Smith as a potential coach while he led the Rabbitohs' reserve grade side in 1979. 'I could tell from his leadership and his analytical mind that Brian was destined to coach,' Anderson recalled. 'From the moment we gave him the under-23s, he warmed to the task. Coaches sometimes need to be able to spin players a yarn—to make them believe in something—and that was among Brian's strengths. He could really get through to the players on a personal level. He gave them confidence to perform at their peak and there are few more important jobs in coaching.'

The under-23 premiership triumph earned Smith a promotion to reserve grade for 1982, but his coaching career suffered an abrupt setback at the end of the season despite his team finishing equal fifth. 'They sacked me and when they did, Bill Anderson quit as first grade coach,' Smith recalled. 'I was never told why I'd been sacked and still don't know. But I think that it was because they'd re-signed Bill mid-season and suddenly decided he had to go. When they axed me, they knew he would quit too and that's the way it turned out. The following year Ron Willey came into the place and I went back to coaching the kids at school.'

Anderson says he had no hesitation in quitting the club despite some good results in his time with the Rabbitohs. 'I wanted Brian on my team and the committee knew that; what they did was a direct challenge to my authority,' he said. 'I felt he was the right man for the job but, more importantly, that I, as head coach, had the right to choose my staff. Brian had spent some time away from the club as coach of a junior representative side, but that would be viewed as an advantage nowadays. When they sacked him, resigning was the only option as I saw it.'

As it turned out, both men moved on to bigger and better

things after the sour finale to their time at Redfern. Anderson coached Balmain for several seasons before going on to a career as a television commentator. After a year back with the kids at James Cook, Smith got his big break when offered the Illawarra coaching position in 1984. 'The club had only been around for a couple of years but it was the sort of opportunity I'd been looking for,' Smith said 'They were young and keen and it was first grade . . . I jumped in.' A young Steelers side defied the odds in Smith's first season, staying in the finals race until the final round clash with Manly. The Sea Eagles dismissed the challenge, but it was the closest Illawarra had come to the finals in the club's short existence. 'They all underrated us,' Smith reflected. 'We kept going along quietly, winning enough games to stay in touch with the leaders. It would have been a monumental shock to all and sundry if we reached the finals, but we fell just short.' Even Manly coach Bob Fulton, a man not known for heaping praise on his rivals, was impressed. 'I've never met Brian Smith, but he is my choice as coach of the year,' Fulton said at the time.

'That first season was fantastic but overall, the four years at Illawarra were a real struggle,' Smith said. 'We won the wooden spoon for a couple of years and holding the place together was very hard. For the coaches, administrators and players, it was a tough time. We really battled competing with the big name clubs. Like the Newtown experience, while it wasn't all that pleasant at the time, it was good for me. It toughened me up and made me realise that you can't shift the buck off the table, that it's always going to end up with you as coach. I think that in the long term it made me a better coach. At the end of 1987, I decided I had to get out. I didn't have a job to go to and it was a hard decision to make, but I knew it was the right one. Both for me and the club. It had got to the point where Illawarra needed a new coach and I needed some new surroundings. And I think both parties benefited in the long term. The Steelers went through another dry spell after I left under Terry Fearnley and then Ron Hilditch but then turned the corner under Graham Murray. I like to think that a couple of schemes I put in place down there like the talented youth programs and development work began to bear fruit. I spent a lot of time working in those areas, along with Neil Lovett, one of the Steelers' officials, and it gave me a lot of satisfaction to watch the club do well, even though it was a couple of seasons after I had left the place.'

Smith was known as something of a fiery young coach in his time with the Steelers. Confident in his ability, he became frustrated at the club's lack of success. 'It was hard for him,' said Bill Anderson, who remains a close friend. 'When you are coaching and things aren't going your way, it's a natural reaction to get a little paranoid. You start to feel the world's against you. To make things worse, when you're coaching a struggling side, things like the bounce of the ball and controversial refereeing decisions always seem to favour the other team. And Brian, keen to make a name for himself, was an anxious young man. He was—and still is—a workaholic. He puts so many hours into the job. I don't think most people would have any idea of all the behind-the-scenes work. He is always thinking football and looking for any idea to give him an edge. But the Illawarra experience taught him a lot about himself and I think he has mellowed since then. He is more philosophical now. One of Brian's strengths is that he has been able to move with the times. The game has changed, he has seen that and adapted. To be at the top for over a decade like he has, you have to be able to change your methods and Brian has always been capable of doing that. He is a real professional and expects nothing less than a similarly professional approach from his players. For that reason, he has fallen out with some players on occasion. They aren't prepared to give him everything he demands. But by and large, the players know they are on a good thing and follow him all the way.'

For almost a year after he left the Steelers, Smith's career was in limbo. His achievements with Illawarra weren't impressive enough to land him one of the stronger Sydney clubs and he found himself on the outside, looking in. At one stage, he even sold insurance to keep bread on the table for his family. 'I did a bit of everything in that time,' he said. 'I knew I wanted to continue in coaching, but it was a matter of waiting for the right opportunity to come along. Then I got an offer to go to Hull in England and it was perfect for me. It was a big step to uproot the family from Wollongong to go over there to a battling club, but it proved great in the long run. I had two-and-a-half years there and it was a real confidence rebuilder for me. I'd become a bit jaded by the experiences with the Steelers and the success we enjoyed in England helped me get back on an even keel. But things didn't start real well. It took me a while to get to know them and them to understand me. We lost four of our first five games and for a while, I thought I was going to be on my bike back home. But we recovered to win 11 in a row and go all the way to the premiership final, where we were beaten by Widnes. I brought over some players who I'd been associated with back home—players like Greg Mackey, Craig Coleman and Jeff Hardy—and they all did well in Britain. We made the playoffs again the following year and then it was in January 1991 that I left to come back home. We were leading the league at that stage; Noel Cleal took over the reins and we went on to win the title. That was a great result, even though I wasn't there to see it.'

BRIAN SMITH

A frantic SOS from St George, the club that had brought him to the big city as a player nearly 20 years earlier, prompted Smith to pack his bags to return home. At the end of 1990, Saints were in crisis. The Dragons won just eight games that season, finishing in 12th spot, their worst performance since joining the competition 70 seasons earlier. Craig Young, once a favourite son of the Dragons, was sacked and Saints were on the lookout for a new coach. Chief executive Geoff Carr, himself a relative newcomer to the club, approached Smith, whose excellent results in Britain stamped him as a coach of real quality. While his win–loss percentage in four years at Illawarra would not have earned him such a prestige job, Smith's performance in turning Hull from battlers into a real force won Saints over. Carr knew Smith well, having played alongside him in the Dragons' ranks in the early '70s, and the pair had remained firm friends. Nonetheless, Smith knocked back the approach. Desperate, Saints then chased Rod Reddy, another favourite son who was achieving good results at Barrow. 'I appreciate your call, but Brian Smith's your man,' Reddy told Carr. 'He's the one you need.' Carr resumed the chase for Smith, this time in more earnest fashion, and met with success. Smith accepted the offer, was granted a release by Hull midseason, and brought Reddy back with him as his deputy.

Carr saw the signing of Smith as a well-timed move by both parties. 'Basically, we needed him and he needed us,' Carr said. 'There had been some lean years at Saints and we were desperate for a coach to get us back where we belonged. And from Brian's point of view, he never had the success at Illawarra he wanted because he didn't have the cattle. He showed what he could do at Hull and in Saints, he was given a team with the ability to make an impact if handled well. When I first rang Brian after the board sacked Craig Young, it was initially for advice as to which coaches we should approach. I knew he was under contract so he wasn't on our list. But I think that call whetted his appetite and he showed some interest. When I called "Rocket" Reddy, who was close to Brian, a few weeks later, he suggested I ring Brian again because the time was right—and that's how it worked out. Brian was able to negotiate a release from Hull and came on board.'

Smith quickly re-established the Dragons as a finals contender in his maiden season, bringing the club to within a whisker of its first semis appearance since 1985. Just as in his debut season at Illawarra, Smith found himself entering the final round needing a win to reach the playoffs. But fate left the Dragons the toughest match of the year—away to Canberra—and they were duly thrashed 40–8. But the emergence of talented young players like Wayne Collins, Tony Priddle and Scott Gourley set the scene for a ground-breaking year for the Dragons the following season. 'That season was an important one to re-establish the club,' Smith said. 'Saints had had a few years in the wilderness but were now back on track . . . and we knew good times were ahead.'

Smith's hard-line approach to discipline and structured play saw the Dragons beat many more-fancied teams in 1992. But it didn't sit all that well with former Saints greats, several of whom had 'digs' at the Smith coaching style. 'I guess you have to expect that sometimes in a club with great tradition like St George,' Smith said. 'The likes of Ian Walsh, Johnny Raper and Reg Gasnier all took pot shots at us from time to time. But really, they are just outsiders, and what they said never worried us. We knew we were on the right track. Geoff Carr was an astute chief executive and with his help, I was able to put together an outstanding coaching team. Guys like Max

Ninness, Matthew Elliott and David Boyle, right down to Brian, our doorman, ensured we had all angles covered. We had a great year in '92 but I'll be the first to admit we had our fair share of luck in the playoffs. We beat Newcastle 3–2 in the elimination semi and then Illawarra 4–0 to win a grand final berth. They were probably two of the most exciting games I've ever been involved in. It was a fairytale to get to the grand final. But when we got there, Brisbane were light-years ahead of us. There can be no denying it. In fact, they were streets ahead of everyone that year. We held them for a while but they ended up winning the grand final by 20 points. It was a disappointing finish, but still a marvellous year for the club.'

While many thought the Dragons didn't deserve to be there on grand final day in 1992, Smith confounded the critics by again piloting his side to the premiership decider against the Broncos 12 months later. This time, everyone had to agree Saints were a force to be reckoned with. The proof was especially evident in the finals series. In contrast to their two dour wins the previous year, Saints thrashed Canberra 31–10 and Canterbury 27–12 to throw down the gauntlet to Brisbane. 'We were a much stronger and more mature outfit in 1993,' Smith said. 'And for all of July, August and September—bar one day—I thought we would win the competition. Sadly, that one day happened to be grand final day. We were the best team in the premiership for those three months and our record showed it. It was without doubt the best team I've ever coached. We were red-hot, playing good football week in, week out. But not on the day that really mattered. We came a lot closer to the Broncos than 12 months earlier, but the fact remains we were very flat. They beat us 14–6 and I'm still at a loss to explain what went wrong. Our preparation was good and we had everything to play for.'

The media had a field day playing up the so-called feud between Saints and the Broncos over the two-year period in which they fought out the grand final. To add fuel to the fire, the Broncos were captured on video celebrating after the '92 premiership decider singing a tune of their own composition— 'St George can't play'. But Smith conceded the feud was a very real one and more than mere media hype. 'The rivalry was very intense in the time I was at Saints,' Smith said. 'It was fierce and some of the stuff that came out of it was very personal, particularly towards me. But it just toughened my resolve. It wasn't nice, but on the field it was never spiteful. It was like the rivalry between Souths and St George in the '60s or Parramatta and Canterbury in the '80s. It was two high quality teams who rose to the occasion when they came up against each other and wanted to show who was boss. We had a couple of great wins over them, but they won the two games that really mattered.'

Smith found himself the centre of an unwanted controversy at the end of 1992 following the retirement of long-serving centre Michael Beattie. Beattie was keen to play on for another season, but quit after a showdown with Smith. The media grabbed hold of the story and a public slanging match ensued between the pair for several days, spread across the back pages of the newspapers. 'That whole episode really disappointed me,' Smith said. 'Without wanting to get right into it all again, Michael had the opportunity to leave with some dignity. He chose to go the way he did and it caused a lot of friction and problems in the ranks. The fact that we were able to overcome that and put together such an excellent season in '93 speaks volumes for the players.'

Other controversies have dogged Smith, but he has ridden them out. Like his penchant for selecting younger brother Tony at five-eighth in the big games. A steady, tradesmanlike player, Tony Smith always did his job but critics cried for the inclusion of a more flamboyant player like Phil Blake in his place. 'That situation was always going to be difficult, for both of us,' Smith said. 'But the fact is Tony was there on his merits. When he was in the team, it invariably functioned smoothly. No coach can afford to play favourites, especially with his own brother. If you don't put the best team on the field every week, you soon end up feeling the flak.'

After coming so close to taking the title in 1993, the Dragons dropped their bundle the following year. Fans could barely recognise the team that pushed the Broncos in the grand final only six months earlier. Lack of form and a terrible run of injuries resulted in the Dragons finishing well down the ladder. 'Things went against us in '94 without doubt,' Smith said. 'The injuries were horrific and seemed to hit us all at once. We lost confidence and morale dropped a bit. I also feel I have to shoulder a lot of the blame. My own performance wasn't as good as it had been in the two previous years. But it wasn't wasted; I learned some valuable lessons. The main one was just how important the senior players in your club are to the overall success of the team. Mark Coyne was establishing himself as our new club captain, replacing Michael Potter, who had retired. It wasn't so much Michael's play that we missed, but the example that he set. And the control he had over some of the more wayward, but still important members of the team. After Mick left, these guys just didn't perform. That made me realise the importance of having quality people as the senior players in your club. Their value is much more than just the form they show on the field.'

Geoff Carr believed the Dragons became victims of their

own spectacular success in 1994. 'I think everyone would agree we over-achieved by reaching the grand final the two previous years,' he said. 'By '94, other teams were fully aware of our potential to knock them off. Also, after two such good years, our depth was eroded. We had to put the players who'd done the job for us on better contracts and as a consequence, couldn't afford to keep other players. Our depth eroded and when the injuries hit, we really felt it.'

Although the Dragons only just scraped into the finals in 1995, Smith has never been more proud of his players. Saints started the year with a horror draw, meeting every top contender in the opening two months of the premiership. After the disasters of 1994, it was the last thing the club needed in its attempt to re-establish itself. Saints lost six of their first eight games, finding themselves in a dreadful position so early in the season. To make matters worse, Saints were thrown into the middle of the Super League war, their ranks torn to shreds as key players defected to the rebel code. Mid-season, Smith himself made the difficult decision to leave at year's end, while merger talks with Sydney City were in full swing. 'We certainly had a lot to contend with—it was probably as difficult a year as any the club has faced in its long history,' Smith said. 'The luck of the draw gave us a really tough patch to begin the season but the thing in our favour was that we never panicked. We retained our morale and kept our minds on the job at hand. The merger speculation was a killer. It's hard for players to give their heart and soul knowing their club may not be around next year. It was a dramatic time; after a couple of games the fans staged emotional on-field rallies and it all made it hard to stay focussed. But we began to win a few games and without doubt the turning point was the match we played against Wests at the SCG. It was a promotional match with a lot of nostalgia but that meant nothing to our players; our only interest was survival. Wests were among the leaders at that stage and we knew if we didn't knock them off, we were finished. I remember driving to the ground and the phone in my car rang three times; on each occasion it was a player dropping out. We had one of those shocking weeks with injury and really put a bits and pieces team on the field. Rocket Reddy's reserve grade side had to get kids out of the park just to make up the numbers, that's how bad the situation was. There were 19 players out in both grades and we were looking at going out the back door if we lost. But the team performed enormously. Gorden Tallis had a big game and we won 25–12. I'd have to rate it one of the most memorable performances in my time at the club. Not so much for the football we played, but for the spirit we showed. That game really got us going and we won seven straight to come into the finals full of confidence. Unfortunately, in the semis, Canterbury just edged us out 12–8 and they went on to win the whole thing. The wet conditions didn't suit us that day and a couple of decisions went against us. We also bombed a couple of tries that proved very costly. But you can't take it away from Canterbury, they did a great job to go on with it and win the title. The campaign in '95 gave me a lot of satisfaction, though. In some ways, it was even more enjoyable than our grand final years in 1992–93. We certainly had a better time as a group and the emergence of players like Gorden Tallis, Nathan Brown, Anthony Mundine, Nick Zisti and Jason Stevens really gave me a kick. They graduated into established first graders in the last couple of years I had there and that was great to see.'

Smith stunned the league community by announcing mid-season in 1995 his decision to quit the Dragons for English club Bradford. At the time, few could understand the motivation behind his decision. But in the months that followed, it quickly became apparent why Smith felt compelled to leave. The highly professional set-up that he had constructed over the previous five years vanished before Saints' fans eyes, with the club virtually back to square one. Chief executive Geoff Carr, a key man in Saints' success, was forced out after a disagreement with the board, while many of the Dragons' top players decided to bail out for Super League. The club lost its major sponsor of nearly 20 years, Penfolds Wines, and budget constraints prevented the Dragons signing any top class players to fill the void. 'It wasn't easy to leave after five years but the time was just right for the move,' Smith explained. 'I had a lot of respect for the people at Saints but there were a lot of things there that time has shown weren't done right. They had the chance to blossom, both financially and by getting players, but chose not to do it. The picture was painted to me by senior administrators in the club that I'd done my bit and could do no more for them. They had respect for me and felt they owed it to me to explain the situation. They couldn't guarantee that the club was going to be the powerful force that I envisaged and that we'd been in my time there. I've had a lot of years of coaching now and I didn't want to be in a place that could be in the bottom tier of clubs. It was very disappointing. We had a great coaching staff and had put together a first class football team. The whole operation worked smoothly, but I could see it all falling apart around me if I stayed.'

Carr believes Smith may have stayed with the Dragons had it not been for the proposed merger with Sydney City, which hung over the club like a dark cloud throughout the first half of the season. 'I must say that Brian received huge offers from both Bradford and Leeds before the merger speculation began,' Carr said. 'But he told the board about them and may well have hung around had we matched those offers. When the merger looked like becoming a reality, I told Brian that at the end of the day, there would only be one coach of the merged club—either him or Phil Gould.' Smith knew Gould, who had been a key man in the ARL's battle with Super League, was too well connected to miss out. Days after his talks with Carr, he requested—and was granted—a release.

Although Smith's association with the Dragons officially ended in the controversial semi-final against the Bulldogs, the quietly spoken coach received a stunning send-off the previous week. In an emotional final home game that the Dragons needed to win to reach the finals, Saints downed the Western Reds 36–18. Sensing the end of an era, the near 20,000 crowd stayed long after fulltime, giving Smith a standing ovation as he took the field to congratulate his players. More cheers followed as players chaired their coach from the field in a heartfelt tribute. In a sport in which most departing coaches are all but run out of town, Saints' tribute was a rare show of appreciation for the man in charge. 'That was a very special day for me,' Smith agreed. 'Just getting to the finals after the long journey we'd been through was a marvellous achievement. And then for the players and crowd to spontaneously send me off with such warm feelings was superb; it's something I won't forget. I had a similar farewell at Hull when we beat Leeds in a TV game, so I've been lucky. I haven't been sacked from first grade yet . . . the trick is to keep moving before they can set their sights on you,' he added with a grin.

At time of writing, Smith was preparing to lead a new-look Bradford Bulls side into the historic maiden British Super League season. 'It's a new challenge; we're virtually starting from scratch,' he said. 'The player turnover has been huge and it's a different situation from what I've been used to. But the rules are different; I've never had this flexibility and I am acting as chief executive as well as coach. Now the task is to get all these people together, both as a football team and a social unit. It's a big challenge.'

Smith is stumped when asked to describe the attributes that make up a successful coach. 'That's the hardest question in the game . . . one I don't think there is a definitive answer to,' he said. People with so many different personalities get into football coaching and are either successful or are not. Probably the two great coaches in the modern era have been Jack Gibson and Warren Ryan. And you'd never meet two more different individuals. One was very scientific and technical, while the other based his coaching on his personal experiences and values. You've got to find your own particular style and refine it. I believe there is no recipe for success as such.'

Something of a coaching nomad, Smith has already determined he will be back in Australian football at the end of his two-year contract at Bradford. 'If I get the opportunity in the right place, I'll be very keen to return,' he said. 'I'm a believer in fate; I know if I keep getting the results, I'll get a job back home and it will be the right one. I enjoy the different type of football and the different lifestyle in Britain, but Australia will always be home. There's more emotion in the British game. The highs are much higher and the lows are a lot deeper. Thankfully, I haven't had to contend with too many of the lows yet. People have a far closer relationship with their clubs in England, a greater commitment to the game. But Australia is the number one place for rugby league and the standard between the two countries is very different. I want to keep proving myself and doing it every week. And the only place to

BRIAN SMITH

do that is in Oz. Britain has some top players and teams, but the week-to-week intensity just isn't the same.'

So fair warning, Aussie clubs—Brian Smith is heading home in the not-too-distant future. More than one club could do worse than to already sound him out about a coaching role for 1998.